VALUING MUSICAL PARTICIPATION

For Eileen Pitts
who was always a good listener (although concerts made her cough)

and for Dorinda Robertson
with love

Valuing Musical Participation

STEPHANIE PITTS
University of Sheffield, UK

ASHGATE

© Stephanie Pitts 2005

Published by
Ashgate Publishing Limited
Gower House
Croft Road
Aldershot
Hants GU11 3HR
England

Ashgate Publishing Company
Suite 420
101 Cherry Street
Burlington, VT 05401-4405
USA

Ashgate website: http://www.ashgate.com

British Library Cataloguing in Publication Data
Pitts, Stephanie
  Valuing musical participation
  1.Musicians—Psychology 2.Music—Performance—Psychological aspects
  3.Music appreciation 4.Participation
  I.Title
  781.1'1

Library of Congress Cataloging-in-Publication Data
Pitts, Stephanie.
  Valuing musical participation / Stephanie Pitts.
      p. cm.
  Includes bibliographical references (p.   ) and index.
  ISBN 0-7546-5095-2 (alk. paper) ✓
  1. Musicians—Psychology. 2. Music—Performance—Psychological aspects. I. Title.

  ML3838.P58 2004
  781'.11—dc22

                                                                2004025743

ISBN 0 7546 5095 2

Printed and bound in Great Britain by MPG Books Ltd, Bodmin, Cornwall

Contents

List of Tables and Figure

Tables

Figure

Acknowledgements

This project was made both possible and enjoyable by the many people who participated willingly and thoughtfully in the research: students at Lady Manners School, Bakewell and at the University of Sheffield; performers, audience members and organisers at the Gilbert and Sullivan Festival in Buxton; the management, tutors and participants at the COMA summer school; and Music in the Round administrators and audience members. I learnt a lot from them, and sincerely hope that they find themselves to be fairly represented in my accounts of their musical activities.

Financial support was provided by the British Academy, who generously funded the research at Music in the Round: for that project I thank Karen Burland for being a brilliant research assistant, and Susan Pennington for spending hours deciphering questionnaires. Thanks also to Simon Clements for allowing me to use one of his sketches for the book's cover: these were done while listening to Music in the Round concerts and capture perfectly the spirit of participation which this book celebrates. Additional funding for the case studies came from the University of Sheffield, who also gave me a semester of study leave in which the first draft of the book was written. My thanks to colleagues for covering my administrative and teaching work during that time, and to Gordon Cox, co-editor of the *British Journal of Music Education*, for keeping a careful eye on our editing duties while my energies were focused elsewhere.

I am grateful to the readers who commented on the work in progress; in particular to Lucy Green and Chris Spencer for their helpful critiques of chapter drafts, and to Nikki Dibben and Eric Clarke for being a constant source of encouragement and the best colleagues anyone could hope for. I have also benefited from conversations with audiences when I have spoken about this work: staff and students on the MA in Music Education at the Institute of Education, in the psychology departments of Sheffield and Keele universities, in the music department at Bangor, and members of the British Forum for Ethnomusicology at conferences in Edinburgh and Aberdeen. The editors and reviewers who have read aspects of the work already published have also made useful comments, and I owe particular gratitude to Nicholas Cook and Tia DeNora for their various roles in supporting the project. And working with staff at Ashgate has been a pleasure throughout, as Heidi May, Anne Keirby and Pete Coles have been consistently efficient and helpful.

Finally, to my parents and to all those friends who have provided support or distractions whenever I needed them; much love and thanks.

CHAPTER ONE

Introducing musical participation

A school student animatedly describes the music college where she hopes to spend the next three years of her life; a man holds his head in his hands as he recalls the humiliating descent of a critical part of his costume on stage the night before; a group of composers who first met two days previously engage in heated debate about the direction their electroacoustic piece should take; and over interval drinks in a crowded foyer, members of an audience share memories of the vast chamber music repertoire they have heard together during the preceding twenty years. Musical participation shapes people's lives, drawing on their emotional, mental and physical energy. Its activities are valued highly and demand great commitment, sometimes to an extent that seems incomprehensible to those who are not involved. Participants often cannot say just what it is that matters to them about music – but they know that it does.

This book explores the musical involvement of participants in a variety of settings: a school, a university, a residential summer school, and two music festivals. Its aims are to understand the motivations, values and experiences of the musical participants in each of these settings, and so to theorise more widely about the contribution of music to social and personal fulfilment. Understanding the experiences of adult participants will lead to questions about how such engagement can be fostered at an earlier age, and so there will be discussion too of the educational implications of the case study settings, and of the social responsibility that exists to ensure that musical involvement is widely accessible. Throughout the book, the participants whose stories contribute to the discussion address the question 'Why make music?', which has been surprisingly neglected in the research literature until now. Inevitably, there is no single clear answer, but the interwoven personal, social and musical motivations that emerge from their reflections offer new insights on the role and potential of musical involvement.

Why does music matter?

The uses and experiences of music in contemporary Western life have attracted recent attention from researchers in sociology and psychology of music, and are also becoming a more central part of the musicological discourse, which has traditionally concentrated on musical texts rather than the behaviour which surrounds their performance. Classical music – broadly defined here to embrace the contemporary music and Victorian operetta included in my case studies – has been particularly prone to research that prioritises understanding of the text and biographical knowledge of its composer above consideration of its social context. With 'new' musicologists and cultural theorists now beginning to consider more carefully the interaction between musical works and their social settings, there is a need for a detailed picture of how and why performers and listeners engage with the music of their choice. This book aims to inform current debate through analysis of the experiences of performers, listeners and amateur composers in a range of contexts.

Several recent investigations of how people in Britain use music in their daily lives were influential in prompting this study; prominent among them Tia DeNora's (2000) *Music in Everyday Life*. In her pioneering book, DeNora reports on studies exploring listening activities in the home, exposure to music in shops and other public places, and the uses of music to change and maintain emotional states. DeNora shows how music is an integral part of daily life, acting as 'a technology of the self' by contributing to the way in which individuals react to and understand their world:

> Music is an active ingredient in the organization of self, the shifting of mood, energy level, conduct style, mode of attention and engagement with the world. ... Music's 'effects' come from the ways in which individuals orient to it, how they interpret it and how they place it within their personal musical maps, within the semiotic web of music and extra-musical associations. (DeNora, 2000: 61)

DeNora's research illustrates the considerable extent to which individual listeners are able to govern and respond to their musical contexts, so countering the doom-ridden commentaries that suggest over-exposure to music in public arenas is damaging the ability to listen attentively (e.g. Johnson, 2002).

Another recent indication of the extent of listening activity in daily life can be found in the study by John Sloboda, Susan O'Neill and Antonia Ivaldi (2001), in which eight volunteers were given an electronic pager to carry for a week, and were prompted at random intervals to complete a report of their current activities, including their response to any music heard within the previous two hours. This 'experience sampling method' revealed music to be present in 44 per cent of the recorded episodes, but showed a relatively low level of attentive listening:

> Music occurred very frequently while participants were travelling, or in public places (such as shops), moderately frequently at home, and less frequently in other locations. It tended to accompany active leisure (e.g. going out with friends) and maintenance activity (e.g. housework, washing, shopping) more than deskwork or passive leisure (e.g. reading, watching TV), and tended to accompany activities undertaken by choice rather than for duty. (Sloboda *et al.*, 2001: 22)

These findings are consistent with DeNora's, and also with the work of Michael Bull (2000), who investigated the use of personal stereos in city life and interaction, noting similar roles for music as a source of increased personal autonomy in routine or time-consuming tasks. Susan Crafts, Daniel Cavicchi and Charles Keil (1993) provide further individual illustrations of these patterns, as their interviewees recall the emotional impact and connotations of their preferred repertoire or listening behaviour. The case for music listening as an important component in navigating contemporary life is emerging as a convincing one.

Despite this growing interest in the functions and effects of music in modern life, few researchers have investigated the experiences of active musical participation amongst British communities. The literature on leisure studies (e.g. Argyle, 1996a; Cohen & Taylor, 1976/92) tends to mention music only in passing; the notable exception being the work of Robert Stebbins, who includes a study of barbershop singers (1996) among his extensive writing on 'serious leisure' (e.g. 1992; 1998). Other genre-specific studies include Sara Cohen's (1991) account of rock musicians in Liverpool, and Niall MacKinnon's (1993) work on the British folk scene. Both of these elaborate on elements present in Ruth Finnegan's influential book, *The Hidden Musicians* (1989), which revealed for the first time the extent of music-making in a single town through an ethnographic study of music groups and activities in Milton Keynes. Finnegan's work illustrated the value of musical participation in the social, personal and cultural lives of those who have regular involvement in a performing society, and revealed the potential for comparative studies of diverse communities around Britain.

Alongside those qualitative studies, attempts to quantify the extent of musical activity amongst the population have produced variable results: 'the National Music Council reports that at least 600,000 people actively participate in amateur and voluntary music-making' (Everitt, 1997: 39), whilst the *Arts in England* report (Skelton *et al.*, 2002) found 7 per cent of the population playing or singing for performance, and in answer to a slightly different question, 'less than half (45 per cent) of all children claim to be able to play a musical instrument compared with a quarter (26 per cent) of adults' (Cooke & Morris, 1996: 127). Of the 8.5 million attendances at classical concerts in 1997, amateur performances accounted for around 1.4 million, and the 2,000 amateur opera companies in Britain gave around 18,500 performances in the same year (Dane *et al.*, 1999: 23-5). The combination of available qualitative and quantitative evidence on contemporary musical life illustrates that although musical participation may be 'a minority pursuit' (Policy Studies Institute, 1991: 33), its value for those involved is considerable and still demands further investigation (cf. Finnegan, 2003).

Concert attendance has been the focus of at least two ethnographic studies: Christopher Small's (1998) analysis of the orchestral concert is critical of the power relationships implicit in the venues and practices of art music listening, while Daniel Cavicchi (1998) is more sympathetic to the gradations of fan behaviour evident amongst Bruce Springsteen audiences. Research in popular music also provides insight on the experience of attending live music events (e.g. Thornton, 1995; Walser, 1993), but across the literature the separation of genres, and of performing and listening experience, makes it difficult for readers from different academic disciplines to forge connections between the available evidence.

This brief literature review has not aimed to be comprehensive: these studies and other related writings will be interwoven with discussion of new empirical evidence throughout this book. However, the research context is clear – a growing recognition of the value and impact of musical participation has yet to be systematically supported with accounts of the experiences of those involved. This book aims to narrow the gap between existing theoretical and empirical perspectives by considering four case studies which shed new light on specific musical events or locations.

Case studies of musical behaviour

Questions of musical identity, involvement and value are explored here through discussion of four empirical projects carried out at musical establishments and events between 2000 and 2003. These projects are case studies of musical participation, in that each sought to investigate a specific location or event in considerable detail, using a combination of research methods to generate rich data and make fruitful connections with the existing literature. The questions and methods of the four studies are inter-related, with each project designed to generate a greater understanding of how participation contributed to the lives of those who were in attendance. The focus was on individual experience within a group context, as participants reflected on their perceptions of the event in question, their interactions with other participants, and their own sense of musical engagement.

The choice of events to be included in the project drew on my local knowledge of established musical events occurring in Sheffield and the surrounding area of Yorkshire and Derbyshire, in the North and Midlands of England. As such, the events chosen show connections with my own musical experiences and behaviour (although not always with my preferences), as I selected festivals and similar events which I knew to be prominent in the lives of the musically active local community, but with which I had no previous personal involvement. I have inevitably omitted a vast number of the varied activities that flourish in this location, and there is obvious potential for longitudinal and comparative research to further inform the ideas presented here. However, since my aim was to document individual experience across comparable musical situations, the project was deemed to be complete when ideas could be clearly cross-referenced between studies, rather than when I had exhausted the opportunities for similar projects. This book therefore serves a different purpose from the local studies conducted in Sheffield by Eric Mackerness (1974) and in Milton Keynes by Ruth Finnegan (1989), both of whom aimed for comprehensive accounts of the wealth of musical activity present in their localities. My intention here is to look through a more closely focused lens at the roles of music in the lives of some 600 or so people who attend and give concerts and stage performances, study music at school and university, or come together to compose and perform music at an annual summer school. These people have each participated in one of the four case studies outlined below, and their accounts and experiences of music in their lives will form the basis for discussion throughout this book.

Study 1: Music students in transition

The smallest of the four studies, this was nevertheless the catalyst for the others, raising questions of musical confidence, preference and sense of identity that prompted further investigation. At the time of this study, I was teaching part-time in a local secondary school and lecturing part-time at the University of Sheffield, a dual existence which meant that I taught eighteen-year-old music students in two quite different circumstances, each with particular norms of behaviour, expectations and pedagogical style. Becoming concerned by these apparent differences and the challenge for students of moving between them, I began some research into the transition between school and university (cf. Pitts, 2002), and asked my Advanced-Level (A Level) students and first year undergraduates to participate in an interview study designed to investigate their perceptions of school and university music education.

Twenty students agreed to participate in the study: eleven A Level music students (7 female; 4 male) in their final year at a Derbyshire secondary school, and nine first year undergraduates (8 female; 1 male) studying music at the University of Sheffield. Each student was asked to complete a questionnaire asking for details of their musical experience to date and their predictions or intentions for their future involvement, as well as some more reflective questions on their definitions of the term 'musician' and the extent to which they felt themselves to belong to that category. The questionnaires were followed up by interviews, which provided an opportunity to return to and clarify ideas. All participants in this study were currently active as performers, each playing at least one instrument, usually to a high standard, and having between them interests which included African drumming, folk guitar, jazz and composition, as well as widespread membership of choirs and orchestras.

The most striking finding in this study was the clear division between those school students who intended to go on and study music at university, and those who expected to cease their involvement when they completed their school education. Those who had auditioned and secured places in a university or college music department seemed secure in their sense of 'self-as-musician', and were confidently optimistic about the quantity and quality of performing activity that they expected to find in those departments. School students who had other intentions for work or study were much more modest in their appraisals of their own playing ability, and tended to view music in higher education as a rather eccentric occupation, populated by extrovert, talented individuals with whom they appeared to feel little connection. This would be a bright enough picture of music in higher education if it were sustained into the reality of first year undergraduate study, but in fact the university students interviewed were much less certain of their own abilities and many expressed doubts about their capacity to complete the course. For some, an unsuccessful audition for the university orchestra had knocked their confidence; for others, there was no specific event to which their unease could be attributed, but rather a feeling that being one among many music students was less enjoyable than the active, privileged role they had occupied as the 'star' musician at their secondary school or college.

From this first study it became clear that musical identity, behaviour and confidence vary according to context, with a supportive environment and ongoing feelings of achievement and success necessary to sustain a sense of musical self-worth. This view, demonstrated in students' self-evaluations, was also evident in their attempts to construct generously inclusive definitions of the word 'musician', whilst at the same time expressing doubts about whether they themselves 'deserved' this title. Close connections between demonstrable achievement and musical identity were beginning to emerge, suggesting that to be a 'musician' involves not just ability and experience, but must also incorporate a degree of recognition from others and a strong sense of self-identification with the values and skills attributed to this label. With a university music department proving *not* to be the obvious location to find people secure in their roles as musicians, the other three case studies in this project looked at events outside mainstream education, to see whether voluntary, non-assessed participation in musical activity might provide the security these students seemed to be lacking.

Study 2: Performers and audience at a Gilbert and Sullivan festival

This study was carried out in August 2001 at the Eighth International Gilbert and Sullivan Festival, a three-week festival held annually in Buxton, Derbyshire. Performing societies from Britain, America and occasionally elsewhere gather to celebrate the music of Gilbert and Sullivan, resulting in a near-complete cycle of their Victorian operettas in the picturesque setting of the recently-restored Buxton Opera House (see Pitts, 2004b). For the purposes of this project, the festival provided an ideal opportunity to meet a large number of comparable performing societies in one location, and to interact with an audience who are passionate about the genre that is its focus. The festival therefore has a very intense feel, which was to be found again in the remaining two studies, illustrating the importance of familiarity, shared focus and single-minded purpose in generating the short-lived musical communities that typify such events.

As with the first study, questionnaires and interviews were used in combination, with the addition this time of a week of fieldwork observations, when I attended the performances, masterclasses and post-show cabarets which make up the festival, as well as noting the behaviour of participants and the impact of the festival on the local town. My main focus in this study was on the performers, and before the festival I contacted each of the performing groups who would be appearing during the week of my attendance to ask them to participate in my research. All were willing and helpful, and I was able to gather 41 questionnaires from across four performing groups, as well as arranging interviews with around 20 of the performers and organising staff. Interviews with the performers usually took place the morning after their show, necessitating a very flexible group interview style, but proving successful in capturing that moment of post-performance reflection that holds real significance for performers but is rarely articulated or documented.

Through the combination of questionnaire, interview and fieldwork data I gained a clear picture of the varied experiences and motivations of these performers, many of whom had comments to make about other performing societies that were equally revealing of their own. Reasons for participating included the sense of 'being someone you're not' which appearing on stage could offer, with the enhancing of everyday life through musical participation forming a substantial part of the discussion. Some performers claimed to find this equally well through rehearsal, valuing the sense of personal development and social connection that belonging to a performing society gave them. All had a light-hearted affection for the music of Gilbert and Sullivan, enjoying the lively character of the music and plots, and finding the four-part choruses and challenging solo roles satisfying to sing. It was clear that loyalty to a local performing society was stronger than that felt towards the festival, which for most performers was only one aspect of a busy musical schedule throughout the year.

Questionnaires completed by the audience revealed a greater sense of commitment to the festival and the genre it celebrates, with some describing it as 'the highlight of the year', not least because of the friendships and sense of belonging associated with their regular attendance in Buxton. The audience questionnaire was distributed before each evening and matinee performance by front of house staff, and included a number of 'tick-box' questions designed to gather information about attendance and musical preferences, as well as some opportunity for more detailed reflection on the festival. In all, 174 questionnaires were returned, with response rates varying between 20 per cent and 44 per cent across the week. Whilst this provided a convincing picture of a loyal audience, enthusiastic about the music and particularly committed to preserving the traditional standards of Gilbert and Sullivan, the opportunity to understand the audience perspective was limited by the decision not to interview them (a drawback which was counteracted by the audience focus of Study 4). This study clearly illustrated the vital role of the audience in contributing to and sustaining regular musical events, receiving in turn a sense of belonging which the performers generally appeared to find elsewhere. Questions were also raised about the relationship between musical genres, behaviours and values, as the nostalgia and tradition of Victorian Englishness found in the Gilbert and Sullivan operettas seemed to be welcomed and preserved by those audience members who felt most comfortable at this festival. Music, performance, location and social interaction were inextricably linked in their responses, and were to show similar connections in the remaining two studies.

Study 3: Participants in a contemporary music summer school

Like the Gilbert and Sullivan enthusiasts at Buxton, the participants in the Contemporary Music-making for Amateurs (COMA) summer school had interests lying slightly outside the musical mainstream, and were tremendously committed to their chosen genre of improvised and recently composed music. COMA brings together amateur performers and composers for a week-long summer school (with weekend and one-day options) at Bretton Hall, a campus of the University of Leeds located within the inspiring landscape of the Yorkshire Sculpture Park. In August 2002, I attended the summer school to carry out fieldwork, interview and questionnaire studies, becoming a participant observer for the one-day course, when I joined in improvisation sessions, attended a 'Composing for Beginners' class and soaked up the atmosphere of this very energetic and intense week of activity. Questionnaires were given to all participants, and replies received from

10 out of 17 (59 per cent) on the weekend summer school, and 26 out of 59 (44 per cent) attending the full week. In addition, twenty participants were asked to keep diaries during the week, in the hope of capturing the day-to-day changes in energy, enthusiasm and evaluation that would seem inevitable in a week of this kind. Fourteen diaries were completed, and proved to be invaluable for the insight they offered on the classes and interactions I had not observed, and the new perspectives on events that I had witnessed but might have understood differently from the participants.

The summer school participants had strong individual motivations, seeking to develop their composing or performing skills, but finding greater enjoyment through pursuing these goals in a group context rather than alone. They were appreciative of their tutors' commitment to the summer school and respectful of the achievement and professional standing held by many of them, but were equally willing to learn from other participants, valuing one another's diverse skills and interests. United by a commitment to contemporary music, these participants had something of the crusading enthusiasm familiar from the Gilbert and Sullivan festival, being similarly keen to share their own musical preferences with young people through education outreach work, and to increase the audiences and performers willing to engage with their music. Unlike the Gilbert and Sullivan audience, who assumed a distinction of quality between the amateur and professional performances available to them in the Buxton festival, the COMA participants were proud of their 'amateur' label, seeing this as a valued part of their group identity.

Mealtimes at the summer school were characterised by lively discussions about the week's music and activities, and diary and questionnaire respondents wrote of the sense of belonging and friendship that they associated with the summer school, second only in importance to the new skills and ideas that would sustain their musical activities through the next year. These were demanding participants, keen to extract full value – in every sense – from their attendance at the summer school, and quick to evaluate their tuition and the contributions of other participants and to challenge these where they were found wanting (cf. Pitts, 2004a). Like the music students in the first study, these performers and composers sought to reinforce their musical identities through continued activity and some measure of recognition, but their sense of conviction in the worth of their activities was arguably stronger than for those students within the educational establishment. Avoiding the competitive, assessment-driven concerns of the music students, COMA participants were motivated by their own commitment to contemporary music and to the importance of finding time for music in their busy lives.

Study 4: Performers and audience at a chamber music festival

For the final study in May 2003 I returned to the concert hall setting, visiting the Crucible Studio Theatre in Sheffield for the Music in the Round chamber music festival, hosted annually by a resident string quartet. Originally a two week festival, now a more manageable eight days, Music in the Round consists of two or more concerts daily with additional social events and lectures, with around half the concerts given by members of the quartet and the remainder by their 'friends', many of whom are regular performers at the festival. Usually themed by country or composer, this year an 'audience choice' programme had been devised to celebrate the twentieth anniversary of the festival, making it an ideal occasion to focus on the opinions and experiences of audience members. A detailed questionnaire was distributed at performances throughout the festival, yielding 347 responses (a 47 per cent return rate), around 20 of which were followed up with interviews. Thirteen audience members kept diaries of their concert attendance, recording their responses to the music, the venue and the social interactions which formed part of their festival experience. Once again I attended all concerts and made fieldwork observations, this time with a research assistant, Karen Burland, who made independent fieldwork notes which were compared with mine after the festival. In the small venue of the Crucible Studio, with many repeat attenders amongst the audience, informal conversations with audience members were plentiful and proved another valuable source of insight.

The timing of this study was fortuitous for another reason; the host string quartet had recently announced their imminent retirement and there was obvious concern amongst the audience that the festival which many had enjoyed since its inception now had an uncertain future. This made some respondents more willing to make suggestions for changes and continuity, whilst perhaps also heightening the sense of celebration and appreciation that was characteristic of the questionnaire responses. Whilst valuing the comfortable familiarity that the informal performing style and regular audience bring to this festival, some respondents were concerned that this was a barrier to growth, recognising that the audience as a whole was ageing, and that the 'cosy' atmosphere might be off-putting to newcomers. Some interesting discussions on the nature of chamber music audiences resulted from this concern, with several interviewees putting forward the suggestion that chamber music is 'for the third age', in other words, something to grow into in later life. Comparisons were also made with church attendance, with a number likening their experience of these concerts to real or imagined membership of a church congregation, with the sense of belonging and spiritual connection that might afford.

Just as the Buxton audience had shown a high level of knowledge and commitment to Gilbert and Sullivan, so attendance at Music in the Round involved for some audience members a level of preparation and concentration that made the week an intense and often tiring experience. Interviewees expressed diverse views on the relationship between live concert attendance and recorded music, with some deliberately collecting recordings of the works they had heard, and others feeling that the live experience would be somehow diluted by hearing the music again at home. Few of the audience were performers, with many expressing regret about this, but those who did play or sing spoke of learning from the performances they had watched, particularly in seeking to emulate the relaxed performing style and spoken introductions they had witnessed at Music in the Round.

Audience members were sometimes cautious in their tastes, avoiding concerts with too many modern or unfamiliar works, and showing a dislike for song recitals and a strong preference for performances by the host string quartet. The accessibility of these performers – who were often to be found mingling with the audience during the interval and after the concert – seemed more important than interactions amongst the audience, which were often limited to people who already knew each other or who were members of the fundraising 'Friends of Music in the Round'. Some interviewees spoke of recognising other audience members for twenty years but never speaking to them, whilst others had made deliberate efforts to hold impromptu post-festival gatherings to allow such acquaintances to flourish. Loyalty to the festival as a whole was clearly present amongst this audience, but most claimed a greater commitment to the music itself, and to the development of their own knowledge and enriching of their listening experiences.

Connections and themes

It will have become apparent from the separate introduction of the four case studies that there are some valuable points of comparison and overlap between them that can help to inform a discussion of musical participation and experience. A wide definition of 'participation' is clearly appropriate, given that the audience members at Buxton and Music in the Round were active and involved in the festivals they attended, and saw them as an important part of their musical lives. The notion of what makes a musician, though, remains open to question (see Chapter 2), as few of the people in these studies felt comfortable in claiming that label for themselves, and definitions seemed to shift according to context.

Musical activity was valued by all participants in these studies for different and interconnected reasons:

- As a potential source of confirmation and confidence (Studies 1, 2 & 3)
- As an opportunity to demonstrate or acquire skills (Studies 1, 2 & 3)
- As a way of preserving and promoting repertoire (Studies 2, 3 & 4)
- As an opportunity to perform with others (Studies 1, 2 & 3)
- As a forum for social interaction and friendships (Studies 2, 3 & 4)
- As a way of enhancing everyday life (Studies 2, 3 & 4)
- As a way of escaping from everyday life (Study 3)
- As a source of spiritual fulfilment and pleasure (Study 4)

Articulating the value of musical participation is a tremendous, perhaps impossible, challenge, since part of its appeal lies in the wordlessness with which it connects participants more deeply with themselves and with other people. Engagement with music is not always positive, however; the students in Study 1 had experienced the destructive frustrations of feeling musically inadequate amongst apparently more skilled peers, and the audience members in Study 4 were conscious of excluding new listeners through the very actions that made regular concert attenders feel welcome. Music plays many complex roles for people who participate in live performance, and this book will uncover and explore some of these, in the hope of articulating more clearly the value of musical participation in education and society.

Referring to participants: codes and terminology

Referencing individual aspects of the empirical data in a way that is transparent without being cumbersome has been a challenge, and some readers will inevitably wish I had chosen an alternative solution. Wanting to assure my participants of the anonymity they were promised, I have given each questionnaire, interview and diary a numerical code, stated in square brackets wherever direct quotes from respondents are used. Pseudonyms might have seemed more personal and elegant, especially in a study focusing on individual experience, but in the large quantities required this approach would quickly have become unwieldy. This solution should allow readers who wish to track the distribution of responses to do so, while those who are more interested in the narrative and discussion can skip across the brackets without being unduly interrupted.

The codes given to each item indicate the study from which the data arise, the research technique that was used – questionnaire [Q], interview [I] or diary [D] – and the participant number, as in these examples:

Study 1:   Undergraduate student questionnaires [UGQ 1–9]
Year 13 A Level student interviews [Y13I 1–11]

Study 2:   Buxton audience questionnaires [BUXQ 1–174]
Interviews with performing group A [BUXI A1–4]
Interviews with individual performers and organisers [BUXI 1–3]

Study 3:   Questionnaires for weekend COMA participants [WEQ 1–10]
Questionnaires for full-week participants [FWQ 1–26]
COMA participant diaries [CMD 1–14]

Study 4:   Audience questionnaires [MitRQ 1–347]
Audience diaries [MitRD 1–13]
Audience interviews [MitRI 1–19]
Follow-up interviews [MitRI 1b etc]

Deciding how to refer to the people in my studies in more general terms also required some thought. Lucy Green (2002) and Ruth Finnegan (1989) both use the term 'musician' unproblematically to describe the participants in their accounts of 'popular musicians' and the 'hidden musicians' of Milton Keynes, respectively. For many of my case study participants, this label had the overtones of a value judgement (see Chapter 2), and so it seemed inappropriate to apply it as a blanket term and so lose the nuances of their usage. Iona Opie's (1993) work offered a pragmatic and attractive solution: researching playground games and activities, she noted that 'children call themselves "people", rather than "children"' (p. 3) and so adopted their terminology throughout her study of 'the people in the playground'.

Participants in my case studies were less consistent in their labelling of one another, but where possible I have noted and reproduced their terms, avoiding the 'musician' title where they did, and using it where they appeared comfortable with its implications. Where clarity in indicating research methods is necessary, I have also used 'questionnaire respondents', 'diarists' and 'interviewees', so offering a reminder that my view will necessarily affect the presentation of theirs (Burr, 1995: 160).

Throughout the book, analysis of the four case studies is integrated under themed discussions, and reference made to relevant literature from a range of academic disciplines. Each chapter considers an aspect of musical participation that emerged as a prominent theme across the case studies, including notions of musical identity and being a 'musician' (Chapter 2), individual motivations for participation (Chapter 3), and the effects of the group context on musical experiences (Chapter 4). Chapter 5 considers the musical values exhibited in participants' behaviour and discourse, such as the impetus to preserve Gilbert and Sullivan for future generations, or to promote contemporary music to a broader public. The audience experience is the focus of Chapter 6, enabling comparisons to be made with the views of performers, so illustrating the extent to which audience members feel themselves to be participant in the musical event. Educational implications and perspectives are discussed in Chapter 7, before more general conclusions are drawn in the final chapter.

This project is concerned with 'valuing musical participation' in both senses: affording recognition to an activity which currently receives limited attention from researchers and policy-makers; and examining the ways in which such activity is valued and understood by its participants. The case study data provide a framework for discussion of musical interests, identities and intentions, in an exploration of musical contexts which have previously been under-researched. Readers familiar with the literature and methods of ethnomusicology will notice some similarities of purpose but differences in approach here, as the relevance of key questions asked in that discipline have informed my project, even while the finite nature of the events under consideration has made lengthy fieldwork impossible (see for example Merriam, 1964; Nettl, 1983; Kaemmer, 1993). The project does not claim to be the first to investigate musical participation, but it joins a limited number of published studies which have focused such an enquiry on Western art music practices (cf. Cottrell, 2002; 2004; Born, 1995). These participants and many others like them have not previously been given a clear voice, despite the relevance of their experiences and opinions to research and practice in education, psychology, sociology and musicology. This book aims to remedy that omission, and to learn from the perspectives on musical behaviour that are offered by those who make a significant but largely unrecognised commitment to such activity in their daily lives.

CHAPTER TWO

Becoming a Musician:
Dilemmas and Definitions

Throughout the empirical investigations which comprise this project, a tension emerged between musical participants' desire to define the term 'musician' inclusively, and their reluctance to apply that definition to themselves. This was most striking in the responses of the school and university students, whose sense of 'self as musician' had been brought into question by the transition from secondary to higher education. Within these educational contexts, the students perceived 'musician' to be a value-laden term and were tentative about their own right to claim such a title. Western education systems must hold some responsibility for this tendency to privilege expertise and employability over engagement and enthusiasm, but recording industries and performance traditions too have established a clear division between 'professional' and 'amateur' performers which makes many active music-makers feel excluded from an inner circle of experts.

> Music is with us all the time, but is made by relatively few, and most of it is not heard as live performance at all. Professional musicians are socially distinct; full-time performing musicians rarely play with rank amateurs. (Chanan, 1994: 24)

The sense of dislocation from live musical performance reported by Chanan was – by definition – largely absent from my case study settings, which were chosen for the potential they held to shed light on the experiences of active participants in musical events. Certainly, there were distinctions made by respondents between amateur and professional status, musician and 'would-be musician' [MitRQ 62], active and retired participant; but all felt connected with the musical events of their choosing, and valued the contribution the events made to their lives.

It is reasonable enough that the word 'musician' was not felt to be adequate in expressing all the facets of musical life reported here, but attempts to define the term and relate it to participants' own experiences were fruitful in exploring the levels of commitment and engagement in evidence across the case studies. The discomfort and insecurity with the term 'musician' that was felt to varying degrees by the majority of respondents suggested a strong effect of context on participants' self-perceptions and levels of musical confidence. Further discussion of these dilemmas and definitions follows, focusing mainly on the school and university students' responses, as presenting the most obvious tensions between self-perception and external recognition.

Self-as-musician: music students in transition

The music students in Study 1 offered the most detailed reflections on what it is to be a musician, often evaluating their own sense of 'being a musician' by considering the extent to which their musical activities had prominence in their lives and by making comparisons with their peer group. Through their interview and questionnaire responses, these twenty students showed varying levels of confidence in their own musical ability, often seeming to aspire to 'musicianly' status, rather than feeling securely located within it.

In making the transition from school to university the students were having to decide whether the musical roles and identities they had forged at school would come with them into the next phase of their lives. For the first year undergraduates looking back across the transition, their final years of school appeared to have been a high point in their musical lives, when they had felt 'special' [UGQ 5] or 'different from other people' [UGQ 9] by virtue of the amount and quality of musical activities in which they had participated:

> Music was extremely important. Lunchtimes were spent rehearsing and there were lots of concerts and musicals to get involved with. I also got the chance to conduct the Y7 choir for a year. [UGQ 4]

> Because not many people studied musical instruments to a high standard at school I felt very advanced. I was therefore expected to participate in every musical concert/ensemble. I got a kind of special attention from my music teachers. [UGQ 5]

This level of involvement had social implications too, as the small number of musically active students in a school were likely to form friendships by virtue of their shared interests and the amount of time spent together:

> It was really nice at our school, because we had like a separate music department, which was away from the rest of the school, and it was like a little school in itself. It had a common room, and all the teachers were really friendly, and we were all friendly with everybody, and all the pupils knew each other because of all the rehearsals and everything. It was a place you could go to at lunchtime and just hang out, just chat to your friends and things. I mean the majority of my best friends at school I actually made through music; it was really great. [UGI 3]

There is evident nostalgia amongst these responses from students who clearly valued the opportunities they had been given at school, even if at times they had felt over-worked or isolated as one of a small number of advanced performers. Most appeared to have been single-minded in their pursuit of musical expertise above their other studies, with one admitting that 'it was the only thing I could really excel in' [UGQ 9]. Only one student had hesitated over her higher education options, before concluding that 'I'd become far too stressed if I did art, because I get really annoyed with it, so I decided I'd do music' [UGI 8]. The decision to study music at university had been almost inevitable for many of these students, and some resented having been written off by the school careers service at that point: 'everybody in my school seemed to see it as if I would just go and sit on a toadstool and play the flute for three years' [UGI 8]. Against this sense of being misunderstood by teachers and other students, the strong communities of school music departments stand out, and give further colour to the memories of being part of a small, committed body of music students.

Students at both levels relished the eccentricity that was judged to be a characteristic of musicians, although one undergraduate was disappointed to find that her peers were 'not quite so bizarre in a lot of ways' [UGI 6] and appeared to feel isolated even within the music department. In one of the few comparable study of university music departments, Brian Roberts (1991) reports that students describe themselves as 'weird, different or otherwise deviant' (p. 45), and uses the word 'insulation' (p. 32) to describe the effects of this self-perception; a word that has more protective and cocooning overtones than 'isolation', but conveys the same sense of distance from outsiders. Making adjustments to the idealised image of a university music department, founded in part on the positive experiences of school musical participation, appears to be one of the greatest challenges of the transition into higher education for music students.

Like the undergraduates, the school music students in the study were unanimous in their mention of highly active musical lives, but were not surprisingly more matter-of-fact about this: still sharing their context and activities with their peer group, they had less need to describe this in colourful detail. However, these Year 13 students were more likely than the undergraduates to mention the emotional expression that they found through playing music, particularly as a release from the pressures of their A Level studies:

> If I've got any worries or anything, or problems, then it's a good way of just escaping from them. I just sing or play or whatever to help me forget about what's happened during the day. [Y13I 1]

> I play the piano quite a lot, it's like my release, if you know what I mean. You can take your stress out on it, if you want to play a bit of Rachmaninov or something, depending on your mood, you can express yourself in things like that, and when you're sat on your own in a little room, it's nice to be able to do that. [Y13I 3]

Music was clearly a part of their lives with which these school students felt strongly connected, and even when they had chosen to pursue other activities beyond school, they were likely to have given some thought to continuing their musical involvement. For most, this meant returning to participate in the county ensembles of which they were currently members, rather than joining university or other groups in their new location. Perceived obstacles to continued involvement included the amount of time students predicted their chosen studies would consume, the physical distance between their own department and the music facilities, and the difficulties of finding new friends with similar interests. It seems that being a 'musician' without being a 'music student' was difficult for the respondents to imagine.

Those Year 13 students who had opted to continue their music studies beyond school conveyed a real excitement at the atmosphere they expected to find in their new environment, often basing this on existing knowledge of departments they had visited:

> It's got an atmosphere – you remember *Fame*, the dancing school? Well it's just like that, it really is, just this atmosphere. It's just musicians, actors and dancers, that's it. And you take part in anything of that sort of nature, and when you've got 500 students that are all like that, it's just fantastic. There's nothing that can describe it, really. I mean when we do the musical here in school, there's a fantastic buzz afterwards, and it's just like that constantly. So I'm really looking forward to going. [Y13I 11]

> I don't know, I suppose it's just the fact that you can't go anywhere without hearing music all the time, and the fact that everyone is just so, so in love with the music and everyone is so talented that it inspires you. I mean I don't really know about universities as much, just music colleges, but they seem to completely submerge you [...] so that you can't escape from it, and that's what I really want. [Y13I 5]

These students – planning to study at the Liverpool Institute for the Performing Arts and at a London music college, respectively – anticipated fitting in well to this atmosphere of intense involvement and commitment, and did not foresee any potential disadvantages, their concerns focusing rather on financial matters and living away from home. It is disappointing then, but perhaps not surprising, to find that the undergraduate respondents, having already made the transition anticipated here by the Year 13s, were feeling much less certain about the pleasures of being amongst a large group of musical peers for the first time:

> I think I consider myself to be less of a musician than I did at school. This is because I am now surrounded by other musicians – I also do not get the chance to play as much with others. [UGQ 4]

> I have realised that there is so much else to know, and so much better I could be (perhaps because there are so many other people around who are far better than me in lots of ways, I've realised I'm not as good as I thought I was. Life experience has shown me that although I thought I was the best at school, that was nothing; I was really a complete nobody!). [UGQ 6]

Starting a music degree had, for these students, turned out to be less of a performance-filled idyll than they might have anticipated. In some cases this could be traced to a specific event – not getting into the orchestra, for example – but for others, the vague sense of university not being quite what they expected had coloured their experiences of the first year. The limited existing research on school-university transition suggests that this is not uncommon (cf. Booth, 1997), but the problems of forging a new role or identity at university seem to be exaggerated for music students, for whom self-doubts about their ability touch not just their academic work but also the performing activities that have been such a significant part of their lives until this point (cf. Pitts, 2002). Henry Kingsbury's (1988) study of musical conservatoires reveals a strong discourse of possessing or lacking 'talent' that makes the problem even more acute for students in that environment, noting that 'for many students, there was a great deal of ambivalence, concern, and social or personal tension relating their musicality to their most elemental sense of self and identity' (Kingsbury, 1988: 3).

The picture from the case study data was not entirely bleak, and some students were enjoying the advantages of being amongst a larger group of similarly skilled performers:

> I've always compared myself with other people, but it is strange, because I was always like the best at school, and now I'm just the same, as it were, which is nice, because I can play like in the flute quartet, and it's nice to be able to play hard things with people, and not to have to practice loads and loads so that other people get up to your standard or whatever, so I do like that aspect. [UGI 2]

> There are so many really talented people here, and from a composing point of view that's great, because all my school compositions were for flute and piano, because it's all I actually had, but here I can compose for what I want and there will be someone around to play it, which is great. [UGI 3]

Both these students had apparently found an outlet for their musical involvement, and were feeling confident in at least this aspect of their departmental activities, whatever insecurities they might have expressed at other points in their interviews. In finding a new role, they had recaptured some of the distinctiveness that had made them feel more certain of themselves as musicians while at school.

This was not a longitudinal study, and so it is impossible to judge whether the students quoted above had started out with more realistic expectations than their peers, or had simply made the adjustment from their busy school lives more effectively. What seems clear, though, is that all of the undergraduates involved in the study had been forced to reappraise their sense of self-as-musician, sometimes in the process questioning their past achievements and self-perceptions. Notions of 'being a musician' had become more complex, as they compared themselves with others who had different but equally advanced skills and interests, or worse, overlapping interests that made their own individual contribution seem less significant. Students attempted to judge their musical strengths more realistically or to define them more specifically; perhaps as a composer, or an academic, who would then have legitimate reason to be 'not the world's best player' [UGI 3]. By refining their strengths and priorities, these students were exploring their hopes and fears for their future musical development, or 'using their possible selves as psychological resources to motivate and defend themselves' (Cross & Markus, 1991: 231). This notion of the 'possible self' is helpful in incorporating individuals' perceptions of their potential futures in their understanding of themselves, as illustrated in this hypothetical description:

> [An] adolescent who has been praised for her musical abilities may develop images of herself as an accomplished pianist, performing in the all-city talent show. Such possible selves become the incentives that fuel long hours at the piano practicing scales, new techniques and chord patterns. With time, she may begin to define herself not just as 'someone who plays the piano', but as a 'musician' or as a 'pianist', and this label will provide a focus and organization for an increasing number of her actions. (Cross & Markus, 1991: 232)

In seeing these 'labels' or self-definitions as motivating forces in a young musician's development, Cross and Markus demonstrate the importance of acquiring a strong self-concept that will sustain the effort necessary to succeed as a musician. The students in my sample generally saw 'being a musician' as something to aspire to, rather than something they already were, although most partially accepted the label for themselves, albeit with doubts and provisos. Becoming a musician still seemed to be a 'possible self' (Markus & Nurius, 1986) for them, in ways that it had ceased to be for the school students who had selected other career and study options. However, evidence from Maria Manturzewska's (1990) biographical study of professional musicians in Poland provides a dispiriting context for these students' self-appraisals: she suggests that an uncertain sense of being a musician during this period of 'formation and development of the artistic personality' is a poor foundation for future performing success (p. 134).

Defining 'musicians'

School and university music students alike were asking questions of themselves in relation to their musical identities and, in this study, were being asked to consider more deliberately whether this made them 'a musician', and how they would define that term for themselves and others. Definitions from the Year 13 students fell into the categories shown in Table 2.1:

Table 2.1 Year 13 students' definitions of a musician

	Sample responses
Attitude	[Y13I 2] You've got to be dedicated as well, and to want to do it, not like some people who have to do it or are made to do it. [Y13I 3] It's not just whether you're a brilliant performer or something like that, it's your general attitude towards music and how involved you are in musical things.
Quantity of activity	[Y13Q 4] Played a lot, knows a lot, has taught, music is their life. [Y13I 5] I think the amount you're immersed in the activity is more important than the standard you do it to. [...] I mean it's got to be good, obviously, but it's more to do with your commitment to the music.
Type of activity	[Y13I 2] Well you could compose or play or anything really, as long as it's based around music. [...] Not just listening; you've got to be able to play something on an instrument, to a certain standard. [Y13Q 8] Playing, conducting – or a performer who makes money out of performing.

Advanced skills – listening	[Y13I 1] Performing's an important part of me being a musician, but I think that people could be a musician if they listened to music and understood it, could analyse it properly. [Y13I 3] I mean listening to a CD at home, I wouldn't say necessarily made you a musician, because everybody does that, but if you listened to a piece, and then went to see it in a concert, and read up about it and all that, then you'd be genuinely interested in it. I think that's part of being a musician, but not necessarily completely being a musician.

Table 2.2 Undergraduates' definitions of a musician

	Sample responses
Status/context	[UGI 3] I mean really just because I'm studying music at university, I think that makes me a musician. [UGI 6] There's a difference between studying music and being a musician. Generally people define a musician as someone who plays for a living, so you don't define a music teacher as a musician, really, you define them as a music teacher. [UGI 7] I think of it more as a career – musician as a career.
Emotional engagement	[UGQ 2] I think that if people can have individual reactions to music, they can be considered to be a musician. We all have an element of 'musician-ness' in us! [UGQ 4] Someone who understands or feels the music they are playing i.e. playing accurately is not enough. [UGQ 8] A talent for feeling and expressing music. An understanding (as far as possible) of music.
Specific skills/ activities	[UGQ 1] Being able to read music. Being able to play an instrument. Having a sense of musicality. [UGI 3] I think you have to have a certain amount of expertise, if you want, in music, whether you're a performer, a composer – I think it refers more to the practical, rather than the academic element, so I don't know really. It's a difficult word. [UGQ 6] The ability to play (quite well usually) and understand music, and be able to say why something is the way it is; why a composer has put a dynamic marking in a certain place; to be able to know why it is there, what it means and how to go about producing what the composer wants. [UGQ 9] To be 'a musician' I think is not just about being able to play an instrument, but playing in groups and performing.

Comparison of the school students' (Table 2.1) and undergraduates' views (Table 2.2) reveals a connection between the respondents' own circumstances and the values they prioritise in their definitions. For the school students, quantity of activity was more important than quality, and they placed great emphasis on attitude, seeing motivation and enthusiasm as vital qualities. The undergraduates were more precise in their call for emotional depth as performers, perhaps beginning to recognise that technical skill is not an end in itself, and so becoming less tolerant than the school students of aspiring instrumentalists.

Although the general assumption amongst the undergraduates was that practical skill was essential to being a musician, the definitions that sought to include knowledgeable listeners were thoughtful, showing recognition of the fact that 'there are a lot of people who know a lot more about the music I'm playing than I do myself' [UGI 5]. One student was particularly keen to include her father in her definition, and so by implication the many other active and intelligent listeners who have not had opportunities to learn instruments:

> When you're a kid you just say, oh 'someone plays an instrument – they're a musician', don't you? But like my dad, he doesn't play any instruments or anything, but his dad was very musical, and like he can pick up songs easily and things, and sing them or whatever, and he doesn't consider himself a musician at all, but I think he is, because he's definitely musical, you know. I think it's unfair to say, oh if you're a composer or something, then you're a musician, and I think there's definitely more to it. [UGI 2]

There are some elements of contradiction and confusion amongst the students' definitions, perhaps reflecting the unsettled nature of their own self-concepts as musicians. Evidently all are committed, experienced and skilled individuals who value their music-making, but seek some reassurance about whether they have really 'made it'. Entering a music department seemed to have revealed to some the many obstacles between their current status and professional success, replacing their view of the eccentric, driven musician with something more serious and unattainable, consistent with Bruno Nettl's (1995) ethnographic study of American departments of music:

> Contrary to the popular image of musicians as people who care little for the conventions of society, live only for art, or are rebels who symbolize this role with sloppy dress and long hair, musicians in academia more frequently stress the importance of social categories as indicators of status and of stages in an order of events. (Nettl, 1995: 49)

Nettl's work as an ethnomusicologist offers a reminder that the definitions explored by the students are culturally specific, strongly affected by a hierarchical notion of musical competence that is largely absent in other cultures (cf. Nettl, 1989). It has become almost a cliché to note the peculiarities of Western attitudes to music-making, but the summary below presents a range of examples from around the world to illustrate the continuum of musical accessibility:

> In some cultures, such as the Venda and Flathead, music learning is widespread; virtually everyone learns to sing or play or even compose as an integral part of social behaviour. In other cultures, the status of musician is ascribed to certain families (as for example, in North India), or, as in the West, is the rare achievement of only the most talented individuals. (Rice, 1994: 42)

Locked within this Western system, some of the case study participants appeared to have found that taking A Level music or starting a music degree had given them the confidence that they needed; for others, their doubts and insecurities seemed set to continue for a good while yet.

The myth of the 'non-musician'

Attempting to assign clear parameters to a category such as 'musician' demands that some people be placed outside those boundaries, implicitly classified as 'non-musicians'. This term has in the past been used quite freely in educational and psychological literature, and the notion of labelling children as 'unmusical' has only recently been closely questioned. Tales of 'growlers' being told to mime at the back of school choirs might seem to belong to an earlier age of music education, but while working as a schools inspector in the 1990s Janet Mills witnessed children being separated into 'choir' and 'non-choir' (Mills, 1996), showing that the blunt judgement of musical potential is not as anachronistic as one might hope.

The prevailing educational philosophy in today's music classrooms is that all children should have the opportunity to experience, create and enjoy music, whatever their level of ability, and the expansion of the curriculum to include a wide variety of musical genres and activities has played an important part in making that possible (see Pitts, 2000a for a historical review of twentieth century ideas on music education). Authentic and engaging musical experiences do not conform well to the demands of assessment and accountability that typify the current educational climate – and nor should they, even if the sense of being a curriculum misfit is a continuing frustration for those involved in music teaching and learning. The intention that all children should become musical participants is worth defending, particularly against the charge that music is an elite subject that should not claim curriculum time and resources. Schools may not be able to turn all children into 'musicians', in the senses discussed above, but they have a responsibility to ensure that children are not made to feel that they are 'non-musicians': 'thinking of oneself as a musician can be an important step on the road to becoming one' (Hargreaves & Marshall, 2003: 272).

Evidence of the limited extent to which the majority of young people are encouraged to think of themselves as musicians comes in recent research reports suggesting that music is the most unpopular curriculum subject for secondary school students (ages 11-18). In two projects for the National Foundation for Educational Research (NFER), John Harland, Kay Kinder and Kate Hartley (1995) report ambivalent attitudes to the arts amongst school-leavers recalling their educational experiences, and Harland *et al.* (2000) found music to be 'the most problematic and vulnerable artform' (p. 568) in their survey of over 2000 secondary school students. Both these studies take 'arts education' as their focus, possibly disadvantaging music through the stronger association with visual arts that this term might have for school students. However, theoretical perspectives on the problems of school music support the findings of the NFER studies: Malcolm Ross (1995) has questioned whether music can in fact be taught, especially by a teaching population of 'disillusioned classical musicians' (p. 189), and John Sloboda (2001) has suggested that 'classroom music, as currently conceptualised and organised, is an inappropriate vehicle for mass music education in 21st-century Britain' (p. 252).

Debate about the purpose of music in education is of course a vital part of the discipline's development, but the relentless negativity of its portrayal risks obscuring the life-changing individual experiences that also occur in the music classroom (cf. Finney & Tymoczko, 2003). It is encouraging, then, that a study by Alexandra Lamont *et al.* (2003) presents a more hopeful picture, with children showing an open-minded attitude to musical involvement: 'those pupils who were committed to music demonstrated a relatively firm commitment, many of those not actively involved in music seemed interested in pursuing this at some later stage, and very few pupils ruled themselves out of any lasting involvement' (Lamont *et al.*, 2003: 239). The fragile relationships with music education indicated there make it all the more important that young people are made to feel that they have musical potential, even where they may not yet have acquired extensive skills or experience. Whilst the term 'non-musicians' may be a useful short-hand for children not learning instruments or taking post-compulsory classes in music (cf. Lamont, 2002), such blunt terminology is symptomatic of the hierarchical way in which musical involvement and achievement is classified, and points to a 'gulf in meaning' (O'Neill, 2002) between the definitions used by researchers and the complex self-perceptions of young people. That some children show a greater aptitude for music or achieve higher levels of musical skill is undeniable, but the many factors that contribute to this – family support, financial investment in lessons, hours of practice, selection of music over other activities – suggest that amongst the musically inactive members of any class there will be many who *could* participate in music, and may choose to do so outside school or at a later stage in life. Music educators are beginning to recognise that schools do not have a monopoly on encouraging musical development: Lucy Green's (2002) account of popular musicians learning by listening to recordings and practising with peers is a useful reminder of the fact that there are many routes to musical competence.

Amateurs, professionals and audiences

Outside the educational contexts discussed so far, one way in which performers can lay claim to the 'musician' label without feeling unduly immodest is to prefix it with 'amateur' – or more often, 'only an amateur' (cf. Bell, 2002; Peggie, 2002). This term can have a pejorative nuance in English usage: badly organised events are 'amateurish', as are botched DIY jobs and unsuccessful sports teams, and so amateur music-making 'evokes dabbling, the cultivation of a pastime, shambolic goings-on in village halls' (Everitt, 1997: 38). The founder and director of Contemporary Music-making for Amateurs (COMA), admitted in interview to having some initial doubts about including 'amateur' in the organisation's name, but had come to feel increasingly comfortable with its implications:

It's not being used in the sense of 'You're an amateur now and next you will become a professional', it's an attitude of mind, an approach, rather than a division ... A number of professionals come and join our concerts because they just want to, they don't need to but they just want to be with us, so they're an amateur in that context. It's for the love of it, for all abilities. [COMAI 1]

The COMA website (www.coma.org) defines amateur for their purposes as 'anyone who is interested in participating in the creation of new music', and describes how the organisation welcomes music written for flexible instrumentation encompassing a range of abilities and notational literacy. COMA management and participants value the connections with established composers that their commissioning of new works entails, reinforcing a relationship of mutual dependence between amateurs and professionals that has a long history in British music-making:

> In the kingdom of music the amateur is an indispensable part of the constitution: without him *[sic]* the professional could not continue to exist. ... As a composer he is sometimes a nuisance. As a performer (unless he is self-taught) he provides the professional with some of his income, and as a listener with the rest. (Shera, 1939: vii)

Shera's view is of its time in assuming that superiority of musical skill and taste lies with the professional, but he recognises nonetheless the power that the amateur holds to shape the wider musical life of society. A survey of English cultural life in the 1940s asserted that amateurs were central to music-making in a way unparalleled in the other arts, since 'the most important aspect of amateur music-making is that it gives the individual so much pleasure and is a key to appreciation' (Political & Economic Planning, 1949: 98). Responses from the Music in the Round audience, discussed in Chapter 6, will illustrate this close relationship between listening to professional performers and engaging with music as an amateur instrumentalist or singer. This is something that, Lucy Green suggests, needs encouraging in contemporary society, where 'most people are involved as consumers and fans, alienated from the majority of music-making activities, and operating instead as spectators on the sidelines of a game in which, if circumstances were different, many more could play a part' (Green, 2002: 3).

Negotiating the amateur/professional divide

Robert Stebbins has spent several decades researching the musical experiences of amateur performers, and it is no wonder that he is careful with his definitions, refuting the traditional distinction between the amateur 'hobbyist' and the professional who earns a living from making music and stating instead that 'the essence of amateurism lies in the social and attitudinal organization of its practitioners' (Stebbins, 1976: 54). Stebbins illustrates these attitudes through his study of barbershop singers, who are 'committed to a deeply fulfilling serious leisure activity in an era when most people are committed only to the comparatively superficial pursuit of pure fun' (1996: 86). The term 'serious leisure', widely accepted by sociologists, requires the clarification that 'the adjective "serious" embodies such qualities as earnestness, sincerity, importance, and carefulness, rather than gravity, solemnity, joylessness, distress and anxiety' (Stebbins, 1992: 8). However, the double-edged qualities of 'serious leisure' were acknowledged by the participants in my case studies, who recognised the additional stress that their activities bring to their lives, while at the same time valuing the depth of engagement this affords:

> In our case, you're working seven days a week for yourself, so it's a form of enforced relaxation; it's something totally different from what you do in your normal life, so it's a form of relaxation although it is hard work. [BUXI 1]

To be an amateur, then, is certainly not to be only partially committed; participants in the case studies were usually juggling family, work and other pressures in order to make time for what could be considered an 'essential luxury' – extravagant in its demands, but vital to their well-being and enjoyment of life.

Just as 'musicians' are partly defined by comparison with 'non-musicians', so 'amateurs' are set alongside 'professionals' to draw distinctions of attitude, extent of activity, and sometimes quality. The audiences amongst the case studies were the most likely to be impressed by the names and reputations of those who earn their living from music, and to expect different standards and approaches from amateur and professional performances. These distinctions were most striking at the Buxton Gilbert and Sullivan Festival, where the separation of professionals and amateurs was built into the programme, as the weekends were reserved for shows given by 'the Festival's own, fully professional, Gilbert and Sullivan Opera Company' (Festival brochure, 2001). Former professionals were also prominent in the festival, as members of the D'Oyly Carte Opera – once the leading professional company for Gilbert and Sullivan performance – gave masterclasses, lectures and conversations as part of the Festival Fringe. Members of the audience valued these opportunities to hear experienced performers speak, perhaps celebrating also the connection with the original D'Oyly Carte company, for whom Gilbert and Sullivan's operettas were written in the 1880s–90s. Reasons for attending these Fringe events were sought through the audience questionnaire and included the following:

> I admire the people being interviewed. [BUXQ 9]

> Brings back memories meeting the old pros. [BUXQ 30]

> The heart of how G&S should be done by those who know it best. [BUXQ 121]

> I have admired John Reed from childhood and this was a marvellous opportunity to hear him talk about his life and career. [BUXQ 155]

The choice between amateur and professional shows was a small but notable factor in ticket purchasing for audience members: 19 out of the 174 respondents specified their preference for professional performances, with a further 24 saying that they selected their shows by 'company reputation', without stating whether this included professional status. Only one mentioned being 'interested in non-professional interpretation and enthusiasm' [BUXQ 59], but since the festival as a whole celebrates those qualities, it seems likely that this was a more widespread attitude. There appeared to be a healthy appreciation of the assumed differences between amateur and professional performances among the audience, with professional shows accorded more automatic respect, and amateur companies able to build their reputation through past successes and perceived quality.

Charles Rosen is amongst those professional performers who has noted the unreliability of this assumption that past successes will guarantee future quality:

> A pianist should be characterised by his *[sic]* finest work: a pianist who on rare occasions gives a masterly performance but plays like a pig most of the time is still a great pianist. From a purely practical point of view, of course, it is worth knowing if the pianist is generally masterly or only from time to time: that helps one to decide whether to risk buying a ticket. Nevertheless, the occasional great performance seems to me worth incomparably more than a steady assurance of efficient adequacy. (Rosen, 2002: 103)

The confidence that comes with status is evident here: a professional who gives a poor performance will emerge with his or her reputation dented but not destroyed, but an amateur in the same position might find it harder to recover and return to the stage. Perhaps this is why the amateur performers at Buxton were so conscious of the need to support one another, valuing the backstage atmosphere associated with pre-show nerves:

> There's a great buzz also about the backstage part of a performance. I mean people will genuinely go around wishing each other well. People that probably haven't spoken for months will come over and say 'have a good one', you know. I think it's a nervous thing, partly. [BUXI A1]

The experiences of belonging to a performing society will be discussed at greater length in Chapters 3 and 4, but the point to be made here is that amateur performance is perceived by audience and performers alike to be a different type of experience from that of professionals, who are set apart by their greater confidence, whether imagined or assumed. The *process* of performing is itself an achievement for those who consider themselves to be amateurs, whereas professionals are judged solely on their *product*, and expected to have the process firmly under control. Audience members may assume a difference in quality as a result of this distinction, and indeed this may be the case on some occasions, but it is not the defining difference, which is rather one of intention and attitude.

Professionals and amateurs alike seem to be valued most when they emulate one another: amateurs when they give a performance of exceptional quality, and professionals when they reveal an accessible and modest off-stage persona. Instances of both kinds of behaviour were evident at Buxton, COMA and Music in the Round, but most notably in the latter case, where there was a deliberate fostering of connections between performers and audience. Players emerged from the backstage area before and after the performance, and willingly engaged in conversation during the interval, a practice valued by audience members as contributing to the informal atmosphere of the concert series. While only 18 per cent of the audience questionnaire respondents cited 'knowing the performers' as a principal reason for attending concerts, nearly all referred to the host string quartet in first-name terms, and in interview spoke of enjoying the 'unstuffiness' of their stage manner:

> They're so exciting to listen to, you're kind of almost holding your breath, you know, and you feel so literally close to them […] you know, you're hearing it all, just perfectly communicated, but in that completely unstuffy way. They're so casual and relaxed about it, they almost take it for granted, don't they? You know, they sit there in their T-shirts; I love the informality of it, the fact that there's that jokey atmosphere as well. [MitRI 10]

This blurring of the amateur/professional divide was reciprocated in the audience attitude towards the performers: recognised as 'loving' their music-making, they were forgiven the occasional scratchy performance, and shown understanding for their evident tiredness towards the end of the festival.

Audience members who had been attending Music in the Round since its inception twenty years ago had seen the host string quartet age personally as well as flourish musically, and one interviewee confessed rather gleefully to enjoying the 'soap opera element' [MitRI 3] that this brought to regular attendance. Reference was made to some of this personal history within the Festival itself; in the spoken introduction to one concert, the leader of the quartet recalled how his heart attack had led to the partial cancelling of one Festival, and received an audible murmur of sympathy from the audience, many of whom will have shared in the anxiety of that episode. In our 'age of celebrity' there is perhaps a certain guilty pleasure in being on illness-recalling levels of intimacy with performers who have an international reputation. Of course, these exchanges take place on the performers' terms: a visiting artist at the Festival might choose not to speak before playing, and would be unaware of the disapproval this would be likely to generate. And the woman who called out from the audience at the last night concert to request the removal of some helium balloons from the stage won herself few friends through this breach of protocol:

> I wish the balloons had been kept – they were part of the fun of Schubert's Octet. Some people get over-serious! Great music relaxes as well! [MitRD 6]

'Informality' and 'intimacy' – words that recurred frequently in audience descriptions of Music in the Round – were clearly welcomed in this setting for the sense of proximity they brought between audience and performers. The audience may have felt themselves to be predominantly 'non-musicians', but they appreciated the closeness to the music-making process that was part of regular attendance at this festival. In this, they showed themselves to be musically active, musically informed, and musically alive. It is a pity that there is a lack of vocabulary to value these qualities, since it makes them cumbersome to talk about and therefore easy to overlook.

Theoretical perspectives on musical participation

Musical participation has been relatively neglected in the research literature until now, perhaps because it falls between established academic boundaries. Musicology has been slow to recognise the importance of connecting the musical text with an awareness of its cultural uses, although developments in recent years have seen a much greater blurring of these artificial distinctions (e.g. A. Williams, 2001). Studies of musical behaviour in Western society have more often come from within the disciplines of sociology and psychology, such that musical activity (usually listening) is seen as one aspect of human behaviour that sheds light on how individuals and societies function. Throughout this study, literature from each of these perspectives has been considered, an approach which brings its own demands since similar concepts and events are interpreted differently within the various research traditions.

The need to consider the performing act 'itself' needs first to be established, challenging musicology's traditional focus on the written text rather than its manifestations (Cook, 2003: 204), which renders the cultural, social and contextual questions of associated disciplines meaningless and unnecessary. This isolationist position is becoming increasingly antiquated in musicology which, in Rob Wegman's characterisation, at times appears to have 'been exposed as a fruitless pathological delusion' (Wegman, 2003: 140). Discussions of performing (e.g. Dunsby, 1995; Rink, 2002) have broadened in scope, but still place only limited emphasis on the motivations and experiences of musical participation for performers or audience members. Writers in ethnomusicology and popular music studies have shown much greater interest in the social worlds within which music is created and consumed; 'ethnomusicologists pride themselves on tracing the social situation of which musical performance is part' (Stock, 2003: 136). But research into 'classical' genres remains haunted by the historical belief that performances of a work are somehow less important than the written text they recreate, a view fuelled by anxiety over the 'apparent devaluation' (Johnson, 2002: 3) of this music within contemporary society.

These historical limitations in ways of thinking about music make it all the more necessary to bring the tools of more socially investigative disciplines to bear upon musical behaviour. Research in the psychology of music over the past few decades has offered one such route to broadening understanding of musical activities, although until very recently there has been greater focus on the cognition and processing of musical sound than on the social psychology of musical use and engagement. Similarly, in sociology of the arts, interest in musical behaviour is relatively new (e.g. DeNora, 2000), and has so far concentrated predominantly on music listening. The need for more deliberately interdisciplinary research is obvious, but Eric Clarke notes the problems of communication that can occur when such crossovers of interests are attempted:

> All too often the trade-off between broad explanatory power and local specificity leads research in the psychology of music to seem blandly obvious and lacking in bite to musicologists, while psychologists point to the apparently arbitrary particularity of

musicological research, its speculative and discursive character, and raise the inevitable questions about empirical support and 'evidence'. (Clarke, 2003: 115)

Researchers aiming to bridge these conceptual and methodological divides risk multiplying the problems of their 'own' discipline by contact with the challenges of another; but the risk is worth taking in the interests of broadening ideas about multi-faceted behaviour such as musical participation. Whilst academic life is structured into 'tribes and territories' (Becher & Trowler, 1989/2001) that at times seem immovable, the study of real world events must overcome such divisions in order to reflect more accurately the behaviours under investigation.

The problems of interdisciplinary research are countered by its opportunities, not least the possibility of forging links between previously separate ways of understanding a particular event or idea. For this project, ideas from research areas as diverse as lifespan development, sociology of leisure, and theories of identity proved to be helpful in establishing a context for thinking about musical participation. These are introduced in the sections that follow, and some initial connections with the case study data are presented here and developed further throughout the book.

Making musical choices: leisure use and personal development

Developing a commitment to musical participation is self-evidently related to opportunity and motivation, both of which vary throughout the lifespan. These factors are recognised in research on musical development (see Hargreaves, 1986 for a review of literature), but this has tended to focus on the rapidly changing but relatively predictable experiences of childhood and early adolescence, rather than the more idiosyncratic development of older adults (e.g. Swanwick & Tillman, 1986; Swanwick, 2001). Evidence of the continued desire to sustain and develop musical skills was clear amongst the case study participants, as they sought new challenges and outlets for their existing interests. This is consistent with recent research on lifespan development, which has begun to question the established view that there are pre-determined transitional stages through which all individuals must pass (cf. Erikson, 1959), and to recognise instead 'a series of continuous changes that occur across the lifespan' (Hendry & Kloep, 2002: 32). Leo Hendry and Marion Kloep emphasise the role of leisure use in managing these life changes, and cite learning to play the piano as an example of a 'self-instigated shift' where the 'individual is not ... a passive victim of change', but deliberately seeks to move his or her life in a particular direction (p. 43).

This study was not deliberately designed to cover the lifespan, but the typical profile of participants in each of the activities meant that this was an incidental effect: Study 1 investigated the transition from school to university; Studies 2 and 3 included more participants in midlife; and the audiences in Studies 3 and 4 were generally older, often in retirement. Their attitudes towards their musical involvement were broadly consistent with theories of lifespan change, being shaped in part by the competing demands of work and family, and fulfilling different needs according to the context in which participants currently found themselves (cf. McIlveen & Gross, 1999). The choices that can be made by any individual are of course affected by their circumstances, and it must be emphasised in all discussion of 'need fulfilment' that participants in musical societies are amongst those fortunate enough to have 'the resources and the will to try out new and atypical things' (Hendry & Kloep, 2002: 113).

Participation in music is often described by those involved as being compulsive or necessary; this despite its position at the top of Abraham Maslow's (1968) 'hierarchy of needs', whereby physiological and safety needs must be securely established before the 'self-actualisation' of musical engagement can take place (cf. Kemp, 1996: 27; and Paynter, 1997). Performers and listeners alike among the case study participants seemed to feel a compulsion to engage in their chosen activity, such that it might seem trivial to classify their involvement as 'leisure' – indeed, they very rarely did so. However, this classification need not belittle their activities, and can offer help in interpreting them:

> There are some individuals for whom leisure is a central life interest. They design their lives around leisure investments rather than shape their leisure to complement family or work roles. They may be in the minority in contemporary societies, but they do represent a possibility that reveals something of the potential of leisure in adult human development. (Kelly, 1983: 105)

Mihalyi Csikszentmihalyi (1990) speaks out against the 'waste of free time' that leads people to spend hours in 'vicarious participation', watching sports and drama events instead of engaging in them: 'we do not run risks acting on our beliefs, but occupy hours each day watching actors who pretend to have adventures, engaged in mock-meaningful action' (p. 162). Participants in musical societies and regular attenders at concerts are surely among those who have escaped this apparent pitfall of contemporary life, answering Michael Argyle's (1996a) call for a 'leisure ethic to replace the work ethic' and recognising that 'it is leisure which can give life meaning and purpose, and give individuals a sense of identity and fulfilment' (Argyle, 1996a: 280). My case study participants spoke repeatedly of the significant contribution that their musical activities made to their lives, and the chapters that follow will illustrate their experiences with further reference to the literature on leisure and development.

Interpreting musical choices: identity and self-concept

An alternative theoretical framework for musical participation can be sought by looking less at the opportunities and motivations for involvement, and more at the effects and self-perception which are its consequence. Psychological theories are helpful in considering, for example, the way in which participants' sense of 'self as musician' appears to be shaped by current activity and priorities, by comparisons with others, and by the context in which these comparisons take place. These findings are consistent with theories of identity, particularly those which emphasise the transitory and socially-constructed nature of the sense of self. Vivienne Burr, for example, points to the importance of a life narrative in constructing the illusion of consistency and continuity in our notion of 'personality', suggesting that 'we create rather than discover ourselves and other people' (1995: 28). Kathryn Woodward, similarly, holds that 'we are differently positioned by ... social expectations and constraints and we represent ourselves to others differently in each context' (1997: 22). The membership of a performing society or a festival audience therefore contributes to the development of participants' identities, providing a particular context where their behaviour and social relations may flourish in ways that are distinctive from other aspects of their lives.

By encouraging self-discovery (as will be discussed in Chapter 3), musical participation may have an effect on other life areas, since 'self-knowledge is associated with adjustment and self-confidence' (Baumgardner, 1990: 1062). Performers at Buxton and COMA spoke of this sense of expanding their roles and behaviours, a factor in musical participation which François Matarasso (1997) has noted as both an opportunity and a danger. The university music students in Study 1 were still resolving the increasing self-awareness engendered by their new peer group, struggling with 'the preservation of ... uniqueness in the context of so many similarities to other people and shifting patterns of relations with them' (Harré, 1998: 2). Kennon Sheldon and Ann Bettencourt address that dilemma in their account of 'optimal distinctiveness theory', which explains the human compulsion to feel assimilated into a group whilst retaining a sense of distinctiveness (2002: 26), a balance which the undergraduates were finding problematic after its easy resolution in the school context. The theory of 'possible selves' already discussed alongside the students' views suggests that their partially formed view of themselves as musicians will be 'particularly sensitive to those situations that communicate new or inconsistent information about the self' (Markus & Nurius, 1986: 956; see also Markus & Ruvolo, 1989). A level of personal confidence is necessary to claim a 'musical identity', and its social reinforcement is also important, as peer and group recognition bolster the sense of self-affirmation.

Ruth Finnegan, whose study of musicians in Milton Keynes (1989) was pioneering in its recognition of the extent and variety of musical participation, notes the potential for research with musical societies as 'arenas in which people develop their sense of identity' (1997: 137):

> Not only is there the investment of the self undoubtedly involved for those people who choose to commit so much of their time, energy and creative abilities to their music-making. There is also the opportunity for identification with specific named groups, offering yet another vehicle for a sense of personal expression and control. (Finnegan, 1997: 137)

Currently, the only book to address questions of musical identity directly is an edited volume, *Musical Identities* (MacDonald, Hargreaves & Miell, 2002), which in its variety of focuses and approaches reveals many of the confusions surrounding this topic. Identity is a contested term, variously signifying self-concept and social belonging; and in music, used in discussions of musical behaviour, preference, and self-perception. Discourse in the popular music literature, for example, tends to focus on people's identification with a particular genre, using 'identity' to mean the sense of collective engagement that is experienced through the display of shared musical preferences (e.g. Bennett, 2000; Frith, 1996). For young people, in particular, 'music preferences give the adolescent information about others and knowledge of popular music can be used as a coin of exchange in peer interactions' (Roe, 1987: 224; see also North & Hargreaves, 1999). However, Christina Williams (2001) raises doubts about this well-established view of young people's engagement with popular music: teenagers in her study 'articulated the significance of popular music in their lives in terms of its usefulness within the context of their daily routines, rather than as a meaningful source for identity investment' (p. 223). Williams' sample was small and not reliably generalisable, but nevertheless offers a useful reminder that even behaviour judged to be typical is open to individual variation, and that these personal stories lie at the heart of what it means to participate in music.

Discussions of music in society also tend to emphasise the power of music to increase collective identity and foster social cohesion (e.g. Leyshon, Matless & Revill, 1998; Born & Hesmondhalgh, 2000). Dave Haslam (1999) illustrates this through his portrayal of musical life in Manchester, and Sara Cohen's account of the Jewish community in Liverpool concludes that 'the consumption and production of music ... draws people together and symbolizes their sense of collectivity and place' (Cohen, 1998: 273). However, Keith Negus and Patria Román Velázquez (2002) caution against the assumption that music automatically generates this sense of belonging, since it is equally capable of building 'sonic walls and bridges' (p. 142). The relationship between music and social identity is still open to question, and researchers perhaps need to consider 'thicker and more nuanced, less reductionist, less determinist notions of how music may connect with, become part of, or be totally irrelevant to our sense of self and collectivity' (Negus & Román Velázquez, 2002: 134).

The difficulties of theorising about musical identity reflect reality to a certain extent, in that clear definitions of what it means to hold a musical self-concept, to be a musician, are confused in the minds of many participants. Sophia Borthwick and Jane Davidson (2002) illustrate the mixed messages that many young instrumentalists receive from their parents, who might provide encouragement for music learning and practice during the school years, but then withdraw this support when the child considers music as a career, preferring instead to afford music the status of a pleasurable hobby for adult life (p. 66). Similarly, several existing studies support the experiences of the music students in my case study, whose general confidence and sense of purpose was closely tied to their musical success, and so easily damaged by insecurities about their performance (cf. Dews & Williams, 1989; O'Neill & Sloboda, 1997; O'Neill, 2002). For students and others feeling doubtful about their musical identity, it seems that continuity is vital in reinforcing the self-concept: past glories are just that – memories that make a limited contribution to an ongoing sense of 'being a musician'.

The case studies explored in this book revisit many of the complexities of musical self-perception and engagement revealed through this brief outline of theoretical perspectives. The aim here is not to construct a new theory of musical participation, but rather to reflect the reality of everyday engagement for this sample of participants, so documenting a facet of musical life that has received comparatively little research attention until now. Consideration of the individual and group experiences of performing (Chapters 3 and 4) will be followed by discussion of the musical interests and loyalties demonstrated by performers and audience members, with comparisons drawn across the case studies where appropriate.

CHAPTER THREE

Music and Individual Experience: Learning, Self-Discovery and Development

Participation in musical activities has the potential to satisfy individual motivations and goals, with new aspects of learning and self-discovery enriching the lives of participants in a variety of ways. Performing on stage, composing an original piece of music, or acquiring new knowledge of repertoire all offer sources of individual satisfaction, as participants identify and meet challenges that allow them to feel musically and personally fulfilled. Much of this individual development takes place within a group context, and belonging to a performing society or a regular audience provides support and encouragement for participants, as friendship and solidarity are generated through shared enthusiasms and a sense of common purpose.

Individual and group experiences of musical participation are closely intertwined, not just in the obvious senses of practical necessity – such as an aspiring singer needing the rest of the cast in order to get her opportunity to appear on stage – but also for the sense of collegiality and validation which a network of similarly motivated people offer to one another. In discussion with case study performers, personal and social motivations were variously highlighted according to context: COMA participants, for example, focused mainly on the development of their individual skills, whilst the Gilbert and Sullivan performers gave greater emphasis to the pleasure of belonging to a performing society. Personal development and social interaction are closely connected in musical experience: participants do not make choices between these two aspects, but rather seek a balance which allows them to satisfy their personal motivations and musical needs. Figure 3.1 illustrates how this search for balance applies to many aspects of musical participation:

Figure 3.1 Balancing individual and group experience in musical participation

Individual experience		*Group experience*
Personal goals		Social goals
Musical aspirations		Musical achievements
Escape from everyday responsibility		Acceptance of corporate responsibility
Self-discovery and development		Group coherence and development
Individual satisfaction		Friendship and support

These elements of participation rarely act in direct opposition, but rather present a continuum of musical experience, within which participants will be differently located according to their current needs and context. The process of preparing for a public performance might see participants moving along this continuum, encompassing initial social motivations to be involved in a group event, with perhaps a mid-point anxiety about their individual ability to meet the challenges of their role, before a return to a shared sense of group responsibility and satisfaction in the final event.

Although separating the personal and social experiences of music-making is a somewhat artificial device, to ensure thorough coverage this chapter and the next address each in turn, and should be seen as complementary in their analysis of these two sides of an interconnected whole. The focus in this chapter is on the individual motivations and experiences of participants, covering the ideas on the left-hand side of Figure 3.1 primarily through accounts of the COMA participants, who had a strong interest in self-development and learning, and used the summer school as a source of sustenance for their independent musical activities during the rest of the year. In the next chapter, greater emphasis is placed on the group experiences listed on the right-hand side of the figure, and performers at the Gilbert and Sullivan Festival provide insight on the pleasures of rehearsing and performing together. In both chapters, as throughout the book, opportunities for comparison between the case studies are taken, in order to illustrate the richness and complexity of musical experience.

Musical struggle and satisfaction

Despite the close connections between the individual and group facets of music-making, their deliberate separation can occur: independent practice is, for classically trained musicians, an accepted part of learning to play an instrument, and the challenge of connecting this isolated musical world with its more social manifestations is widely recognised (e.g. Kemp, 1996). Published accounts of wholly individual music-making are rare, but Alan Rusbridger (2002) vividly recounts his experiences of returning to piano lessons in adult life, hoping to build on his adolescent ability to 'play the piano plausibly, if not accurately' (p. 1). As an adult learner, his determination to progress is stronger than it was in childhood, but the demands on his time are more pressing, and his knowledge of music more extensive, resulting in a greater impatience with his own limitations, especially on the days when 'spirit and fingers aren't on speaking terms and the result is fumbling, dismal, depressing' (ibid.: 1):

> Am I any good? The honest, objective answer is no, I'm not very good. But if the questioner is not especially musical a plausible answer might be – not bad. I recently played a Bach prelude and fugue to a friend who knew little about music and the friend didn't run from the room. The notes were the right notes. There might even have been flashes of phrasing and touch. But I know that anyone even moderately knowledgeable about music would have tiptoed off to make the tea. (Rusbridger, 2002: 1)

Rusbridger has no desire to perform publicly, but reports nonetheless that 'playing the piano – or trying to play the piano – is now such a part of my life that a day now feels incomplete without having sat at the keyboard for even two minutes' (ibid.: 3). His acknowledgement of the value of such self-directed musical activity is rare: respondents amongst the Music in the Round and Buxton audiences (Studies 2 & 4) often dismissed their adult attempts to practice as being only marginally relevant to their musical lives, comparing themselves unfavourably with professional performers rather than emphasising the greater appreciation of music that their practical insight might afford. Rusbridger's attempts to conquer the practical challenges of the piano seem to offer him a stronger engagement with music than would otherwise be possible, and mean that his private musical experiences are connected at least in his own mind with a wider musical world.

Engaging in musical learning and development as an adult arguably demands greater effort and perseverance than is the case for children and adolescents, who are more reliably supported by parents and teachers, and are often able to play alongside their peers in school and regional ensembles. Fluctuations of enthusiasm and commitment are inevitable at any age, and the phenomenon of young people 'dropping out' of instrumental learning as they transfer to secondary school has been widely observed (Sloboda, 2001). Nonetheless, the friendships and sense of community recalled by the school and university students in the previous chapter must be sought out with greater determination by an adult who wishes to make music with others. Peter Cope's (2002) interview study with Scottish traditional musicians emphasised the need for supportive group music-making sessions in which informal learning could flourish, even while noting that 'the scarcity of contexts for continuing to play into adulthood and the formality of those that do exist do not encourage continued participation' (p. 104). Adults participating in musical groups must have the confidence to display their musical abilities and potential in public, and those who choose to play only in private will need intrinsic motivation and a sense of satisfaction to sustain their solitary music-making.

The COMA summer school offers the clearest example from amongst my case studies of an event where individual learning and development is prioritised by participants. This is not to say that the group experience is not valued: the discussion below will illustrate the importance of the supportive context which results from a group of like-minded individuals pursuing similar goals alongside one another. The concentrated experience of a summer school results in different kinds of social interaction from those found in a performing society that meets regularly over a longer period of time: more immediate negotiation of inter-personal difficulties is necessary, and the personal aims which members bring to the group have less time to be assimilated into shared goals, and so remain clearly articulated in participants' discourse. Discussion of the summer school will begin with an investigation of this balance of personal and social motivations, revealed through the participants' declared reasons for attending.

The COMA Summer School: 'a concentrated experience'

The Contemporary Music-making for Amateurs (COMA) Summer School, by its very nature, attracts participants who are keen to develop their musical skills and interests through an intensive week of workshops and rehearsals, culminating in evening concerts at the end of the week. For these participants the individual motivation to develop as a performer or composer is likely to be stronger than the social desire to be part of a group; social needs are fulfilled more effectively through the regional activities of the COMA organisation, which offer regular meetings and more stable group membership (see Service, 1999).   In the questionnaire given to all participants in the one week summer school, respondents were asked to place the following reasons for attendance in order of priority:

  i.   To develop my interest in contemporary music
  ii.   For the social aspect of rehearsing and performing with friends
  iii. To develop my performing skills
  iv.   To develop my composing skills
  v.   To meet like-minded people

Most participants chose three or four options from the list, with the result that cumulative totals for the five given reasons were roughly similar; between 19 and 22 responses for each, with a further 9 choosing the 'other' option and giving reasons of their own. The various aspects of the summer school are shown by this measure to be equally important, as participants attend with a hope or expectation that musical, personal and social aims will all be fulfilled. Choices in first place were also roughly balanced, with the development of composing skills and the meeting of like-minded people leading by a small amount, suggesting a body of self-directed learners who were looking forward to forging new friendships and connections.

Participants' own sense of balancing social and individual motivations were revealed in the open-ended question that followed: 'What are your main expectations or hopes for the week?'. Here, 85 per cent of the respondents made reference to learning, improving skills or receiving tuition, demonstrating the extent to which they had come with clearly-defined challenges and a determination to develop existing skills:

> To know new repertoire, to challenge myself in learning new repertoire in a short period of time. [FWQ 14]

> To play my violin a lot and hopefully improve/learn something, particularly in the field of improvising. [FWQ 16]

Returning participants, in particular, gave answers that encompassed the full range of summer school experiences, illustrating the importance of a social context for their individual challenges in their hope of being 'broadened emotionally and intellectually in new unforeseen ways, by music and musical people' [FWQ 9]. The variety of aims and hopes expressed here capture the participants' desire to get full value (in every sense) from the summer school; as one said, 'it is my life-blood, and I am up here for another injection' [CMD 7]. The supportive ethos and shared goals of the participants led one to describe the summer school as a 'very safe environment in which to take musical risks' [WEQ 8], so summing up the way in which compatible individual goals generate a feeling of communal endeavour.

COMA participants appeared to enjoy their sense of individuality, not seeking to subsume their aims within the group context, but rather enjoying the feeling of being able to indulge their self-perceived idiosyncrasies amongst like-minded people. Participants clearly valued the exchange of ideas and sense of community offered by the summer school, and were notably lacking in the competitiveness and self-doubt that had proved problematic for the university music students (Study 1). Very few made reference to the more advanced skills of other participants, seeming to relish the diversity of their backgrounds and interests, and the opportunities this afforded for collaborative learning. In fact, the exchanges with other participants that were most highly valued were intellectual, rather than musical, as discussions over meals and in the workshops were for one 'the first time for ages that I've really engaged with *ideas* at a higher level than the mundane' [FWQ 24], and for others an opportunity to share ideas with 'lively, intelligent, interesting people' [FWQ 7]. Only a few were 'intimidated' by the intensity of debate and discussion that characterised the meal breaks but, as some noted, it was possible to find quieter moments in the week by retreating to a hostel room or walking in the sculpture park that surrounds the campus.

In their attempts to describe a 'typical' participant, respondents showed an awareness of the opportunities and challenges of social exchanges amongst their diverse membership:

> Very varied in age, social background and musical experience, mostly white. Mostly very friendly, thoughtful and open-minded, but there are always a few people whose main aim seems to be to promote themselves, and who find it hard to work in groups. [FWQ 21]

> No 'typical' participant. Some retired, looking for something interesting to do; some 'regulars'; some students etc. Some get on well in workshop groups, some try to take over and dominate. [FWQ 24]

References to potential difficulties in social interactions were quite frequent, suggesting that participants saw the group dynamics of workshops and rehearsals as another aspect of their learning, rather than something that could be taken for granted. Such problems were usually observed in other people's behaviour, but some participants recognised their own attempts at conflict resolution, one stating 'I became more tolerant of an awkward person' [FWQ 17] and another that 'I have become more confident in my own vocation as a composer and also exercised social skills in situations where emotions are inevitably involved – I feel I have grown up' [FWQ 10]. This self-awareness of success in group interactions offers another example of the conceptual separation of individual and social goals at the summer school: opportunities to learn from one another were recognised and welcomed, but where unsatisfactory group dynamics threatened to disrupt individual learning, participants were pro-active in resolving tensions and monitoring their own behaviour (see Chapter 4 for examples; also Pitts, 2004a).

These musicians (and the COMA participants are the only ones amongst my case studies to use this word with any ease) were striving to fulfil challenges that they had set themselves, whether this was a determination to sing solo, lead the orchestra, have a composition performed, or develop specific skills and techniques. Their respect for the tutors – variously described as 'heroes' [FWQ 7], 'important composers and performers' [WEQ 10] and 'excellent tutors' [WEQ 4] – meant that securing their approval and praise was also important, as this diarist's summary of her achievements during the week shows:

> I would have to say that it's all to do with the piano course. 1. I got to write 4 pieces of music. 2. I got one of them performed. 3. I have a chance of getting some of them published in a COMA book of short piano pieces. 4. I have a chance for some of them to be used in the book of piano composing techniques that [the tutor] is writing! [CMD 11]

This participant had a tangible individual achievement to take away from the summer school, but for most the sense of development was more general, bringing for one respondent of 'a resolve in my own work and its importance to me' [FWQ 1], and for another 'the satisfaction of doing something you've never done before and it enhancing your general or artistic outlook' [FWQ 20]. Having started the summer school with clear individual goals, there was a strong element of self-evaluation in participants' summaries of the week, in which they held themselves, as much as their tutors and peers, responsible for their levels of enjoyment and satisfaction.

The overall picture given by the questionnaire responses is of a lively group of participants, focused on their own goals and development but recognising the contribution that like-minded peers could make in fostering new ideas and connections. The social network provides a context for individual learning, rather than being the main reason for attendance, and participants engage in high levels of self-evaluation rather than making comparisons with or judgements of their peers. This could be considered an ideal – although perhaps unsustainable – learning environment, where the stamina and energy of all participants is directed towards the shared goal of the final performance, through which individual challenges are met. Participants are fully immersed in the group context during the week itself, but to be satisfied with the experience they must have individual achievements and insights to take away into their next year of contemporary music-making. Some reflected on the new resolve that the summer school had given them: 'I shall plan a better practice routine into my day and week. Maybe take lessons' [CMD 12]. Without a follow-up study it is impossible to tell whether these good intentions were realised, but certainly the summer school appears to provide an impetus and renewed enthusiasm for many participants, making it 'something of an anticlimax to return to other (real?) life' [FWQ 9].

Further insight on the individual experiences of participants emerged in the diary study, where 14 members of the summer school kept a daily record of their activities, thoughts and feelings. All diaries were filled in with great detail and included some highly articulate and colourful reflections on the week; diarists were asked to respond to two or three questions each day, as well as using the space provided for additional comments. Diaries were completed by 4 male and 10 female participants, who between them covered a range of ages, interests and previous COMA experience. Volunteers were sought by approaching a random sample as participants arrived on the first day, and all were assured of confidentiality and could request a copy of their diary on completion. The sample is small but rich in data, as the daily reflection encouraged a level of detail beyond that of the questionnaire responses, and allowed the high and low points of the week to be represented as they happened. To give a sense of the depth of description the diaries offered, some extracts from one diary (under the pseudonym Sarah) are discussed below.

Sarah's diary: impressions of a COMA convert

Sarah was unusual amongst the full week participants in being a first-time attender at the summer school, although she had previously played with a regional COMA ensemble. She is an art therapist in her 60s, and describes herself as being 'always excited by new, unusual rhythms and sounds'.

Diary entries on the first day of the summer school show Sarah feeling 'an initial sense of being a newcomer', but soon finding a place amongst the returning participants, helped by the course administrator who 'was particularly good at making me feel at home'. Sarah makes several references to the need to pace herself in order to last the week, and draws a smiley face next to the comment 'mustn't *try too hard*'. Her summary of the first day is enthusiastic and full of anticipation for the rest of the week:

> *Saturday 20th July*
> I shall have to resist the wine – much as I like it – as I shall not be able to function properly – also late nights in the bar – though tempting – will spoil my ability to cope and I will get overtired. I missed one workshop in the afternoon (bearing in mind [the] advice to leave a little space) and was glad that I could rest and therefore enjoy the late concert – which was superb. [...] I enjoyed the first three performances and workshops enormously – I like the mix of players with composers and singers. Don't know if I shall fit in the practice that I feel I need to take part in performance later. I always doubt my own ability.

In her Sunday entries, it becomes clear that Sarah has befriended many of the weekend participants, and is feeling slightly anxious about how the course will change once they leave. She expresses further doubts about her energy levels and musical ability, saying that 'there seemed little time' to get the results of one weekend workshop 'up to performance level'. Sarah has already found the art rooms on campus, where she intends to spend part of the week, and has engaged in conversations about 'art, philosophy and music' with 'many, many people – all interesting'. She ends the diary entry by stating that 'I got a bit pissed in the bar tonight – not a good idea – I'll regret it in the morning probably'.

Monday's writing records no such ill-effects, and Sarah feels 'that today has been the serious start to the school'. Having said goodbye to some friends made at the weekend summer school, she is 'expecting to bond with the longer term players now', and seems to be finding a balance between time spent on her own in the art room and time interacting with participants and tutors. She has joined an additional workshop to replace the weekend option, saying 'I felt that I should play the compositions of members and get the feel of their different talents and ideas'. Finding the evening concert of electroacoustic music 'too loud and painful on the ears – an agonising hum', the next day sees Sarah discussing this with the tutors who had performed in that concert:

Tuesday 23rd July
I discussed the sound problem I had [... and] was told that their audience was usually very young. 18-30. I was surprised! They apparently like the louder sounds; even if they do lose their hearing. [...] We agreed that some people find free improvisation impossible to sit through. We are probably brought up too conventionally and not encouraged to try less measurable experiences.

Sarah appears to be finding a comfortable level of familiarity with tutors and other participants, but still values the time spent on her own: 'I found myself painting the shapes of sculpture in the park – colour seen through sweeping arches and curves – very satisfying'. The pace of the week is catching up on her however, and she notes with annoyance that she missed one concert by sleeping in her room, and on attending another 'I slept through that, too – even though it was very good at the beginning'. Returning to her room for an early night she 'dreamt of getting fatter and fatter because the food filled me out twice as fast as it normally would. (So much for people's praise of the meals and their stories of not being able to get into concert clothes at the end of the week).'

On Wednesday, Sarah remarks that the unseasonably cold weather 'has made us rather serious', and indeed her own thoughts seem to be more self-critical than has been the case on previous days. Asked about her 'hopes and concerns for the rest of the week', she responds with this appraisal of her own abilities:

Wednesday 24th July
My concern is that I cannot learn the music fast enough or well enough to record or to perform it – and that I will come in on a rest. This may be just vanity; but alongside people who play better – or sight-read better than I do I can lose confidence rather than gain it and be tentative. My sight-reading is fine on easier things but high and fast my violin can be very untidy until I have learnt the music. Hopes are still that I am inspired to go back and attend more lessons and that playing music will take a more central place in my life and become more of a pleasure than a worry.

This rare example of comparing herself to others appears to mark a low point in Sarah's energy and confidence, but the next day's entry begins brightly with a compliment from the conductor of the orchestra; 'This felt good as he usually stops me from tapping my foot. However, I found the next pieces extremely difficult so his praise was cancelled out'. The concentrated nature of the summer school experience comes across here, as casual comments and small events affect Sarah's moods and her capacity to cope with the day. In need of some revitalising conversation, Sarah did not find it over lunch:

Thursday 25ᵗʰ July
Lunch time – my first boring one. I sat with 3 men who talked psychology with great conviction. I don't like men who know with *certainty* how other people think. I did not bother to argue with them. I believe that the human DNA is full of much more memory and possibilities than one self-opinionated man can conceive. (Am I right in thinking that, if unravelled, it could stretch to the moon and back?)

There are possible clashes of gender, as well as art and science, here; inevitable, perhaps, amongst such a diverse group of participants, but obviously a disappointment to Sarah after more interesting exchanges earlier in the week. Concluding her diary for that day, she reflects on the similarity between amateur musicians and artists, where in both cases the amateurs 'are not jaded or arrogant – what they do is *human*, not done for effect'. Clearly, the overall impression of the summer school is still positive, as Sarah demonstrates the next day in answer to a question about returning to 'everyday' life:

Friday 26ᵗʰ July
The very intense and concentrated musical space will be hard to leave behind. It cannot be sustained in everyday life. It is wonderful just to let all the details of practical living be taken care of by somebody else. No phones, post or advertising. No telly. I shall have to take responsibility again – to do things that cut across my concentration as an artist and musician. I met many people who taught me different skills, ideas and attitudes to music. It was also good to discuss ideas with like-minded people and not to feel I had to tone down my enthusiasm so as not to bore or overwhelm.

The sense of feeling at home in the COMA environment comes across strongly in the second half of Sarah's diary, and is a remarkable change for someone who felt a 'newcomer' at the start of the week. There are several references to 'next year', and she resolves to 'try to persuade some to try the experience' when she returns to friends and family at home. Summing up the week as 'an intense and wonderful experience which will change the way I concentrate my energies in daily life', Sarah comments that she has valued the discussions with participants but 'felt less happy when politics were introduced'. It seems that the abstract, 'arty' discussions she has enjoyed best epitomise COMA's character, and anything more socially or politically charged is intrusive, perhaps demanding too much of a connection back to the 'real' lives that participants do not share with one another. Sarah's final diary entry is a tribute to the opportunities represented by COMA and its summer school:

Saturday 27ᵗʰ July
COMA is probably unique in what it has offered to amateur players/performers which is of very, very high quality. The maturity of most of the participants is one of its advantages. Everyone is here because they really *want* to be here and little time was

wasted having to cajole people into attending groups (as far as I know). I made many new friends.

Sarah's diary reveals the depth and intensity of the summer school experience, and shares with the other diarists an honesty and level of self-evaluation that would have been hard to find through other research methods. The fine balance between the summer school's strengths and frustrations is apparent: praise from a tutor quickly destroyed by self-doubt at a difficult rehearsal; open-minded discussions that make more opinionated exchanges harder to tolerate; great output of energy that takes its toll in the middle of the week; and good food and wine that lead to nightmares about over-indulgence! There are no half-measures in a residential course of this nature, and participants who engage fully with the personal and social, the musical and intellectual, and in Sarah's case, the artistic and visual too, are drawn into the intensity of the experience in a way that cannot fail to make an impact.

Individual experience in a group context

The level of involvement demonstrated through Sarah's fluctuating confidence, energy and optimism was evident in the other diaries too, as participants recorded their immersion in the summer school activities and their reluctance to leave them behind at the end of the week. The sense of belonging and participation was shared by all diarists, but what comes across strongly in reading them together are the differences in their individual experiences. This diversity was built in to the programme of the summer school: participants had to choose from a variety of workshop and rehearsal options, and so it was unlikely that many would share an identical timetable. When asked about how the social networks of the summer school seemed to function, most diarists stated that meeting people in workshops was the strongest way of forging friendships, because 'we share feelings' [CMD 6], and many enjoyed the flexibility of interactions between participants: 'There clearly are people who cling to their friends or a small group but a large number of people mix well, or at least are happy to chat when approached' [CMD 14]. One participant summed up her peers as including 'people with a strongly developed individuality who are at the same time very much aware of what is going on socially in the world they live in' [FWQ 22], and indeed this sense of individuals moving within a fluid but supportive network is a useful way of understanding the group dynamics of the summer school.

Belonging to the COMA group allows participants to assume a high level of shared values, so leading to the interesting conversations and like-mindedness that many comment on appreciatively. In this sense, the organisation gives a unity to the activities of its individual members, of which the summer school is one manifestation; fluctuating membership is relatively unimportant, so long as the ethos is understood and preserved by those who do attend. To have a year without attending the summer school would be devastating to some participants, but perfectly acceptable to others, since the role it plays in participants' lives varies according to their broader musical context. Through its finite timescale and physical separation from 'everyday' life, the COMA summer school frames the activities that take place there, and connections between that week and the remainder of the year are made by participants if they choose to pursue them. Friendships forged during workshops and rehearsals were left behind as the participants dispersed at the end of the week, and one diarist noted that she 'forgot to say goodbye to many people' [CMD 6]; resuming those friendships or their equivalents next year is one of the pleasures of return attendance. As the next chapter shows, membership of a performing society gives regular attendance and consistency of personnel a much higher priority, since the society is defined and shaped by its regular members and relies on their continued presence to fulfil its musical functions.

Experiences of the summer school varied enormously according to the intentions and expectations of each participant. Some came as composers wanting to 'promote' their own compositions, some as performers wanting the opportunity to play a wide variety of repertoire, and almost all to expand their listening, knowledge and engagement with contemporary music. Participants – in all but a very few disappointed cases – took away from the summer school that which they had hoped to find there, and so were renewed for their independent lives as performers, composers, teachers, musicians in the forthcoming year.

Escaping *from* and escaping *to*

Participants at COMA and Music in the Round spoke of a contrast with 'everyday life' that distinguished the heightened experience of the summer school or festival from the routine of the surrounding months, and this term is also widely used in the research literature (e.g. DeNora, 2000) despite being 'the most self-evident, yet the most puzzling of ideas' (Felski, 1999: 15). David Hesmondhalgh (2002) notes that 'everyday' has almost replaced 'popular' in discussions of widespread cultural practices, a move which he suggests 'reflects a shift in media and cultural studies away from a concern with meaning and interpretation ('reception') and towards a greater interest in how media fit into, and help to constitute, the rhythms and routines of people's lives' (p. 121).

Previous research on the uses of music in everyday life has concentrated almost exclusively on listening to recorded music: amongst the most notable examples are Tia DeNora's (2000) study of the musical soundtrack to daily life constructed by adult women, Michael Bull's (2000) work on the ways in which personal stereo usage allows listeners to cope with the pressures of urban living, and Crafts, Cavicchi and Keil's (1993) interviews on musical meaning and experience. Each of these studies illustrates the ways in which listeners make use of recorded music to enhance and change their moods, forming musical identities through their affiliations with particular genres or performers. Connections between everyday life and musical performance are more scarce, comprising mainly the biographies and autobiographies of professional musicians, and tending in those cases to be anecdotal rather than reflective, concentrating on specific events rather than contemplating the effects of music or its imagined absence. Even Ruth Finnegan's

(1989) study of musical activities in Milton Keynes focuses mainly on the pragmatic functioning of performing groups – their organisation, membership and practices – rather than on *why* music is important to those who make it.

The extent to which musical participation is 'everyday' is an underlying theme in much of the case study data: participants across the studies sought continuity between the values and experiences of the annual event and their more routine engagement with music, and yet distinctiveness from daily life was also an important part of their musical experiences. Arguing for the 'special' nature of musical activity can be counter-productive, although it is frequently attempted in educational debate, where the pressure to justify the role of music in the curriculum encourages claims of uniqueness. Other academic disciplines reinforce this notion that music is inherently different from other human activities, often by conflating the cultural value that is attached to particular musical works with the sociological benefits of music-making:

> The physical, emotional, and pleasurable quality of music and music-making cannot be experienced in quite the same way through any other form of social or creative and artistic activity, which is why music is so popular and valued so highly. (Cohen, 1991: 191)

The musical pleasures that Sara Cohen outlines were certainly echoed in the accounts of my case study participants; but had I interviewed actors, footballers or rock-climbers I might have found similar results. Not everyone will find their source of satisfaction in musical participation, and although Mihalyi Csikszentmihalyi suggests that 'singing in a choir and playing in an amateur string ensemble are two of the most exhilarating ways to experience the blending of one's skills with those of others' (1990: 112), it is clear that this would not be true for someone with little liking for disciplined rehearsals or classical repertoire. For the case study participants, musical involvement satisfied their need for 'optimal distinctiveness' (Sheldon & Bettencourt, 2002: 26), whereby their contribution to musical activities left them sufficiently separate from the group to feel necessary and valued, whilst at the same time offering them membership of a like-minded community. It is true, of course, that many other active leisure pursuits fulfil the same function: belonging to a football team would bring many of the same experiences and pleasures, but would appeal to those who prefer running to singing. The importance of music in the lives of participants cannot simply be explained by its difference from other activities.

It is perhaps more helpful to see music not as being objectively unique or special, but rather as becoming so to participants through continued engagement, gradually assuming an embedded role in their lives that makes it seem irreplaceable. The multifaceted nature of musical experience allows individual participants to engage with it in ways that best suit their needs and temperament, setting their own goals and achieving satisfaction from fulfilling them. As the COMA participants demonstrated, these goals might become specifically musical once participation has become habitual, but the initial impetus to participate seemed often to come more from a desire to seek personal or social development, with music offering one possible vehicle for such fulfilment. Participants in the case studies struggled to articulate what was unique about musical experience, unable to pinpoint those characteristics which would persuade others of its distinctiveness. They were more certain, however, that musical involvement did make a distinct contribution to their lives, enabling them to demonstrate or explore personal qualities that they felt to be under-used in other aspects of their work and leisure. In this way, musical participation became both 'special' and 'everyday', with this dual function contributing to its appeal and sustainability.

'A break from everyday life'

The relationship between 'everyday' life and musical participation varied across the case studies: from the university students in Study 1 adjusting to the fact that music now was their main focus instead of competing for their attention, to the audience members at Buxton and Music in the Round putting other commitments aside to prioritise their festival concert-going. Participants in the COMA summer school were the most direct in their desire to 'escape' from the daily routine, in some cases citing this as their main reason for attendance:

> To have a break from my life in a safe environment that's completely different from my normal surroundings. [FWQ 16]

> Having time and opportunity to focus on music-making away from the demands of home and work. [WEQ 2]

Participants sought the 'total immersion in music' [FWQ 5] that a residential summer school can provide, with attendance implicitly demonstrating a need for a concentrated period of music-making that for many might not be possible in their daily routine. In this respect, the contrast between the week's musical involvement – described by several as 'like being on another planet' [CMD 5] – and the return to everyday life was the greatest of all the case studies, and the end of the week marked a significant change of focus. Several participants spoke of the difficulties of describing the summer school to friends and family who had never been: having experienced a shared enthusiasm for contemporary music, this would once again be a minority interest when they returned home, and it would be necessary to 'restrain myself from going over the top; they wouldn't believe me' [CMD 1].

COMA participants were physically removed from their families and work, but even without this factor a similar sense of suspending the normal routine was evident in diaries kept by Music in the Round audience members (Study 4). The audience for this festival was mostly local, and for those who attended the full programme of concerts, the disruption to daily life was considerable. Interview respondents spoke of scheduling the week of the festival to avoid all but the essential aspects of their work, and even for those people whose attendance was partial, most missed concerts because of other commitments rather than to have a night off. For some, the week therefore felt 'like a very active and exciting week's holiday!' [MitRD 10], and it was suggested that 'breaks for rest and reflection would be helpful – especially to an ageing population!' [MitRD 12]. In some respects, the Music in the Round audience remained more embedded in their normal routine than was the case for COMA participants, but the transition from festival existence to the everyday was still significant for some, and the diarists reported various coping strategies:

> One plans a wake (we always do): on the Sunday, whatever the weather, we walk the Peak. [MitRD 5]

> After the concert we spontaneously invited a dozen friends back to the house for soup, bread, cheese and wine [...] and celebrated the Festival and talked and talked and wound down and made the 'withdrawal' from all that music more bearable. We parted at 2 a.m.! [MitRD 6]

Like the COMA participants with their new resolve to practice more, Music in the Round listeners find themselves sustained through the festival-less weeks; 'I shall return to the "everyday" with a wealth of memories and some new things to explore as time goes by' [MitRD 2]. As one reflected, 'you can't live for ever at this level of cultural experience' [MitRD 1].

It may already be apparent that the 'everyday' for most of these participants was far from mundane, and indeed a number commented on the wealth of activities – musical and otherwise – that occupied them outside the events being studied here. In judging music to be 'essential', they were valuing its enriching properties in already sophisticated and fulfilling lives (cf. Maslow, 1968), finding in musical participation a source of emotional equilibrium, intellectual satisfaction and spiritual uplifting. These effects are not confined to those in comfortable social circumstances: Michael Argyle (1996a) suggests that for those in run-of-the-mill jobs, 'leisure may be the more important source of identity and self-esteem' (p. 129), and Betty Bailey and Jane Davidson's (2002) study of a choir for homeless men demonstrates that where work and family identity is completely lacking, musical participation can play a powerful role, as choir members 'experience[d] joy, contentment, increased self-esteem, pride and relief from physical complaints' (p. 239). Whilst there are variations in the money, time and priority that can be given to music in different people's lives, a pattern is emerging of similar roles and values being afforded to participation, such that the singers in the homeless choir and the performers at Buxton might find surprising connections in their shared uses of music.

Engagement in serious leisure activities, including musical participation, can alternatively be viewed as 'resistance to everyday life', although Stanley Cohen and Laurie Taylor (1976/92), as the main advocators of this view, make little mention of music in their analysis of hobbies, mass media and cultural consumption. Nonetheless, many of the COMA participants, particularly, might recognise themselves in Cohen and Taylor's description of the 'scurrying human beings' of contemporary Western society who, 'periodically or permanently dissatisfied with the picture of everyday reality which occupies their consciousness

... busily search for ways of ignoring, distorting or subverting that reality' (Cohen & Taylor, 1976/92: 211).

With typical COMA participants consistently described in questionnaire responses as eccentric, open-minded and intellectual, the notion of 'subverting reality' would undoubtedly have some appeal amongst this group, who are demonstrating the 'resistance and escape' of Cohen and Taylor's argument even through their decision to attend the summer school. Their interest in contemporary music, too, could be seen to fit 'the search for novelty ... [which] for people in our society is often the only way to put themselves ahead of reality, to absent themselves from mindless involvement in routine' (ibid: 69). Music in the Round audience members were often more cautious in their attitudes to unfamiliar music, and devotees of the Buxton Festival were adamant in their preference for the traditional, so the theory can be only loosely applied across the case studies. Nonetheless, the sense of enhancing everyday life is present at each of the musical events, where participants accept new routines, specific to that festival but sharing enough characteristics with other events to feel familiar and comfortable. The balance between the familiar and the strange is well known to be a powerful factor in enjoyment of music (Berlyne, 1971; see also Wilson, 1985: 129), and it appears that this applies not only to musical works, but also to musical encounters and behaviours.

'Being something you're not'

Festival and summer school attendance brings a certain disruption to daily routine, but demands no fundamental changes of the people who participate; they leave the event an enriched, possibly exhausted, version of their everyday selves. For those seeking a more continuous challenge to the daily routine, participation in staged performances can offer an opportunity to 'get out of your own character, to become something else' [BUXI 1]:

> It's a form of unreality − you can be a swashbuckling hero, you can be a cowboy, you can be a sailor; you can be something you're not. And I do find that perhaps a lot of people are in singing, not for an ego trip, but it's a confidence boosting exercise; because once you've overcome any shyness that there might be, or nervousness, when you can get out in front of an audience, and they are all looking, maybe not at you directly, but at the company you are with, there's something which builds you up and you think 'Yes, this is great'. You become a somebody, you might become something you're not. [BUXI 1]

The notion of 'becoming a somebody' was mentioned often by performers at the Gilbert and Sullivan Festival who, whilst deriving much of their pleasure from the group aspects of performance, nonetheless identified some strong individual motivations for going on stage. For some, the escape from everyday life was tangible: a large man who described himself as 'not having the figure for football' turned his size to advantage when he appeared on stage, becoming a commanding presence that meant 'people look at you when they'd pass you in the street normally' [BUXI A1]. Another singer, self-conscious about his receding hairline, enjoyed the chance to wear a wig and be the 'dashing young hero' [BUXI C1]. It is notable that these are male examples, since for women Gilbert and Sullivan's ideals of pretty, identical young 'maidens' were more of a pressure than an escape route since, as one tenor noted, 'with a show like Iolanthe [which features a female chorus of fairies] if one were to have two or three ugly, fat fairies, it doesn't have quite the same effect as all these lithe, pretty young things on stage' [BUXI 3]. Such concerns had caused one interviewee to hang up her costume and join the backstage team: 'I looked at myself one day when I was about forty and I just thought "Oh no, stop", and that was it. I just decided that there were so many other things I could do, all these things where you're not in the spotlight, backstage and all' [BUXI A3].

The adoption of a stage persona which is different in physicality or personality from the everyday brings a source of escape for some, but the opportunities are recognised as being finite: 'there comes a time when in fact you can't perform on stage because you physically can't bob up and down like a policeman or you don't look like a lovesick maiden either when you're 50 years old' [BUXI 1]. Many Buxton participants had noted the problems of ageing participants and audiences, and expressed concern that the future of the festival and the repertoire itself was placed in jeopardy by this profile (see Chapter 5 for discussion of ageing audiences in Studies 2 and 4). For individual performers, the effects of 'musical ageing' can leave them faced with having to retire from the stage, some taking this decision for themselves and others being gradually excluded through failed auditions and decreasing performing opportunities.

There have been few studies of the specific motivations and experiences of older musical participants, one exception being Don Coffman and Mary Adamek's (1999) survey of wind band members in an American Midwestern city, in which they note that the character of the older generation is changing, and expectations of their needs and behaviour perhaps need to be modified:

> As a group, older adults are more educated, healthier, and more active than they were in previous years ... Participation in music is enriching and stimulating for all ages, and this enrichment and stimulation is a necessary part of healthy ageing. (Coffman & Adamek, 1999: 31)

Research on retirement from work supports this view that active leisure incorporating social contacts is an important part of the transition into later life (Argyle, 1996a: 66; McIlveen & Gross, 1999: 71), but there is an irony for ageing musicians, who could fulfil these needs through continued performance, but may find themselves unwelcome or undervalued in their performing societies. Some musical groups appear to find this less problematic than others; male voice choirs, for example, often have a high average age, but make appropriate demands of their members, with little need for solo singing or movement during the performance. Those groups whose ideal age profile would be much younger experience greater difficulties, and staged performances – including Gilbert and Sullivan – hold the potential for real conflict between the needs of the performers and the desire for a polished and commercially viable performance. Of the performing groups studied at Buxton, only Group A (see page 56 for group profiles) explicitly recognised that their society fulfilled important functions for their members that might be to the detriment of the performance, and seemed to feel happy with the balance of 'therapy' and achievement that resulted from this outlook. Where performing groups choose to emulate the professional model of working and focus entirely on the product, the outcome may be more polished, but some difficult clashes between individual and group motivations have to be considered along the way.

If 'being something you're not' has a limited lifespan, so too has the need to perform, at least for some interviewees at Buxton. One woman spoke of not having performed when her children were little, saying 'it wasn't that I couldn't get someone to mind them, it just wasn't important to be in the shows at that time' [BUXI A3]. Other participants noted that members of their societies tended to be 'either single, or married and of a certain age' [BUXI A4], suggesting that the desire to perform on stage is strongest in early adulthood and later life, a pattern possibly reflecting the demands of work and family that for many people are dominant in the intervening years (cf. Rapoport & Rapoport, 1995). One respondent went further in describing performance as 'a kind of therapy', such that the need for participation would vary throughout people's lives:

I don't know, I think you do actually eventually grow out of it. It's a phase you go through, and at some point you feel that whatever demon you had inside you that needed to be worked through has worked through. It's almost like a psychologist, and you reach a point where you don't need it any more. In some respects it's like a substitute for Prozac, so when you feel normal again you don't have the same urge to get out there and do it. [BUXI A1]

The emotional balance offered by musical participation has long been asserted: the American surgeon (and cornflake pioneer) Dr John Harvey Kellogg wrote in 1931 that 'music must certainly take high rank as a psychic remedy, because of its power to inspire cheerful and hence healthful trains of thought [which] thereby counteracts worry, apprehension, fear and other depressing emotions' (Hunter, 1999: 133). Whether the need to perform is as transitory as the performer quoted above suggests, the emotional energy and release that is found through performance was widely recognised amongst participants (cf. Clift & Hancox, 2001). These feelings seemed to come partly from the validation offered through audience applause and recognition; 'people have paid money to come and see us, and as I say, if you're good at that – obviously everybody wants to be Pavarotti or whoever it is, and you can be that for a brief hour' [BUXI A1].

The opportunity to demonstrate a talent that might otherwise remain hidden is highly valued by these participants, and is an aspect of performance that does appear to have longevity, as illustrated by Alison Oddey's (1999) interviews with successful female comics and actors, for whom 'performing is an exercise in vulnerability, but always with the possibility of both giving and gaining satisfaction' (Oddey, 1999: 280). The continual challenge of performing 'provides the opportunity for identity construction or the expression of multiple personalities' (ibid.: 279), such that the self is discovered by the performer as well as revealed to and recognised by the audience. That 'being someone you're not' might be a route towards being more completely who you *are* may seem like a contradiction. But the process of 'becoming a somebody' – Pavarotti or otherwise – offers the chance to reflect on the differences between that assumed persona and that of the everyday, opening up the possibilities for change and development off-stage as well as in performance. Participants are not escaping *from* their everyday lives and personalities, so much as deepening them through exploring aspects of their behaviour that might have no other outlet.

'What I would do if I wasn't doing this?'

The lights, make-up and costumes of staged shows bring a dimension to musical performance that is not generally found through instrumental playing or choral singing. Those Gilbert and Sullivan societies that also do choral work acknowledged that not all participants enjoyed the stage experience, and some would join them only for Christmas concerts or similar events that did not require any acting. One Buxton participant, recently launched on a professional singing career, reflected on the different demands of oratorio, where expression must be achieved solely with the voice and face as 'you're not supposed to wave your arms about' [BUXI 3]. For him this resulted in a more spiritually engaging experience – 'I get more of a shiver down the spine singing oratorio than I do anything else' – and a greater focus on the words and music. Singing in another context was thus a qualitatively different experience, offering an alternative emotional and musical satisfaction to that found on stage.

If there are differences between staged and non-staged musical performances, how much greater then is the gap between musical activities and other kinds of recreation or 'serious leisure' (Stebbins, 1992). Some participants attempted to explain their involvement in music by comparing it to other activities, particularly those they had rejected as potential pastimes:

> I mean I don't know what we would do if we weren't doing this. Margaret likes gardening, but for heaven's sake, I don't. [BUXI 1]

In his evident disgust at his wife's use of her leisure time (and see Bhatti & Church, 2000, for discussion of gendered attitudes to the garden that might explain this) the singer quoted above shows that a chosen pastime must have a certain credibility for participants, even if this choice cannot be justified to more sceptical outsiders. Those involved in a leisure activity 'voluntarily submit to its rhythms and demands' (Cohen & Taylor, 1976/92: 115), increasing the incomprehension felt by those who are not participants. No wonder then, that families and friends sometimes find it hard to understand the experiences of musical participants:

> I remember one night coming home from a show, and I sat with tears streaming down my face, and my husband said to me 'Why do you do this?', and I said 'Because I love it'. [BUXI A5]

Musical participation is understood by some to be slightly crazy or obsessive, as illustrated by the tendencies of Gilbert and Sullivan and COMA members alike to describe their peers as 'eccentric' or 'social misfits'. Just as the COMA participants anticipated difficulties in conveying their summer school experiences to friends at home, so the Buxton performers felt a sense of loyalty and closeness to one another, embracing their shared values and excluding those who fail to understand them. Individual participation is therefore supported and validated by the group context; the sense of being a 'misunderstood musician', still evident in some of the university students' responses (Study 1), is reduced by the contact with others of similar persuasion. Robert Stebbins' research in a wide variety of 'serious leisure' settings has led him to conclude that such conviction in the value of leisure activities is widespread: 'Serious leisure participants seem quite undisturbed by the marginality of their activities. They see them as harmless social differences of which they are rather proud' (Stebbins, 1998: 116).

Some participants' accounts convey a sense of inevitability in their musical involvement, similar to that found amongst the university students who felt that they were destined to study music because that had always been their main interest: 'I don't think I ever decided to do music, I just decided not to do anything else' [UGI 6]. The point at which music is prioritised over other potential pastimes often happens early in life, this being the point at which instrumental tuition is offered, practice habits are founded, and opportunities for performance are first encountered. Adult participants then come to feel that they have 'grown up with music', a phrase used often across the studies to explain the central role of music in someone's life. This is of course insufficient explanation; the population of amateur performers would be far greater if force of habit was itself enough to guarantee a musically active life, and so some level of commitment has clearly been necessary to sustain musical involvement beyond those initial educational opportunities. Nonetheless, the sense of affinity with music which childhood experiences can generate shows the importance of providing such opportunities for young people, within and beyond school. (See Chapter 7 for further discussion of educational implications.)

The Buxton performers, in common with participants in the other case studies, agreed on the importance of having a central activity in their lives that was distinct from the demands of 'ordinary' life: 'as you get older, you do need an interest otherwise you just vegetate' [BUXI 1]. This motivation to have 'an interest' is widely recognised in literature from sociology and psychology which addresses the functions of leisure, albeit with only infrequent reference to musical participation. However, greater research attention has been paid to 'casual leisure' (Stebbins, 1997; 2001), perhaps because activities such as watching television, going to the cinema, reading newspapers, eating, drinking and conversing are all far more widespread than musical participation amongst the populations commonly studied (see e.g. Kubey & Csikszentmihalyi, 1990). Participants in the case studies tended to be fairly dismissive of these low-energy activities, perhaps recognising that a distinct 'interest' of the kind valued by the Buxton participants is unlikely to be found through casual leisure:

Few people are likely to proclaim to the world that they are, for example, inveterate nappers, television watchers, or consumers of fast food. To the extent that faceless casual leisure dominates the free time of people, this less than optimal balance of leisure activities deprives them of one or more leisure identities that they could otherwise have. (Stebbins, 2001: 307)

There is a certain social snobbery attached to those activities which are widely available, despite the high level of critical insight that can be brought to bear on consumption of many aspects of the mass media. Some COMA participants commented on the pleasant absence of television at the summer school, while Music in the Round members saw complex and not wholly positive relationships between their concert attendance and their use of recorded music (see Chapter 6). Just as 'faceless casual leisure' steals time from more active and potentially fulfilling activities, so musical participation squeezes out the default pastimes of home-based media consumption. This, in turn, raises participants' expectations of the satisfaction and pleasure to be achieved through active leisure, encouraging continued self-development through further participation.

Re-connecting individual and group experience

Discussion in this chapter has shown how participants bring a variety of personal and musical aspirations to their chosen activities, using music for self-discovery and development, or to ward off ageing and boredom. Music holds a role in their lives that seems essential or irreplaceable: contemplating other leisure activities clearly horrified some participants, and all were prepared to invest considerable time, effort and resources in the pursuit of their musical interests. Participants come across as determined, committed and energetic in their search for musical fulfilment.

The next chapter considers the effects of the group contexts within which these individual experiences are located. Just as the individual elements of musical experience discussed here need placing in the group context to be fully understood, so too the participants appeared to find greater satisfaction in their music-making through pursuing their individual goals within the mutually supportive ethos of a performing society or workshop group. The shared interests and priorities of participants have already become apparent, and these will be shown to be a highly valued aspect of interactions with like-minded group members. Inevitably, though, the strong individual characters present in these groups mean that some negotiation of shared aims has to take place, and the frustrations and challenges of making music together are also present in participants' discourse. Group membership is shown in the next chapter to provide a generally supportive context for the individual development explored here, and to contribute greatly to the enjoyment and satisfaction that is to be found in musical participation.

CHAPTER FOUR

Music and Group Experience: Rehearsing and Performing With Others

The personal experiences and effects of music discussed in Chapter 3 are complemented in the case study data by a more group-orientated motivation to perform, in which the value of belonging to a performing society and making music with friends assumes great significance in participants' lives. The process of rehearsal afforded as much, if not more, pleasure than the performance itself for some participants, as did the social rituals that contribute to the character of performing groups. Making music with others was shown to affirm a sense of belonging and like-minded endeavour, so sustaining commitment and offering a shared experience that fostered memories and friendships among a diverse group of people.

The impetus to make music with others can be seen as a logical extension of the personal needs and goals already discussed, broadening the opportunities for music-making and countering the isolation of individual practice. Wayne Booth (1999), in his autobiographical celebration of the amateur musician, reports on the experience of learning the cello in adulthood, finding his greatest pleasure through chamber music evenings held regularly with friends. The physiological challenges of playing the cello make Booth wonder 'what could lead an "over-thirty" man who loves to listen to music to the kind of assignment I gave myself last night: a half hour of practice on one thumb-position passage' (p. 37), but he finds his answer in the informal playing sessions that are sufficient reward for such effort. Of course, playing with others is not always so pleasurable, and in his account of learning to improvise jazz at the piano, David Sudnow (1978/2001) reports becoming self-conscious in ensemble playing, with the result that 'the music wasn't mine – it was going on all around me' (p. 33). Frustrated at his inability to use his recently acquired improvisation skills, Sudnow was driven back temporarily to the safer isolation of practising alone, having experienced all too vividly the potential for public embarrassment that lurks amongst the social pleasures of performing.

In the discussion that follows, most case study participants find themselves closer to Booth's enjoyment of collective musical endeavour than to Sudnow's public anxieties, but the risks and frustrations of group participation are sometimes visible nonetheless. In this chapter, the experiences of the Gilbert and Sullivan performing societies will be presented alongside those of the COMA workshop participants, in a discussion of the extent to which group intentions support or conflict with individual ambitions. The wider musical group, comprising performers and their audiences, will also be considered, with evidence from the literature and the case study data helping to illuminate the mutual understanding – or otherwise – that is at the heart of live performance.

Inclusion and cohesion: the social structures of performing groups

Membership of a performing society requires each individual to work within a complex social structure; shaping, responding to or challenging agreed conventions and behaviours, and balancing the desire for personal fulfilment with a broader responsibility to the group. Finding a valued role within a musical society can fulfil the diverse needs of members from a variety of social circumstances, as Ruth Finnegan (1989) notes in her study of music-making in Milton Keynes:

> The sense of making a significant aesthetic contribution is perhaps particularly emotive for individuals regarded as in some way 'marginal': outside formal employment, say, or somehow at the bottom of the heap. But those 'advantaged' in material terms are often as keen as any to take part in something valued, perhaps balancing their 'profane' success by their intangible but perceptibly real contribution in music – that is, in a pursuit judged worthy, not only by the practitioners and their peers but also, in a very real if elusive sense, profoundly valued by society more widely. (Finnegan, 1989: 328)

Participants across the four case studies showed this willingness to embrace diversity and to value individual contributions to the group, with only the university students (Study 1) and a few of the more self-deprecating COMA performers (Study 3) expressing anxiety about the comparisons of ability that might result. Eccentricity and social difference were widely tolerated and even welcomed, such that a Buxton performer explained that 'there's nobody normal in this society – we're all misfits, yet we gel like we were Siamese twins' [BUXI A5].

Simon Frith has suggested that 'music making is less about managing one's own emotional life than about enjoying being together in groups' (2003: 100), and whilst the individual aspects of musical participation have been shown to be important to these case study participants, the pleasures of group belonging were undoubtedly significant too. Membership of a performing society brings a continuity to the musical involvement of participants, which would be difficult to sustain alone or with sole dependence on the annual summer school or festivals. Between the high points of performances comes the ongoing negotiation and fulfilment of musical aims, much of which takes place off-stage, invisible to the audience, who see only the culmination of the weeks or months of rehearsal:

> Personally I've always said it – I would rather rehearse. There's a great social aspect to it; you go along twice a week every week throughout the year and you rehearse – and then the show comes and it's over. What do we do with our lives? You often hear that – 'What are we going to do now with our evenings? The show's over.' [BUXI A1]

Rehearsals bring pleasures different from those found in performance, but are equally valued as opportunities for making music in a congenial environment.

Table 4.1 Experiences of rehearsing in Gilbert and Sullivan societies

	Themes	Sample responses
Group A	*Organisation of rehearsal*	[BUXQ A1] 2 hour duration; pep talk; one hour music, one hour production. [A5] Warm up – scales etc. Note learning. Tea break. Performance.
	Styles of learning	[A2] Good concentration on work during rehearsal. Little work done at home by most people. Principals always learn music at home. [A4] If music for a show is being taught, each line is played as most members are not readers of music – it is learned aurally; line tapes are given also. Musical accuracy and tempo: it is important that it is learned accurately.
	Enjoyment of rehearsal	[A6] Hard work/lots of laughs and plenty of socialising afterwards. [A8] Good music, hard work and a great social life.
Group B	*Integration of work and fun*	[BUXQ B2] Late start! Good-natured banter. Careful, detailed rehearsal with chorus master. Sociable break. [B5] An evening of hard working, listening, learning and enjoyment. [B8] Rehearsals never start on time. Informal with chance to have a laugh but yet still serious enough to respect our chorus/musical directors. We usually feel as if we have had a good sing by the end of the evening. [B13] Very relaxed atmosphere, but everyone knuckles down when work is to be done. Lots of laughter.
Group C	*Organisation of rehearsal*	[BUXQ C7]We have a full run-through every rehearsal and practice thoroughly bits that need improving. [C8] A run through the whole show stopping at difficult bits and re-rehearsing them. Important to clear up any problems.
	Influential people	[C14] Run through one act, or the whole show, accompanied by piano, conducted by our MD and stopping where necessary for corrections, as instructed by the Director. [C6] We rehearse either all the show or parts of it, repeatedly until it is as the producer wants it.
	Social aspects	[C1] Disciplined meaningful effort. Attention to detail. Happy bunch of people pulling on the same rope in the same direction. [C14] We may stop for a break in the middle, when we have hot or cold drinks and chat, or just take breaks when not required 'on stage' – this social aspect is quite important.

Insight on the rehearsal process was provided through the questionnaires completed by groups performing at the Buxton Gilbert and Sullivan Festival. Three performing societies (coded here as Groups A, B and C) were asked to give descriptions of a typical rehearsal, and their responses variously emphasised the social, organisational and musical aspects of their experiences (see Table 4.1).

There are clear similarities of organisation across the performing groups, familiar to me from years as rehearsal pianist for an opera society: rehearsals lasting two or three hours are led by a director or musical director, and consist of a combination of note-learning and run-throughs, perhaps with a refreshment break in the middle of the evening. Respondents from the three societies placed slightly different emphases on the social and musical aspects of their rehearsals, possibly reflecting the distinct characters of the groups and their status within the Gilbert and Sullivan Festival. A brief description of each will help to provide this context:

♦ Group A – based in Ireland, members of this group described themselves in interview as 'a drinking society who make music' [BUXI A2]. They saw the Festival as a chance to relax and have a holiday together, and claimed to be less interested in its competitive elements. Group A is a 'choral and musical society', performing works other than Gilbert and Sullivan, but enjoying the G&S repertoire particularly for its humour and the chance for some good chorus singing.

♦ Group B – from the Midlands of England, this group is a strong presence at the Festival and has won many awards in recent years. Seeing themselves as 'defending champions', they have a serious approach to the competitive element of the Festival, and are proud of their high standards and quality productions.

♦ Group C – based in central England, Group C was formed specifically to perform at Buxton, bringing together members of several local performing societies for an annual production. They have a committed but not overly competitive attitude to the Festival and are clearly devoted to the music of Gilbert and Sullivan; when I met them on the morning after their Buxton performance they were already discussing the following year's show.

These profiles go some way towards explaining the differences in priorities evident in the descriptions of rehearsals given by group members in the table above. Group B's unanimity in seeing rehearsals as 'hard work combined with fun' is illustrative of their clearly defined goals and shared ideals; wanting to retain their 'champion' status at Buxton, they are like-minded and disciplined in their attitudes towards rehearsing. The clarity of the society's aims and role at Buxton mean that the tensions present in some other groups, where an allcomers policy might conflict with the desire for high standards, are avoided: as one respondent stated, 'peer pressure keeps the standard up (and ensures those who are below standard leave)' [BUXQ B14].

There are greater similarities in the other two groups, where the different priorities of individual members were revealed in the varied focus of their rehearsal descriptions. Their relationship to the Festival differs, though, in that Group A retains a slightly mocking distance from more competitive and focused 'rivals', whilst the members of Group C place the Festival at the centre of their activities, having been founded specifically for that purpose. Leadership roles appear to be stronger in Group C, perhaps because the group has formed recently, and the impetus of the director in securing and developing the membership is still in evidence. There has not yet been time for the group to fall into rigid patterns of behaviour, or to acquire members who do not 'pull their weight' (cf. Stebbins, 1996: 58); indeed, Group C is active in encouraging young chorus members to join, as demonstrated in the number of respondents stating that 'a friend made me do it'!

It appears from these responses that rehearsal practices are broadly similar between the groups, but that attitudes towards the Festival vary, as do the participants' reasons for attendance and their consequent expectations of what membership will bring. Further information on members' reasons for joining their performing society was sought through the questionnaires, with respondents asked to select their main reasons from a given list:

i.   I enjoy the social aspect of rehearsing with friends
ii.   I enjoy making music to a high standard
iii.   I want to develop my performing skills
iv.   I am a Gilbert and Sullivan enthusiast

For each group, the social aspect of rehearsing with friends emerged as a strong reason for participation, balanced in Group B by an enthusiasm for high standards, and in Group C by a desire to develop performing skills and a love of the repertoire. Results were consonant with the group descriptions given above: Group A were clearest in the priority given to social elements (100 per cent of responses), Group B had least need to develop performing skills since most were already highly accomplished (14 per cent of responses), and Group C presented an almost equally weighted set of responses, perhaps reflecting the spread of age and experience amongst their membership and consequent diversity of needs.

These results hold some limitations in understanding the societies and their ways of working; not only in the small sample size, but also in the timing of the research, which emphasised the effects of the performance as questionnaires were issued a few weeks before the Festival and interviews conducted the day after each show. A longitudinal study would be necessary to monitor whether the responses given at those peak times in the performing life of a society are replicated throughout the rehearsal season. It might be predicted that commitment would be reduced at times when there was no imminent performance to prepare for, but that societies might have strategies for maintaining enjoyment and enthusiasm during these periods. Certainly the Gilbert and Sullivan groups I interviewed recognised the 'post-show' feelings of anticlimax and withdrawal, and one described how a local school had offered counselling to pupils after a school production to help with the readjustment to 'normal' life [BUXI A]. Recent studies including those by Robert Stebbins (1996), Colin Durrant and Evangelos Himonides (1998), and Gage Averill (2003) have not convincingly identified such a cycle of emotional engagement through interviews or observation, tending instead to record the 'average' experience of belonging to performing societies. Given the rapid changes in energy levels and enthusiasm demonstrated by the COMA participants within their week-long summer school, it seems likely that a study following the progress of concert preparation from the planning stages to the aftermath would yield a more differentiated picture of musical participation.

The risks and rewards of rehearsing

The rehearsal practices of the performing groups discussed here are consistent with those found by Ruth Finnegan (1989) in her study of the 'hidden musicians' of Milton Keynes, which documents in detail the organisational structures of groups performing in a wide variety of musical genres. Amongst the choral and operatic societies she observed, there are some striking similarities with the balance of social and musical priorities noted in the Buxton groups, as illustrated by this description of a choir rehearsal:

> There were also the concurrent but conflicting desires of choir members, on the one hand to get on with the rehearsal, on the other hand to exchange news with their neighbours or comment on the bit of music they had just been trying to sing – they'd come partly for a social night out, not *just* for the music. The result was some element of hidden struggle between conductor and choir, the conductor trying to keep people's full attention throughout the practising, the choir accepting this in principle but still wanting just to make their own personal remark to their neighbours. (Finnegan, 1989: 242)

Groups A and B in my study mentioned the comparable problem of late arrivals at rehearsals, another instance in which the group experience is compromised by the individual habits of its members. Making the rehearsal a top priority for all members is a challenge (cf. Finnegan, 1989; Stebbins, 1996), especially as many participants have responsibilities in other aspects of their lives that can be hard to reconcile with punctual and whole-hearted rehearsal attendance. Rehearsals make their own demands on participants, and were seen by some as presenting a greater performing challenge than the final show:

> It's the toughest place you'll ever perform, is in the rehearsal room, where all your folk are sitting around looking at you. [BUXI A2]

> Yes – 'he didn't get that note' or 'she didn't get that', or 'gosh, that duet was terrible, they were flat'. They're terribly critical. The urge then is to do it better, to get it right by the end of the rehearsal. [BUXI A1]

Here the pressure of taking risks in front of potentially critical peers and friends is in evidence, such that earning colleagues' respect becomes of more immediate concern than the audience's reaction to the end product of these rehearsals. Mistakes that might be seen once only by the audience are more obvious when made repeatedly in rehearsal, and there is clearly a sense of pride attached to maintaining standards and reputations within the performing group. However, the appraisal of group members rarely strays beyond this focus on specifically musical skills, and so can be seen as contributing to group cohesion by avoiding comparisons of wealth, employment or social standing that might separate members in everyday life (Argyle, 1996b).

Attitudes towards the competence of other members varied: one Group A interviewee stated quite cheerfully that 'in this society we have people who can hardly sing at all' [BUXI A2], demonstrating the balance of social, personal and musical needs that members of that society bring to their participation. Other groups might be less tolerant of this multiplicity of functions, and so find themselves discouraging their weaker members, or losing their 'stars' to groups perceived to have higher standards. One such outlet for ambitious performers at Buxton is the Festival Production, where singers from all societies can audition to be part of a cast that rehearses and performs during the final week. A tenor who had sung with a number of amateur societies and was beginning a professional career at the time of the study commented in interview on the pitfalls of established societies, largely avoided in the Festival Production:

> With societies that have been established for 60 or 70 years, you're going to have people who are only in there because they've been pestered, or who are just a bit complacent, but you don't tend to get passengers here, that's most unusual – everyone tries and really pulls hard, which I guess, although I've never seen a Festival production, but I think it probably does show when people are having a good time and really concentrating on working hard. [BUXI 3]

The combination of hard work and good fun leading to a polished performance clearly contributes to this singer's enjoyment, a view echoed in the small sample of five questionnaires returned from the Festival Production participants; one characterised the rehearsals as 'intense run-throughs with good humour (and tea break)' [BUXQ D4], and another saw them as being 'like other rehearsals, only better' [BUXQ D1]. Participating in the Festival Production brings with it expectations of high standards and commitment, leading to the clarity of purpose that was also observed in the descriptions of Group B rehearsals. The shared interests that characterise any performing group are here refined into clearly articulated aims and goals, such that all those participating are aware of their role and willing to make a full contribution.

Social negotiations in musical workshops

At the COMA Summer School (Study 3) there was a similar sense of participants being conscious of their individual skills and their responsibility to the group goal of the imminent performance. Groups there were largely made up of people who did not know one another, so heightening the challenges of group interaction, and potentially increasing the anxiety of playing or singing in front of one another. Roles within the groups had to be settled quickly to ensure the effective functioning of each workshop, often through hasty and sometimes difficult power negotiations:

The facets of social life have a very wide range on this course and it is not always easy to know who is a likeable person or who you had better avoid. The social games that some people play remind me of public schools. [CMD 13]

COMA participants were faced with the same personal and social challenges as any amateur performing group, magnified by their compression into a one week summer school. As the process and product of their interactions were brought closer together by the finite timescale, so the pleasures of each had to be finely balanced; the week itself must be enjoyable, but the outcome must be achieved to the highest possible standard. With no time for slow negotiations of power and responsibility, participants needed to be sophisticated and self-aware in their dealings with other group members, and some were explicit in recognising the need for this skill:

I do try and make an effort to talk to new people; as someone who's been here before, I think it's partly up to me to make new people feel at ease, not to be cliquey. [CMD 14]

I have made a point of not sitting with the same people twice until I have tried to meet everyone. There has always been someone interesting to talk to. As a new participant I have heard and learnt a lot from people who have been coming here longer. [CMD 12]

New and returning participants alike seemed to recognise the need for social skills in ensuring a comfortable and friendly environment at the summer school. Within the workshops and rehearsals themselves, however, relationships were sometimes more strained:

Monday: Irritated with flute player next to me – no good reason.

Tuesday: Irritated with the flute player because she knows best and tells me what to do. [CMD 7]

The frustrating flute player does not appear again in this diarist's account of the week, so the problem was presumably resolved or tolerated over the course of their rehearsals. COMA participants generally seemed very accepting of one another's differences – even eccentricities – but became more critical when tutors seemed unable to accommodate these satisfactorily within workshops or rehearsals. One composing workshop suffered from an 'invasion [by] some men who were not beginners' [FWQ 8] and another generated the complaint that 'one or two individuals are taking too much time and consequently others are being excluded' [CMD 5]. In the latter case 'quiet words were spoken to the relevant parties, and some resolution found' [CMD 5], demonstrating that participants were more assertive in their role negotiations when they were felt to be jeopardising their learning and enjoyment (see Pitts, 2004a for further discussion).

In their criticisms of tutors the COMA participants demonstrated their expectations of clear leadership within a traditional model of teacher-directed small group learning, whilst retaining their right to intervene where relationships were breaking down. The lack of direction noted in the composing classes described above was in direct contrast to another workshop where the tutor was seen as excessively controlling, a characteristic that was strongly resisted by members of that group:

[The tutor] started by being ultra-democratic with the group and has now become totally autocratic, making all decisions himself without consultation. I can't decide whether to protest or let it go. I half want to fight it and let us into the choices, but this takes energy and may not be worth it. I'll see how easy it is, or not, to take part in the editing of the music we have recorded. [CMD 7]

The group with the 'autocratic' tutor were writing music for a radio play, something the tutor had already done professionally and clearly had strong ideas about. His single-minded approach would almost certainly have resulted in an impressive outcome, but the determination of the participants to retain some influence in the finished product illustrates their intention to learn and contribute, rather than merely to observe. The process of musical participation was valued at least as highly as its product across the case studies: just as the performers here and at Buxton were willing to be physically tired and emotionally committed to their performance, so too these workshop participants refused to take the easy route and demanded instead a more complete involvement in the preparation for performance. Their determination meant that the performance of their piece was cited as the highlight of the week by the participant quoted above, whose insistence on being present for the editing of their improvised sounds had given her a greater sense of ownership and pleasure in the completed piece.

Musical participation at COMA seemed to be viewed as a form of problem solving, with satisfaction and frustration prompted less by the sound of the musical outcome, and more by the processes by which it was generated. Composing workshops offered the greatest opportunity for debating matters of musical taste, and the group collaborating on an electroacoustic piece had many heated discussions on the direction their work should take. As the tutor observed several times during their sessions together, 'we're having to compose by committee here, but we're all adults, so I'm sure we can do it'. Members of the group were often articulate in offering their musical suggestions, although they took different approaches to being heard: one man spoke directly to the tutor on most occasions, another generally stood to make himself heard, while an older woman spoke only to the person sitting next to her. Early attempts at recording material were met with stern critique from the group: 'it's a bit tedious'; 'I wouldn't buy it and I wouldn't play it more than once'; and 'the string sounds are too prominent'. Later in the week, discussions became more hasty as the tutor reminded them that there was 'no time to talk through everything in great detail', but the problems of tutor dominance that had occurred elsewhere were replaced here with a realisation that the tutor could have 'just said what would work' but had chosen to give the group greater control. Despite the interpersonal and musical challenges of group composing, the result seemed to be satisfactory to all involved, and there was unanimous agreement when the tutor asked 'Have we got a piece?'. Participants in this group were modest about their achievements, and recognised the limitations of the time and resources available to them:

> Early on I realised that if I was to try to be creative with electro-acoustic music, I needed to be more technically proficient, and that in spite of great support, it would be too time consuming. But I enjoyed the sessions. [FWQ 21]

Nonetheless, their satisfaction in working together towards a clearly defined goal was obvious, and the contributions made by each participant resulted in some of the most detailed musical discussion that was in evidence during the week.

The Gilbert and Sullivan Festival performers and COMA participants have both been shown here to be determined and committed in their attitudes to working and rehearsing together, expecting to make a useful musical contribution within a supportive social context. Frustrations arise when others, particularly those in leadership roles, are seen to be compromising the likelihood of a successful outcome, or reducing the pleasure to be gained from the rehearsal process. Negotiations of power and responsibility usually take place at an unspoken level, only becoming a more central concern when a significant proportion of the group are dissatisfied. Participants are generally prepared to be tolerant of one another's differences and respectful of members' diverse skills, but are also seen as a potentially critical audience for whom it is important to maintain standards and effort in rehearsal. Rehearsing, in other words, is every bit as demanding as performing.

The shared musical experience

This consideration of the group experience of making music has so far focused on its social effects, including the negotiation of roles and the development of supportive networks. Matters of musical taste and preference were less prominent in performers' discourse, perhaps because common ground was assumed within each event. At the COMA summer school, for example, while all participants were interested in the broad category of contemporary music, few expressed clear or extensive views about the repertoire they encountered as listeners and performers during the week. Diary reflections tended to focus on the social interactions, emotions and challenges of the week, with little detailed reaction to the musical content of workshops or concerts. When invited to spend a day as a participant in the one day summer school, I came to understand this apparent lack of focus on musical preference as being partly dictated by the pace of events: learning vocal and percussion parts for the evening concert took all my mental energy, to the point where I reflected only later on whether the musical product had been enjoyable. If my experience was typical, participants were perhaps so engrossed in the immediate challenges of performing that they had little opportunity to consider their effect.

It may be that the absence of 'purely' musical discussion amongst the case study performers is more a function of the difficulties of putting these shared experiences into words. Paul Berliner (1994) has noted a similar tendency amongst jazz musicians, many of whom prefer to give feedback on their band's performance through their musical actions rather than through spoken commentary, 'due to the difficulties inherent in translating musical concepts into words and the awkwardness of confronting problems' (p. 425). However, evidence from other published empirical studies suggests that participants do occasionally make a conceptual separation between the musical, personal and social in their reflections on musical experience, as in this account from a barbershop singer:

> When you're singing, the sound around you is incredible. You feel like you're being carried away with it. It's absolutely inspiring. But, you know, it seems to take a contest or the annual show to bring out the best in us, to get to that level of perfection where the chords ring and you feel like you're being swallowed up by the music itself. (Stebbins, 1996: 94)

This singer has experienced the sensation of being part of a musical sound that surpasses the individual contributions of the participants and takes on an identity of its own. He makes it clear that this happens on rare occasions, and Stebbins theorises that such events 'motivate the singer to stick with the art in the hope of finding similar experiences again, they demonstrate that diligence and commitment can pay off, and they serve as major turning points in the leisure career' (ibid.: 56).

Barbershop singers have developed a vocabulary to describe the way in which music exists beyond the contributions of the individual performers; they talk about chords 'ringing' when the close four-part harmony of their singing finds a particular resonance, and the frequent use of such language in rehearsal means that all participants are encouraged to be aware of the music 'out there' (cf. Stebbins, 1996; Averill, 2003). Gage Averill suggests that the physical vibrations of closely harmonised singing create a close personal and musical connection amongst participants: 'the relationship of the internalising and externalising of the self and of others in collective musical encounters encourages the production of a powerful, transformative experience of the self as a participant in community, resulting in a greater sense of solidarity and unity' (Averill, 2003: 178). By emphasising the physical, bodily engagement with music that is felt in these moments of heightened experience, Averill goes some way to explaining the aspects of musical participation that lie beyond words and connect the social and personal benefits that are more readily articulated by participants.

Some respondents in Sara Cohen's study of Liverpool rock bands made a greater separation between these elements and 'delighted in the physical activity of producing noises and sounds' even while remaining unconvinced by the musical product: 'some expressed a personal dislike of the music their band produced but nevertheless loved playing it' (Cohen, 1991: 190). There was similar ambivalence amongst some of the Gilbert and Sullivan performers, who appeared to value the performing opportunities generated by the repertoire more highly than its musical content. This raises the interesting question of exactly what it is that participants enjoy about their musical activities. Perhaps the personal and social functions of participation are mentioned more often than the musical aspects not only because they are easier to talk about, but also because they hold greater or more immediate significance for participants.

It is striking that the strongest musical opinions and affiliations across the case studies are to be found amongst the audiences; Buxton regulars with their devotion to Gilbert and Sullivan, and Music in the Round listeners developing their extensive knowledge of chamber music. For those investing emotional and physical energy in the musical process as performers, rather than solely in its product as listeners, opportunities for continued involvement are arguably more important than the repertoire itself, which is readily available through other, easier means, such as recordings and professional performances. Wayne Booth expresses this anxiety about his own musical involvement, since 'for the music lover, the most disturbing theft that playing commits is of time stolen from listening' (1999: 150). He notes that in the chamber music sessions of the pre-recording era, amateur musicians 'risked hearing badly played music as an alternative to hearing none' (p. 150), but for Booth, as for my case study participants, the choices are no longer so stark. Amateur performers choose to engage in the processes and practices of music because that is where much of their enjoyment lies; in the self-development, group solidarity and companionable pleasures that contributing to a musical performance can bring.

The pressures and pleasures of musical involvement

For all the emphasis on enjoyment in participants' responses, the pressures of time and energy were frequently mentioned too: performers in the COMA summer school and the Buxton Gilbert and Sullivan Festival spoke of their exhaustion at the pace of activities, and audience members at Music in the Round often followed comments on their own tiredness with a recognition that the problem must be greater for the host string quartet, who performed at least once daily throughout the festival. This intensity of activities is by no means unusual in musical events, where action-packed festivals are a common phenomenon, and pressured rehearsals as deadlines approach are a widely accepted part of the performing process. These pressures *could* be avoided, but only if participants and audiences were willing to accept a slower rate of performances, prepared over a greater length of time without recourse to the punishing rehearsal schedule observed at Buxton and COMA. The decisions to make the performing experience an intensely physical and demanding one are self-imposed, at least to the extent that 'once people have agreed to participate in a musical event, they must suspend a range of personal choices until they have reached the end of the sequence of action that was determined by their original decision' (Blacking, 1995: 152). Participants may rebel or feel frustration in the midst of this process, as did some of the COMA participants, but their co-operation is rarely fully withdrawn and so their complicity in this pattern of preparation continues.

The need for such intensity of engagement is illustrated by its absence for the undergraduates in Study 1, who cited their busier musical schedules while at school as evidence for their reduced feelings of 'being a musician' once at university. With music the central activity in their studying and often their social lives too, they were no longer having to work as hard for their musical experiences, and so were gaining less satisfaction from their involvement. Orchestral and choir rehearsals during the day were not considered by most to be part of their studies (equivalent to a lecture, for example), but neither were they entirely voluntary, and so the divisions of work and leisure were becoming confusingly blurred for these students. Somehow a timetabled rehearsal appeared less authentic, contradicting the familiar chaos and urgency of preparation that they were used to from school productions and concerts. Musical participation that is not difficult, exhausting and challenging is apparently less satisfying; a self-destructive premise perhaps, but one that sheds new light on the dedication felt by amateur performing groups to their shared endeavours. Meeting the self-imposed challenges of musical performance through collective exertion places high value on the musical product, since the effort and exhaustion of the process must be worthwhile if it is to be entered into repeatedly and willingly.

Musical participation must surely rank amongst Michael Argyle's category of 'seriously committing leisure activities', whose followers are 'happier, and found their leisure more satisfying, though it was also ... challenging and stressful' (Argyle, 1996b: 32). Few case study participants demonstrated the compulsive involvement that Robert Stebbins cautions against, whereby 'amateurism ... engenders in the practitioner a desire to engage in the activity beyond the time and money available for it' (1996: 75); but perhaps their families and colleagues would have offered a different perspective on that subject. Certainly, the rock band members interviewed by Sara Cohen were candid in acknowledging that friendships outside the band were often neglected as a result of their musical involvement, and that 'girlfriends conflicted with, or distracted them from, their band activities, which was why some of them, particularly younger members, insisted they didn't want girlfriends at all' (Cohen, 1991: 32). For the case study participants, experiences seemed to resemble more closely the accounts of Ruth Finnegan's Milton Keynes musicians, who found 'a great sense of comradeship and co-operation' (1989: 99) amongst fellow performers, and valued the practical and emotional support that membership of their performing group afforded.

The challenges of musical participation can take many forms, and in a survey of the social impact of arts projects on participants from disadvantaged backgrounds, François Matarasso notes that 'almost all the projects required people to take personal and social risks of different kinds – not involving physical injury or financial loss, but risks associated with self, identity, capacity, ability, relationships and similar intangibles' (Matarasso, 1997: 59). Despite differences in their motivations and backgrounds, participants in the community arts projects studied by Matarasso reacted to their arts experiences in ways that were often comparable with the case study participants. Like the Gilbert and Sullivan performers, they enjoyed the chance to be noticed and heard more than occurred in everyday life; 'finding their own voice or, perhaps, the courage to use it' (Matarasso, 1997: 17). Similarly, they shared with the COMA participants their valuing of 'a supportive and co-operative atmosphere, where everyone's efforts and ideas were appreciated' (p. 15).

Matarasso's focus is explicitly on regenerative arts projects, with specific social aims, and he points out that established amateur participants are less likely to come from disadvantaged backgrounds, since 'their existing commitment to the arts implies previous experience and, perhaps, a degree of confidence in their own creative abilities' (p. 56). Certainly, the experience and confidence of the case study participants, although variable, was greater than the average, but their personal and social experiences of music-making seem similar in kind to those of the community project members in Matarasso's study. Taking individual risks within a supportive framework seems to be at the heart of the pleasure that is to be found in musical participation, at whatever level and in a variety of contexts.

Perspectives on professional performance

The understanding of rehearsing and performing processes that amateur involvement in music affords holds the potential to inform in turn participants' listening to other performing groups. Respondents at the Music in the Round festival, in particular, readily acknowledged the greater insight that performing experience – at whatever level or stage of life – brought to their chamber music listening. The published literature on professional rehearsing, however, shows marked differences from the experiences reported by case study participants; tales of insensitive conflict-resolution in string quartet rehearsals (Waterman, 2003) or low job satisfaction amongst orchestral players (Levine & Levine, 1996; Allmendinger *et al.*, 1996) might surprise those listeners whose main musical involvement has been amongst enthusiastic amateurs. Attempts to enlighten deluded audiences about the lives of professional performers have a long history:

> Many an amateur in the audience thinks how exciting and delightful an orchestral player's life must be. This is an illusion. The life is one of incessant strain and back-breaking work in which minutes of pleasure are paid for by hours and hours of slogging. (Shore, 1938: 9)

Like their amateur counterparts, professional musicians seek relief from their work in hobbies which balance their everyday activities; gardening, writing, home improvement and aviation were popular amongst the Levines' sample, apparently because these are 'hobbies which provide a high degree of control' (p. 22).

While there is limited published literature on rehearsal practices, the most extensive accounts are of string quartets, so offering a useful connection here with the perceptions of the Music in the Round festival audience (discussed more fully in Chapter 6). Psychological studies (e.g. Murnighan & Conlon, 1991; Davidson & Good, 2002) and biographical accounts (e.g. Blum, 1986; Nissel, 1998) both emphasise the complexity of the decision-making processes that contribute to a string quartet performance, where the potentially diverse views of four highly skilled players must be resolved – at least temporarily – into a coherent interpretation. Styles of leadership and behaviour are critical in ensuring the survival of such a group, and Vivienne Young and Andrew Colman (1979) suggest that this creates particular difficulties for the first violinist, whose musical leadership cannot be assumed to bring with it a psychological dominance: 'although the first violinist is the designated head in a formal sense in every string quartet, he *[sic]* is perhaps not necessarily in every sense a leader since the official position which he holds is no guarantee that he will have the greatest decision-making influence in the group' (Young & Colman, 1979: 15).

Murnighan and Conlon (1991) champion a different member of the quartet, seeing the well-being and role satisfaction of the second violinist as critical to the successful functioning of the group: 'They must have consummate ability that rarely finds complete expression; they must always play the role of supporter during a performance, even if the first violin seems wrong; and they get little attention but nevertheless provide one of the most salient bases for evaluating the quartet as a whole' (Murnighan & Conlon, 1991: 169). Interview discussion with the second violinist at Music in the Round confirmed this view, as he felt his own role to be one of 'enabling people to play better' and expressed frustration at the widespread misconception that second violinists are really aspiring leaders, waiting for their lucky break [MitRI 20]. No doubt viola players and 'cellists could defend the challenges and significance of their own contributions in a comparable way, giving an overall picture of a potentially volatile group composed of four strong individual perspectives.

The audience at the Music in the Round festival (Study 4) seemed to have a surface awareness of the challenges of string quartet performance, but often revealed in their discussion a conflation of the quartet's identity with that of its flamboyant first violinist. Since the leader of the host string quartet is also the Artistic Director of the festival, his role is doubly reinforced in the minds of the audience. He tends to give the spoken introductions to the quartet's performances, with the result that his personality is most clearly delineated for the audience, while the other players remain more anonymous. Many interviews and questionnaire responses mentioned the first violinist only, valuing highly his role as 'impresario' [MitRI 16] and relishing the demonstrative nature of his playing. A few listeners were more alert to the varied contributions of the quartet members, noting that the leader was 'almost a soloist at times and the other three hold him, keep him together' [MitRI 2].

In forming musical judgements of the different instrumental roles, listeners were helped by the visual impact of the performance, in that the movements of the players enabled them to pick out musical lines in a way that they found difficult when listening to a recording:

Is it the Schubert quintet where either the second violin or viola plays these repetitive background chords for ages, you know, and it's absolutely crucial to the sound that's made, and I hadn't realised how incredibly sort of repetitive it is in the background until you see [the viola player] playing it. [MitRI 11]

Visual and aural perception had an obvious contribution to make to listeners' musical experiences, and as the most mobile and demonstrative player, the first violinist was once again frequently prominent. Social links seemed to be important too, in that knowing quartet members individually also helped to distinguish their musical characters and contributions. Interviewees often mentioned personal connections with the players; in the case of the second violinist, for example, 'his kids went to the same school as ours, and he used to play in the school concerts, which goes down very well' [MitRI 11]. Audience members appeared to enjoy these social links, which emphasised the individual lives and personalities of the quartet members; 'we meet their families at school and theatre events and they become part of Sheffield' [MitRQ 203]. Listeners drew variously on the personal, visual and aural information that was available to them in and around the performances, employing a variety of strategies to seek greater connection with the quartet.

Music in the Round listeners often revealed a desire to see behind the scenes and know how musical and social influences interact in quartet playing, and the critical acclaim and popularity of Vikram Seth's (1999) novel *An Equal Music* suggests that this curiosity is not unusual. Seth's narrative about the fictional Maggiore quartet includes accounts of tempestuous rehearsals, decisions over repertoire and recordings, conflicts of interest stimulated by relationships outside the quartet; in short, the trappings of quartet life that generally remain hidden from the audience. The desire for performers to be 'human' and accessible is familiar enough from popular music, where the habits and preferences of performers are well known by their audiences and such knowledge is valued and exchanged amongst fans (Cavicchi, 1998; Rhein, 2000). In Western art music, with its historical notions of the performers as vessels through which the composer's intentions are communicated (e.g. Scholes, 1935: 122), celebrities are rare – although now perhaps on the increase through a crossover of marketing strategies – and information about the temperaments, dislikes or home lives of performers is kept largely hidden. The Music in the Round audience members, however, were keen to observe friendliness, approachability and other desirable human qualities in the performers they heard, emphasising once again the strong connection between the personal, the social and the musical in participation.

Several 'real world' accounts supplement Seth's fictional view of performing life, including those of the Amadeus (Nissel, 1998) and the Guarneri (Blum, 1986) quartets, both of which emphasise the social and interpersonal aspects of string quartet membership; Muriel Nissel from her perspective as the wife of Siegmund Nissel, second violinist with the Amadeus, and David Blum through round-table discussions with members of the Guarneri. Blum's account offers the most direct line to the hidden world of rehearsal processes, as in this comment from Arnold Steinhardt, the first violinist and leader of the Guarneri quartet:

> One mustn't forget that in developing a quartet, personal qualities play as important a role as musicianship; the two can't be easily separated. Each of us has to be strong enough to exert his leadership, strong enough to endure the constant criticisms of his colleagues, and strong enough to let go of cherished ideas when they don't coincide with the majority opinion. (Blum, 1986: 7)

This quote reveals the element of truth in the instinctive connection between personality and product that informs the Music in the Round audience's understanding of their resident quartet. Listeners appeared to relish the spontaneity and variety of interpretation that were part of this quartet's style, enjoying the glimpse this afforded of the 'constant working-out process' reported also by the Guarneri (Blum, 1986: 7).

Nissel's account is necessarily more anecdotal, focusing little on rehearsal and more on the characters, experiences and lives of the Amadeus members. She writes of 'stormy' patches in the quartet's early years which might have caused a less dedicated or determined group to separate, and so gives support to Stebbins' notion of 'continuance commitment' (1992: 51), whereby the risks to professional performers of ceasing a particular musical activity are seen to outweigh the potential benefits, and so frustrations are tolerated and conquered through a greater investment of time than amateur ensembles might willingly give to similarly difficult circumstances. An illustration of what happens when this continuance commitment is absent can be found in Tory Butterworth's (1990) analysis of the Detroit String Quartet, a part-time ensemble for whom dreams of world class careers had been set aside in favour of high quality but less ambitious concert schedules:

> Making beautiful music was far more important to quartet members than critical or commercial success. This attitude allowed the ensemble to plug along at a slow, steady pace consistent with its aspiration of continual improvement coupled with harmonious group relations. (Butterworth, 1990: 221)

So intent were this group on avoiding conflict that they chose to disband rather than recruit a new member when one of their players moved away from the area. Like the Gilbert and Sullivan societies discussed above, the quartet maintained its equilibrium through shared and realistic goals, and when these were fulfilled or no longer possible, the quartet's useful life was at an end. This experience is perhaps closer to amateur performing, where similarly ready acceptance of circumstances sometimes constrains or dictates the future direction of an ensemble or society. In the full-time quartets discussed above, the disjunction between performance as 'work' and as 'serious leisure' was more marked, perhaps creating a distance between the amateur players in the audience and the performers on stage, since both parties have a more limited understanding than they might realise of one another's motives and practices. The contrast between the amateur experiences of the case study performers, the professional views revealed in the string quartet literature, and the multiple perspectives of the case study audiences make it increasingly remarkable that musical activity holds the potential to fulfil such diverse needs and intentions.

Re-connecting the individual and social in musical participation

Discussion in this chapter and the previous one has revealed widely-held personal and social motivations for musical participation, which bring with them a demand for high standards, commitment and energy from all concerned. Musical participation has been shown to offer an independence from the restricted or pre-determined roles of everyday life, rendered safe by the supportive group context within which such self-exploration takes place. Participants clearly relish the sense of autonomy that their musical lives provide, whilst enjoying their membership of what Howard Becker (1982) has called 'art worlds' – virtual communities of people engaged in the 'patterns of collective activity' which contribute to the completion and dissemination of any piece of art work (p. 12).

The social rules enforced within performing groups can be every bit as constraining as those in other spheres of life, since participants must meet the schedules and demands of rehearsing together if the outcome is to be successful (cf. Blacking, 1995: 152). However, co-operation with the rules of musical participation leads to the tangible benefits of a successful performance, and can always be withdrawn by individual participants if or when those rewards become insufficient to justify the effort they demand. The risks of participation are therefore within the control of participants, and the shared challenges of rehearsing and performing contribute to the pleasure experienced by group members.

Participating in music has clear ramifications for the individuals concerned, and for the groups to which they contribute, but Christopher Small holds that active musical involvement also has a broader social significance:

> Music is too important to be left to the musicians, and in recognizing this fact we strike a blow at the experts' domination, not only of our music but also of our very lives. If it is possible to control our own musical destiny, provide our own music rather than leaving it altogether to someone else to provide, then perhaps some of the other outside expertise that controls our lives can be brought under control also. (Small, 1977/96: 214)

Small's sentiments were echoed to a certain extent by participants at the COMA summer school (Study 3), many of whom saw connections between the 'unexpected and imaginative nature of contemporary music' [FWQ 21] and the open-minded world views of COMA members. The summer school included much improvisatory music, as well as flexibly-scored arrangements where levels of difficulty were within the players' own control; both approaches which challenge traditional models of musical power and expertise. Performers at Buxton and COMA were also aware of their relatively marginal position in relation to the musical establishment; each, in their different ways, resisting the most obvious musical choices available to them and pursuing an interest that better suited their outlook and preferences.

Making music with others is a public statement of intent, which invests that activity with a high priority and value assumed to be commonly held by other members of the performing group. Membership of a performing society or a well-established audience was likened by some participants to religious experience, and in particular invited comparisons with church attendance (cf. Gabrielsson & Lindström Wik, 2003: 202). Belonging to a church congregation was either known or imagined to provide the same sense of collective endeavour, shared values and routine, and group identity as did attendance at festivals or membership of performing groups:

> Everyone else is there with the same frame of mind; it's almost like going to church might be I suppose, it's a kind of community [MitRI 11]

The link between religious and musical experience is in many respects persuasive: both involve heightened attention to aspects of daily life that are part of the cultural background, but become foregrounded only through individual intention or public events (cf. Johnson, 2002: 7). 'Both can evoke a powerful and fairly intense emotional response which is generally highly positive. Both have elements which are private to the individual, and occur in a social context such as a public act of worship or musical performance' (Hills & Argyle, 1998: 91). And both involve a combination of intellectual and emotional engagement that makes them hard to translate into words: the indefinable 'extra' quality of religious activity is recognised as 'spirituality', a term sometimes drawn into discussion of the 'special' nature of musical experience, since the vocabulary is otherwise lacking:

> Going to something like Music in the Round is like this little oasis of physically taking time out, but also kind of like, I don't know, not spiritually, but it's like recharging your batteries, you know, and just going and listening to something incredibly beautiful, and really life enhancing I think; I can't say that strongly enough really. [MitRI 15]

Musical and religious experience both offer a reflective space in which participants can look beyond worldly concerns, mirroring the opportunities for a release from the pressures of everyday life that were valued by performers at Buxton and COMA. Once again, this would be inaccurately described as escapism, in that the activities make fresh demands of participants even while they relieve them of everyday concerns. Churches and concert halls alike offer a haven to escape *to*, enabling participants to return to everyday life refreshed and enriched. Musical and religious participation share, too, the fact that they are incomprehensible to – sometimes barely even tolerated by – those who are not involved in them. There are clear limitations in attempting to explain one imponderable with reference to another, but for those who hold at least a religious sympathy, if not an active faith, the comparison of music with an aspect of life that is widely recognised to be 'other worldly' offers some way forward in interpreting its significance.

These two chapters on individual and group experiences of musical participation have illustrated the satisfactions to be gained from individual striving for a self-imposed goal, and collective sharing of enthusiasms and a common sense of purpose. From their personal vantage points, participants make connections between their group musical activities and their individual musical lives, establishing a network of experiences that build or reinforce their sense of being musically active and engaged. So far, there has been little discussion of a third significant element: the kinds of music with which participants become involved and affiliated. The next chapter will therefore explore the musical allegiances and passions expressed by the various participants, and will consider the implications and responsibilities that such choices bring with them.

CHAPTER FIVE

Identifying With Music:
Preservation and Promotion

Discussion in the preceding chapters has focused on the processes of making music, with little consideration so far of participants' attitudes towards the repertoire or genre within which their experiences were located. In this chapter, attention turns to the identification with particular musical practices and styles that framed and defined the activities of participants. Across the three event-based case studies, a strong campaigning instinct emerged amongst participants who were variously concerned with preserving the traditions of Gilbert and Sullivan, making contemporary music accessible to amateur performers, and freeing live chamber music from the stuffiness of concert hall traditions. Questions of musical allegiance and preference emerged which have previously been researched only in relation to listening, and the relevance to the case studies of recent research on fan behaviour and musical preference is considered here. The chapter begins with a consideration of the appeal which each musical world holds for its participants, before moving on to consider the manifestations of and reasons for their collective desire to preserve or promote the genre of their choice amongst a wider public.

Relationships with repertoire

The events studied in this project involve aspects of Western music which attract strong devotees and detractors: contemporary music and Gilbert and Sullivan operetta, although very different, can both be seen as an acquired taste, and chamber music was characterised by several audience members as 'music for the third age', demanding greater maturity and patience of its listeners than, say, orchestral music. Participants in all three events seemed to take a pride in their less than mainstream musical tastes; their musical preferences reinforced by the perceived need to defend or justify them.

Participants' attachments to the genres in which they were active inevitably varied in nature and degree: some came to a particular kind of music out of curiosity, some as a considered and impassioned choice, others by accident or necessity where the events or groups joined were simply the most convenient source of musical activity. Within each genre, 'fanatics' were viewed by the majority with a hint of caution – perhaps least so in the contemporary music environment where eccentricity was seen as being a valid part of the experimental ethos. Clearer hierarchies of enthusiasm could be seen at the Gilbert and Sullivan festival, where the strongest devotion to the genre was to be found amongst the audience, and performers were often more ambivalent about the repertoire, seeing it principally as giving them access to frequent and enjoyable performing opportunities. And at the Music in the Round festival, individual tastes were more in evidence, as audience members acknowledged the boundaries of their preferences and chose to challenge these or remain within them, according to their temperament, time availability, and ticket budget. A closer look at the genres celebrated in the festivals and summer school will highlight these distinctions further, whilst also demonstrating the similar decisions and judgements that inform participants' loyalties and behaviours.

The appeal of Gilbert and Sullivan

The creative partnership of W. S. Gilbert and Sir Arthur Sullivan was unique in generating a substantial body of operettas that set English texts to accessible (but not always easy) music, so allowing generations of dedicated performing societies to enjoy the rich four-part chorus writing, witty solo characters and affectedly English dialogue. But the popularity which has given the operettas a secure place in the affections of audiences and performers has left their creators outside the mainstream of operatic history (Hughes & Stradling, 2001: 225), with Sullivan, in particular, criticised for failing to put his compositional skills to more musically adventurous or conventionally prestigious uses (Headington *et al.*, 1987: 289). The legacy of this divide between apologists and detractors can be seen in the literature (e.g. Eden, 1986; Stedman, 1980), which is generally defensive in its praise of the operettas, whilst occasionally acknowledging that 'they are best appreciated in performance' (Wren, 2001: ix).

Gilbert and Sullivan's operettas have an energy and familiarity which evidently makes them fun to participate in and attracts a loyal audience. Gaining enjoyment from them, however, requires a suspension or denial of contemporary concerns if the Victorian attitudes of the plots are to be tolerated: women, for example, have a uniformly lowly status, and are differentiated mainly by their levels of beauty and sanity, and their success in finding a husband. Critical discomfort with these ideas was notably absent at the Buxton festival; participants were there to celebrate Gilbert and Sullivan, described in the festival brochure as 'the very best of British entertainment for all the family'. Specialist knowledge of the trivia quiz-winning kind was valued and displayed through discussions and Fringe activities, but there was very little interpretative debate, and performances that differed from the traditional models were viewed with some suspicion. The only sustained critique of the genre came in the church service which is an annual feature of the festival, stemming from the local vicar's enthusiasms and on this occasion featuring his own piano playing and a selection of hymns written by Sullivan. Addressing this congregation, William Parry defended the operettas against an assumed charge of being 'frivolous' or 'mere froth', stating that Gilbert and Sullivan's work could 'alleviate our human concerns' by balancing some of the painful realities of the modern world with their invitation to 'take heart in the positive, to be joyful'. Rather than finding unfamiliar, more subtle meanings in the operettas, Parry urged an appreciation of their obvious qualities, so endorsing the relationship that the majority of his audience will have had with this repertoire.

Participants at the Buxton festival seemed to recognise that the genre they celebrated was somewhat removed from the values and concerns of twenty first century life, but experienced that disjunction as a positive feature rather than seeing it as problematic. Performers were more likely than audience members to be ambivalent in their attitudes to the genre; inevitable, perhaps, as the audience had made a clear decision to attend a Gilbert and Sullivan production, whereas performers could be participating for reasons other than a love of the genre. Indeed, performers' views on the repertoire varied, with the responses of one group (Group B – see p. 56 for a description) to the question 'What appeals to you about performing Gilbert and Sullivan, in particular?' showing the multiple factors that had influenced their decision to participate:

Table 5.1 The appeal of Gilbert and Sullivan for performers

	Sample responses
Character and style	[BUXQ B3] The Englishness and the language. Also the satire which is not prevalent in modern operas. [9] Music – a good sing! [11] The humour. Good chorus involvement in every show. The camaraderie. [12] Love the music, humorous, English. [14] Musically more satisfying to perform than musical comedy.
Accessibility and opportunities	[2] Working with quality soloists, director and musical director is the appeal, not particularly the G & S operas. [6] It suits my voice and my performing abilities – good range of characterisation to develop acting skills. [8] Different types of characters throughout the different operas. Plenty of chorus numbers. [13] The amount and quality of chorus work.
Enduring appeal	[4] 130 years on, it is still extraordinarily powerful musical theatre. [14] Shows have had enduring appeal for over 100 years. Enthusiastic audiences.

These performers – possibly among the most devoted to the genre given their 'champion' status at the festival – show a range of enthusiasms for the repertoire, sometimes comparing it with other performing styles to illustrate the unique opportunities that their Gilbert and Sullivan society provides. For some, this provoked a respect for the repertoire by which longevity and 'enduring appeal' was cited as evidence of its value; for others, the suitability of the music to their personal or group needs was the strongest factor in its appeal. Members of the group appreciated the humour of the dialogue and the quality of the music, and some also mentioned 'Englishness', an appeal which was acknowledged with some puzzlement by these performers from Ireland (Group A) in their group interview:

-   But what makes an Irishman love Gilbert and Sullivan? You can understand it with an Englishman, but what does it do for an Irishman?
-   But Sullivan was Irish.
-   But that's beside the point.
-   It is very English, but he was laughing at the Establishment, and that's something the Irish love. I think it's because they liked to take the piss. *[Laughter]* That's exactly what they did – I know it's crude, but we like it because that's what we like to do. We like to laugh at ourselves. [BUXI A1-3]

The 'Englishness' of Gilbert and Sullivan was linked closely with its humour by these performers, and they rejected the opportunity to claim the Irish heritage of the operettas, dismissing Sullivan's ancestry (which was also part-Italian) as 'beside the point'. Later in the interview they noted the 'the difficulty with the accents in the dialogue', and indeed this had been remarked upon by the adjudicator at the end of their performance the previous evening. The operettas resist translation even into a regional Anglophone accent, suggesting that their 'Englishness' is potentially an excluding and insular feature, even if it was not felt as such by these Irish participants, who attempted to make connections with their own perceived national characteristics.

Debates on the Englishness and humour of the Gilbert and Sullivan operettas are inevitably circular: both aspects make sense to those who enjoy the repertoire, whilst contributing to the alienation felt by those who do not. Giving reasons for participation (see Table 5.1), some performers avoided these debates, focusing instead on more pragmatic features: accessibility, quality of solo and chorus roles, and the chance to work with skilled performers and directors. The first of these reasons was elaborated on in interview by a tenor who had performed many Gilbert and Sullivan principal roles:

I think the accessibility is a major factor, because it's something you *can* do – you can watch a performance tonight of *The Mikado*, and in six months' time you can be on stage with your Gilbert and Sullivan society wherever, and you could be Nanki-Poo or the Mikado or whatever. [BUXI 3]

It seems that some performers participate in Gilbert and Sullivan because they *can* – relishing the opportunities to develop their skills and perform with other like-minded people – whilst others are clearer in their devotion to the genre, enjoying its particular brand of humour and social satire. Audience members were more likely to be loyal to Gilbert and Sullivan specifically: 140 of the 174 audience questionnaire respondents (80 per cent) included 'I am a Gilbert and Sullivan enthusiast' in their selection from a given list of reasons for attending, and 116 (67 per cent) had been to the festival before, suggesting a high level of interest in the genre, although 105 audience members (60 per cent) also saw it more generally as a source of 'live music of high quality'. This imbalance of performer and audience commitment to the repertoire might be assumed to be typical; audience attendance at performances is governed by their considered tastes and preferences, whereas the performers may gain their greatest pleasure from participation, with the repertoire making an important, but not exclusive, contribution to fulfilling their musical needs.

For audience and performers alike, the festival provided a larger community that allowed them to celebrate their allegiance to the genre – however deeply felt – amongst like-minded enthusiasts. Many performing societies hired scenery, props and costumes from the same theatrical company, creating a similarity between performances that was welcomed as being true to the traditions of the genre. Sitting amongst the audience for a week, I overheard numerous detailed discussions of the productions and their merits, with audience members often in private disagreement with the official adjudicator who gave her report at the end of each show. Loyalty to the Gilbert and Sullivan repertoire was for many a matter of 'serious enjoyment', and the sense of responsibility to the genre and its continued existence was keenly felt.

The appeal of contemporary music

The questioning and debate that had been absent at the Buxton Gilbert and Sullivan festival was a central feature of the COMA Summer School: these participants were evidently used to justifying and explaining their musical passions, and were happy to explore them through discussions with each other, as well as in their diary and questionnaire responses. Just as there had been differences in the motivations of the weekend and full week participants, so the weekend questionnaire responses showed greater caution and generality in answer to the question 'How would you describe your attitude to contemporary music?'.

Weekend participants tended to express conditional enthusiasm for the repertoire, stating that it was 'fun to do – not for the layman audience to listen to!' [WEQ 5] or that they were 'easily bored by stuff that has no meaning' [WEQ 4]. Open-mindedness was also a common factor in their responses, as they described contemporary music as 'an adventure often worth taking' [WEQ 8] or a 'curious and challenging' experience [WEQ 9]. The only whole-heartedly enthusiastic response came from someone who intended to stay for the whole week 'as soon as the children are less dependent on me' [WEQ 10], and whose work involved proof-reading for contemporary music publications. This woman viewed her participation as 'a vital part of my life – it reflects/interprets how I interact with the world' [WEQ 10], but many others on the weekend course were more uncertain of their relationship with the repertoire; interested enough to invest their time and money in a short course, but cautious about the experiences they might encounter there.

With the exception of one weekend respondent who made a distinction between 'scored' and 'unscored' music, describing the latter as 'improvisation from nothing – musically unsatisfying' [WEQ 3], participants reacted to the generic notion of 'contemporary music', with few specific preferences or experiences identified. This was reasonable enough, since the question had not asked for such a response, but the full week participants gave more detailed reasons for their enjoyment, and also revealed a greater level of enthusiasm for the practices and aims of contemporary music as a whole. Open-mindedness was again prevalent, as participants described themselves as 'perplexed – enthralled – bemused' [FWQ 23] and explained that 'by participating in contemporary music I have begun to understand a lot more about it' [FWQ 21]. Full week participants emphasised their emotional as well as intellectual engagement with contemporary music, feeling 'open, interested, vitalised' [FWQ 2] and 'always excited by new, unusual rhythms and sounds' [FWQ 13]. For one respondent, it was 'the only music possible' [FWQ 15], and many seemed to share this total commitment to participating in and promoting the music of their choice.

Evidence of the continuum between weekend and full week participant attitudes could be seen where respondents gave some background details to account for their growing enjoyment. Amongst the weekend participants, one response showed the early stages of enthusiasm suddenly flourishing in the summer school environment:

> After the first day (Saturday) I returned to my hostel crying out for a real score with real notes – some Mozart. But what we achieved on Sunday was so exciting and exhilarating! I just loved the whole experience. [WEQ 5]

Several full week participants described similar shifts of interest from classical to contemporary repertoire, with comments including the following:

> Until last year, I wasn't a fan of contemporary music, thinking along the lines of it sounds horrible. I am now a big lover of it, choosing contemporary over 'nicer sounding' music to study and listen to. [FWQ 19]

Participants seemed fully aware of having chosen a musical path that is still unusual, and enjoyed the opportunity to feel surrounded by like-minded enthusiasts at the summer school: 'It's wonderful not to have to justify my liking for contemporary music' [CMD 14]. This diary comment came from a founder member of COMA who reflected throughout the week on the unique atmosphere of the summer school, valuing 'people's willingness (and even eagerness) to try almost anything':

> I remember the first COMA ever, 10 years ago; it was incredibly exhilarating to be amongst so many people who were mad keen on contemporary music and that enthusiasm has never really died. I'm prepared to overlook a lot of minor irritations for that sense of purpose and dedication untouched by any considerations of commerciality or 'correctness' or conventionality. [CMD 14]

A few other participants found the 'anything goes' mentality rather limiting, with one finding the 'ethos a little too dated and precious' [FWQ 26]. Several of the tutors had been active in the 1960s and drew on the ideas of the Cornelius Cardew 'Scratch Orchestra' and similar experimental styles in their teaching, which for some participants was not contemporary enough. Others found the same ideas new and unfamiliar, so illustrating how previous experience with the repertoire shaped participants' responses to the workshops and rehearsals: 'My attitude towards music has changed completely since trying some 'scratch' composing and improvisation. I feel more in control and appreciate the need to listen to others more and respond to them' [FWQ 8].

The director of COMA told me that no deliberate effort had been made to cultivate a particular atmosphere at the summer school, whilst commenting half-seriously that 'a drift towards a perfect cadence is not jumped on, but noted' [COMAI 1]. Whereas the Gilbert and Sullivan festival had obvious boundaries of repertoire within which even small changes were noticeable (and not always well received), the approaches and scope of the COMA summer school were much more open to negotiation, and vary each year according to the tutors and participants who are present. Participants commented on the opportunities this afforded to learn from one another, and for the most part relished any challenges to their existing beliefs and behaviours.

Rather than coming to the summer school to have their knowledge and enthusiasms confirmed – as at the Gilbert and Sullivan festival – the COMA participants were intellectually and emotionally alive to new experiences, and engaged in often heated discussions about the concerts, workshops and rehearsals in which they were involved. Concerts, particularly, drew strong and diverse reactions; an electroacoustic performance was a 'feast for the ears' [CMD 8] to one participant, whilst another 'felt the noise was unbearable and left' [CMD 13]. Often, the participants made connections with other aspects of their musical experience, and found that their contemporary music-making made them question more traditional practices:

> It's impossible to say adequately how much I enjoyed the concert tonight […] It makes me think even more slightingly of the conventional type of concert (neat rows of too-small seats, stuffy room, hush …!) and think that music doesn't just need new forms, new music, but also new ways of listening both mentally and physically. [CMD 14]

There are many clear differences between the Buxton and the COMA participants: the former had come to entertain or be entertained, the latter to learn and develop their skills; Gilbert and Sullivan attracts audiences familiar with and devoted to the genre, but contemporary music invites a more questioning approach; Buxton audience members were more homogenous in their age and outlook, whilst COMA participants had the opportunity to display more individual characteristics and eccentricities. It might seem too neat to suggest that participants were attracted to musical environments that matched their temperament and world view, but the two groups would certainly have felt uncomfortable if they had stumbled by accident into the 'wrong' festival, and I would speculate that this would be as much to do with the attitudes and behaviours they would find there as with the music. The two elements *could* be separated: COMA participants could debate the cultural messages of the Gilbert and Sullivan repertoire, and Buxton festival-goers might find unexpected pleasures in contemporary works – but this potentially disastrous disjunction illustrates the function that the festival and summer school serve for the repertoire that is their focus. By providing a clearly-defined environment to which like-minded and enthusiastic participants are attracted, the two events protect and preserve their repertoire and its practices. For the Gilbert and Sullivan repertoire, this is a nostalgic, backward-looking process, since the contemporary analysis of the operettas would disrupt the enjoyment felt by its devotees. For COMA participants, there is a greater willingness to embrace new experiences and engage in critical discussion, but this too is rendered safe by the likelihood of finding social groups within which deeply felt opinions will be recognised and supported.

The appeal of chamber music

The repertoire of the Music in the Round festival was if anything more diverse than that of the COMA summer school, having drawn together elements of the previous years' festivals through an 'audience choice' consultation. In many cases the audience members' principal loyalty appeared to be to the event or to particular performers, and reflective comments about the appeal of chamber music were rare, although individual enthusiasms for particular pieces emerged strongly in the questionnaires and interviews. The intimacy and immediacy of the 'in the round' venue were frequently mentioned, and these qualities seemed to be associated with the repertoire as much as with the event. The pleasure of following the interweaving melodies of a string quartet, for example, drew some listeners into the music in ways that a more forceful orchestral or choral sound might fail to do:

> It's often a revelation, how the music is put together, and I think that's why I like string quartets so much [...] I can't do that in an orchestra, can't really decipher the sound, because there's a lot of people, but you can in a string quartet, you can see the contribution they all make. [MitRI 10]

Chamber music appears to offer these experienced concert-goers a chance to feel fully involved in the music, and perhaps to be taken 'to "a different place", inducing a sensation of peace and tranquillity which is difficult to achieve by any other means' [MitRQ 6]. Others expressed the same sense of involvement in more active terms, valuing the 'passion, energy and tension of the music which is felt by us all' [MitRQ 115].

Despite their current enthusiasms, some audience members acknowledged that chamber music had not always held great appeal for them, and at least one had experienced a 'conversion to chamber music' as a result of the festival [MitRQ 39]. The notion that chamber music is a more challenging listening experience than, say, orchestral music, is evidently a long-lived myth:

> The idea has become established that chamber music, and especially string-quartet music, is difficult to listen to ... True, it is seldom sensational, as a circus is sensational, but does one attend only the circus? ... For clarity of purpose, for ease of listening, and for relaxed enjoyment chamber music has no equal. (Ulrich, 1951: 33)

Music in the Round participants offered several explanations for previous cautious attitudes to the repertoire. One interviewee suggested that chamber music is 'a player's music' [MitRI 2], holding greater interest for listeners who might attempt the same repertoire with friends, or who have a greater understanding of the musical structures and intricacies of these small-scale forms. Certainly, a substantial proportion of the Music in the Round audience were either experienced listeners or active performers, and so there is clearly some truth in the notion that chamber music attracts an audience wanting to be fully engaged, intellectually and emotionally, in their listening experience. The same interviewee was teased by his wife for past concert-going habits: 'You used to go to orchestral concerts because it was better value for money if you saw a whole orchestra' [MitRI 19]. This change in musical preferences appears to be replicated more widely; a study of American listening habits has suggested that smaller ensembles are better able to survive in the current economic climate, such that 'at the same time that orchestras have struggled financially, chamber music is enjoying enormous growth in the US' (Dempster, 2000: 51). Many of the Music in the Round audience expressed a dislike of the venues for orchestral music in Sheffield, and so their interest in chamber music may be partly a result of local circumstances, which encourage them to reject some concert-going options and increase their attendance at others. Even if Music in the Round has attracted some of its audience members through this process of local selection, however, there are undoubtedly qualities in the event itself and the repertoire it promotes that secure the loyalty of the audience once they have begun to attend.

Within the broad category of chamber music, audience members had clear preferences for particular repertoire, instrumentation or performers that affected their attendance (see Chapter 6 for full discussion). Their willingness to refine their tastes within the overall scope of the festival differed from the other case study events; Gilbert and Sullivan listeners being restricted in their choices by the relatively small canon of works lying within the remit of the Buxton festival, and COMA participants seeming almost morally compelled to 'listen to anything – once, at least' [FWQ 5]. Not surprisingly, the enthusiasms of Music in the Round audience members were varied, although there was a general tendency to avoid vocal recitals, a fact sometimes confessed rather guiltily, and much lamented by those who did attend the 'SongFests' in the programme. Audience members were asked to state the factors which influenced them in their choice of concert attendance; inevitably some of these were practical, to do with time, cost and other commitments, but the musical reasons shed some light on the preferences of individual audience members, as in the responses shown in Table 5.2 to the question 'How do you decide which concerts to attend?'. An element of caution in their answers is coupled with a level of willingness to learn; Music in the Round audience members appeared to want some guaranteed elements in each concert, perhaps because investing time and money in an evening out creates some pressure for it to be a pleasurable experience. Some had their own ways of compromising, favouring programmes with one new work amongst several favourites, or being willing to 'risk something different if it is at a lunchtime concert (cheaper for OAPs!)' [MitRQ 105].

Table 5.2 Audience members' decisions on attending concerts

		Sample responses
Musical preferences		[MitRQ 29] By process of elimination. Voice concerts are less attractive to my ear.
		[40] Read prospectus and avoid 'modern' music.
		[55] Most interested in strings so tend to choose concerts involving strings or strings & piano.
Performers		[21] [Host string quartet] preference but normally one played by another group.
		[41] Visiting performers who one rarely gets a chance to hear in live performance.
		[103] Something different/unusual groups.
Familiarity/ unfamiliarity		[69] The programme – both works I am familiar with, and works which I don't know but would like to expand my knowledge by hearing.
		[87] Works I like best. Works I don't know by composers I like.
		[251] I like to attend a concert in which I know some of the pieces and others are unfamiliar to me.

Responses to the opposite question – 'What reasons may make you choose not to attend a particular concert?' – were predictably similar but reversed, although there were fewer references to particular performers. Again the musical reasons offer most insight on the finer gradations of liking for chamber music:

Table 5.3 Audience members' decisions on not attending concerts

		Sample responses
Musical preferences		[MitRQ 5] Don't like more 'modern', 'discordant' style of music.
		[25] Not keen on solo piano.
		[53] I favour instrumental ensembles – not too keen on vocal.
		[70] Too many separate items.
		[81] I would always choose strings and ensembles or voice before piano or jazz or folk music programmes.
		[83] If they involve period instruments, or ultra-modern composers.
Familiarity/ unfamiliarity		[21] Too modern or unknown.
		[41] If I already know the works inside out.
		[51] Concerts must have at least one item I know or believe I shall like e.g. by a composer I like.
		[103] Pieces being played I've heard recently.

Although caution and unfamiliarity are still evident in these reasons, over-familiarity also emerges as a factor which would make participants select a different concert with more unknown – or partially known – repertoire. The strong element of choice, which was largely absent in the other case study events, gives these listeners the opportunity to hone their individual tastes and decide whether they want to be educated or entertained. A small proportion of the questionnaire respondents (8 per cent) avoided all such dilemmas and bought a season ticket, wanting to 'take advantage of the full picture being presented' [MitRQ 48] and stating that only 'injury, sickness, death' [MitRQ 4] would stop them attending.

Concert choice and behaviour in chamber music forms part of the larger debate on the role of live classical music in contemporary society (cf. Cottrell, 2003), about which there has been much gloom-ridden commentary (cf. Johnson, 2002). Music in the Round audience members fit well with the trend identified by Ruth Levitt and Ruth Rennie in their analysis of the classical music industry:

> Despite the well-documented fear that audience figures are falling, in fact audiences for classical music are changing rather than diminishing. Patrons are becoming more sophisticated and choosy, and therefore more demanding, and they are interested in a wider variety of styles and methods of music-making. (Levitt & Rennie, 1999: 24)

Music in the Round audience members are certainly demanding, but generally express their sophistication and choosiness by being loyal to the festival and its regular performers, favouring that concert series above others available locally. There are of course some exceptions to this; the dissenting voices stood out amongst the enthusiasm of the majority, and were perhaps under-represented by the nature of the research carried out. Those who felt least comfortable in the festival were likely to speak critically of the 'cult' following, whereby performances given by the host string quartet sold out almost immediately, and were always greeted with rapturous applause by devoted fans. Where larger numbers of the audience might express preferences for or criticisms of other performers, unquestioning loyalty to the resident quartet seemed to be widespread amongst these listeners who had grown up with them over the twenty years of the festival (see Chapter 6 for further discussion).

Individual preferences for particular repertoire seemed to be accepted as idiosyncratic by participants, and the generic reasons present in the other studies – preserving Gilbert and Sullivan or promoting contemporary music – were less apparent. Couples interviewed together sometimes seemed surprised to discover one another's unexplored musical interests, particularly where one partner had the main responsibility for booking tickets. Others attributed their preferences to past listening experiences, whether acquired through the 'themed' festivals that had run in previous years, or through family influences, particularly parents; a father who was 'a terrific enthusiast for the Beethoven quartets' [MitRI 18], or a mother who 'would have string players around the house sometimes and just play trios, quartets' [MitRI 1]. Few became as frustrated as this participant in the *Music and Daily Life Project* (Crafts *et al.*, 1993), who is attempting to explain the pleasures of listening to Bach's *Magnificat*:

I think it's unexplainable. Maybe the problem is that there could be so many different reasons ... for example, I could say: the relationship I have with my dad is a positive and close one and he listens to it and I have feelings toward him ... positive feelings toward my family and my home. Or I could talk about the technical musical aspect and how the music is intentionally designed to evoke certain feelings. Or I could talk about my high school experiences playing the oboe ... experiences walking through gothic cathedrals, spending the afternoon listening to Bach cantatas ...   And maybe it's partially all of them. Or maybe it's absolutely none of them. I don't know and I never will know. ... It's not a scientific experiment. And I'm glad, because I don't want to know. ... I don't want to know. And I don't care. (Crafts *et al.*, 1993: 98)

While Gail, the 21 year old interviewee speaking above, struggles increasingly in the attempt to explain her musical preferences, Music in the Round audience members seemed more comfortable in the individuality of their tastes and explored them willingly in interview. Where expressing a dislike for Gilbert and Sullivan or for contemporary music would have been heresy in the more narrowly-focused case study events, here participants could enthuse about or reject elements of the repertoire whilst retaining a shared liking for chamber music as a whole. There was therefore much more flexibility for debating and negotiating preferences with listening companions and, given the extent and variety of the repertoire, a preparedness to be surprised by new discoveries or to re-appraise old favourites.

Much more than for the other case study events, it is difficult to separate participants' attitudes to the repertoire from feelings about the festival and the performers, such that the Music in the Round study offers a complex picture of the appeal of chamber music. The majority of listeners appeared to value the concentrated nature of the repertoire, and its capacity to bring them intellectual and emotional fulfilment, with one stating simply, 'life is better after a concert at the festival' [MitRQ 46]. The audience members here were as fully engaged with their musical activities as any of the case study performers, and often linked their love of chamber music with gratitude to the performers and appreciation of the venue, such that the 'intimacy' and 'immediacy' commented on by so many participants could be attributed to any of these factors.   Once again, this event presents a picture of a setting that is highly valued by the majority of the people involved, but would seem alien to their counterparts in the other case studies, illustrating the extent to which musical communities and the genres they celebrate become impenetrable to outsiders even while they fulfil the needs of regular participants.

Musical passions and perspectives

The question of what – if anything – people's musical choices and behaviours say about them is a contentious one, drawing on broader debates concerning the nature and location of musical meaning. It would seem logical to assume that participants engage with musical activities and genres that are consonant with other aspects of their world view, and in the case of the COMA participants this connection was overtly noted in their discussions and diary entries. The experimental nature of much contemporary music reflected and informed their self-proclaimed tolerance and open-mindedness, and the need to make a distinctive contribution to, for instance, an improvised piece of music, chimed with a respect for individuality in everyday life. But what of the Gilbert and Sullivan audience members and their commitment to a genre whose conventions and values are specific to the Victorian age? The overt mockery of the establishment in Gilbert's plots was welcomed as part of the fun of performing, but the more subtle social messages, such as the representation of marriage as the perfect ending to every story, assume a certain perspective on the world that may or may not have been shared by those attending the festival. Julian Johnson (2002) suggests that this potential disjunction between musical preferences and other aspects of emotional and intellectual life is a widespread problem:

> Different musics are not neutral in terms of value systems; they are positioned because they quite literally *do* different things. ... My suggestion is not only that we should be more self-aware of how different musics are positioned, but that we frequently identify with music whose value-position objectively contradicts that which we claim in other spheres of life – such as ethics, politics or education. (Johnson, 2002: 8)

Niall MacKinnon (1993), in his study of the British folk music scene, investigated a musical world that has some direct parallels with the Gilbert and Sullivan festival, not least in the tendency for the music to attract aficionados whose devotion is incomprehensible to non-fans. He explains this with reference to folk music's low media profile, suggesting that 'those who do not attend folk scene events are unlikely to come into contact with folk music except from prior contact during its heyday in the early 1960s, from school, or if they happen to be in town during a folk festival' (MacKinnon, 1993: 33). The same could be said of Gilbert and Sullivan, except that the heyday was longer ago, adding to the archaic feel of the repertoire for those who have not grown up with it. MacKinnon's study includes an analysis of the demographics of audience members at ten folk clubs, where he found participants to be educated to a higher level than the British national average at the time, more likely to be in professional and non-manual work, and more involved in active leisure than the general population. He concludes that folk clubs are composed of 'a group that is especially active, erudite, aesthetically and artistically orientated' (ibid.: 45), and speculates that their involvement in folk music is partly driven by a resistance to the 'cultural passivity of middle-class Britain' (ibid.: 68).

In the absence of matching data on leisure pursuits and occupation, it is impossible to make a direct comparison between the Gilbert and Sullivan audience and the members of MacKinnon's folk clubs. Questionnaire respondents in each of my case studies were invited to describe a 'typical' member of their event, but where the Music in the Round participants approached this task with relish (see Chapter 6), those at Buxton were reluctant to engage in such a search for the archetypal Gilbert and Sullivan fan. Where they did answer, the responses were remarkably uniform: the audience was perceived to be made up of professional or retired workers, with equal gender distribution and a high average age. Of the people who answered this question, 77 (85 per cent) were prepared to say that they fit this pattern, and only 14 (15 per cent) felt – or hoped – they did not. There is a rough sense, then, that the audience at Buxton were older than those in the folk clubs, but otherwise similar in outlook, valuing the role that their musical tastes played in staving off the aspects of contemporary culture most alien to them.

A convincing case could be made for the affinity between case study participants' musical choices and their broader world views, but to assume from this a causality – in either direction – would be too simplistic. The Bruce Springsteen fans interviewed by Daniel Cavicchi (1998) could see the two potential explanations for the feeling that Springsteen was 'reading their minds' in songs that perfectly encapsulated their own life experiences: 'several fans expressed some confusion about whether their views of the world came from Springsteen's music or whether their views were what drew them to the music in the first place' (Cavicchi, 1998: 132). Cavicchi suggests, therefore, that the separation of musical engagement and life experiences is a false one, as listening is 'about making sense of the world in which music is created and shared' (ibid.: 1998: 133). This view seems to fit the evidence from the COMA study, where participants' attitudes to music and everyday life seemed broadly similar; but it has some uncomfortable implications for the Gilbert and Sullivan audience, who would thereby be assumed to share the values portrayed on stage, craving a nostalgic sense of Englishness that is at odds with many aspects of contemporary life (see Blake, 1997 for a comparable discussion about the Proms). Without sufficient understanding of the ethical and political perspectives held by the Buxton audience members, it would be inappropriate to speculate on the extent to which these were revealed or otherwise in their musical affiliations. Further research remains to be done on listeners' and performers' own perceptions of how their musical preferences – as well as their activities – contribute to their broader intellectual values and lives.

The social responsibilities of musical allegiance

Throughout the discussions with performers and audiences at the three events studied, it was clear that the values attributed to performance went beyond the individual or group experiences that were being described, and in many cases reflected a broader feeling of the necessity or importance of particular musical activities. This could be manifest as a straightforward desire to entertain an audience, with performers fully aware of their responsibility to give people who had bought tickets their money's worth in quality performance. But the idea of performing, concert-going and the promotion of particular repertoires as being socially desirable activities was also present, as expressed in interview by the director of COMA:

> People could be having as much joy and pleasure out of contemporary music as they are, clearly, out of going to the art galleries. Everyone's into contemporary art at the moment, it seems, and they don't find it at all difficult to live with some not necessarily very satisfactory work, and meanwhile they're avoiding the concert halls. [...] It's not a

question of whether people understand it or not, people are shying away from it, and they're missing out on enriching their lives. [COMAI 1]

The COMA director's clear mission in founding the organisation and building up the summer school is shown here to stem from a frustration with perceived social shortcomings and a desire to share his own enthusiasms with a large number of people. The social and cultural perspectives that had informed this initiative were shared by many of the COMA participants, who were similarly passionate about the need for more widely accessible contemporary music. Some sought ways to increase the contemporary repertoire used in their own instrumental teaching, while others were active in local COMA ensembles, so demonstrating a strong practical engagement with their musical and social values. The conversations that took place over meals at the COMA summer school often had an 'evangelistic' quality too: my fieldnotes record a number of such conversations overheard or participated in, and (with names abbreviated to initials) some extracts from my notes are given below:

- L talks about attitudes to contemporary music; more of a commitment than art, where you can wander around a gallery with friends instead of having to sit and concentrate for two hours. People need visual stimulation – should increase music teaching to compensate for this.
- Discussion of education with N – 'I really do believe music has everything'; talks of wanting his sons to learn instruments – they're now interested but 'it's too late'.
- Debate over dinner about what kind of people are interested in contemporary music, and why many people are not – 'they wouldn't see what we do as music'. Sense of being misunderstood.
- D tells me he is the reincarnation of Noah. Also says he is interested in a wide variety of music – 'mainly concerned with widening people's boundaries'.

The concern to make the music that they love more accessible to other people is a perpetuation of COMA's original aim, and was often connected in participants' discussions with ideas about improving or increasing music education. For some, these ideals were put into practice through their activities in COMA regional groups or their influence as teachers or parents, whilst for others, the discussion of social changes that would benefit contemporary music was intellectually satisfying in itself, but seemed unlikely to have any practical implications in their own lives.

A similar range of topics were covered in interviews with the Music in the Round audience, who were also likely to draw parallels with the greater popularity of contemporary art compared to music, and to see the need for investment in school music education. A number of interviewees mentioned the educational outreach initiatives of the festival as making an important contribution, widening access to musical events whilst at the same time ensuring the future of the festival. Visits to the 'Music Box' project run by Music in the Round for pre-school children allowed me to see evidence of this commitment to fostering musical interest beyond the established festival audience; other projects linked with the festival cover the full primary and secondary school age range, and work in both musically active and less privileged schools across Sheffield, often encouraging collaboration between young people from a range of musical, social and economic backgrounds. One interviewee shared the ideals of the Music in the Round education team when he spoke of the social imperative to spread the beneficial effects of the organisation's work as widely as possible:

> I think that for people who are playing chamber music or classical music to have some degree of educational energy and activity is desirable almost to the point of being morally desirable [...] People, especially kids, are living in a context in which the music and other forms of culture that they are exposed to have already been highly mediated by very strong influences, market influences and media influences that are self-motivated and that tend to skew what people are exposed to towards what is the auditory equivalent of fast food [...] and so forms of educative activity carried out by people like Music in the Round have at least a degree of compensatory effect. [MitRI 1]

Others among the audience saw outreach work as being more directly related to enculturating a future generation of listeners, and particularly valued initiatives aimed at bringing young people to the festival. Since the introduction to music as a child had formed such a valuable part of their own lives, the hope was that young children encountering music through the Music in the Round projects would find something 'marvellous and awesome and wonderful, which they just might take with them through life' [MitRI 17].

The challenges of youth and ageing in musical participation

In feeling that their music should be more readily available to a broader public, COMA and Music in the Round participants seemed to be motivated mainly by a desire to share the experiences that had brought them so much pleasure. While this motivation was shared by the Buxton participants to a certain extent, their campaigning to increase access to Gilbert and Sullivan had a greater urgency, given the potential for interest in the repertoire to die out if it becomes less frequently performed:

> We've got to get more and more schools, youth establishments, education authorities, putting it back into schools, because our generation will not have been brought up on it, unlike our parents' generation, who were part of church societies or whatever. [...] So it's important to get new people into it, and the educational initiative that we launched last week I hope will do that this year. [BUXI 2]

Whereas the Music in the Round outreach programme has broad musical aims, focused on the process of music-making rather than on a specific genre, the founding of the Gilbert and Sullivan Educational Trust (re-launched in the festival's January 2003 Newsletter) was driven by the fear that 'in 30 years' time G&S may have disappeared from the repertoire' (Newsletter, p. 15). In aiming to provide scores, simplified orchestral arrangements, and expert tuition for school productions, the Gilbert and Sullivan education programme places the repertoire at its heart, seeing it as 'the ideal vehicle for introducing youngsters to the joys of music-making through its melody, spectacle and humour' (ibid.). With the

Educational Trust still seeking financial backing to become fully established, its effects cannot yet be evaluated, but its intentions reveal the strong preservation instincts which are more subtly displayed in the festival itself. Like the COMA members who wanted more people to be aware of the pleasures of contemporary music, the directors of the Gilbert and Sullivan festival see in their musical passions a broader social responsibility to increase and perpetuate the availability of the activities and repertoire they value so highly.

The fear that the Gilbert and Sullivan repertoire has a finite lifespan, the end of which may be fast approaching, provides a vivid illustration of Christopher Small's (1977/96) critique of Western society's urge to preserve and restore past works of art, something that Small sees as a threat to contemporary creativity:

> If an art work is thought of as in any way alive it should be allowed to die when its time comes, and, if necessary, to be mourned. ... Our art galleries, and especially our concert life, are choked with past works, many of them, like Leonardo's *Last Supper*, being kept alive by methods that do as much violence to the artist's vision as do the oxygen tent and drip feed used to prevent the dying nonagenarian from ending his [sic] life in peace and dignity. (Small, 1977/96: 92)

The sense of anxiety expressed at the Buxton festival about the future of the Gilbert and Sullivan repertoire suggests that it falls well within Small's 'dying nonagenarian' category, even if the strategies used to preserve it seem at times more like embalming than life support. It is understandable though, to continue Small's analogy, that love for someone (or something) approaching extinction will in many cases prompt a strong urge to preserve life for as long as possible, even if the cause is apparently hopeless. Small is keen to point out that he is not advocating wilful murder (of either works of art or elderly people); his view is rather that the life cycle of musical works should be respected, and that the insistence on preservation and restoration of older repertoire should be at least open to question.

The audience and the repertoire are ageing together at Buxton, as many participants observed, and in some ways the resistance to this trend disturbs what could otherwise be a fitting and tranquil coincidence of life transitions. The presence of ex-D'Oyly Carte performers at the festival reinforces the sense of preserving past glories and has significant appeal for audience members, as it forms a direct connection back to the first performances of the operettas, and to the professional productions that a number of audience members recall from their childhood. Yet this visible reinforcement of the D'Oyly Carte legacy also has a stultifying effect; offering a reminder of a company that used to make 'performance in the traditional manner' a condition of granting licence to perform the works to amateur companies (Political & Economic Planning, 1949: 115), and regulating the quest for authenticity by placing ex-D'Oyly Carte performers in the adjudicating role. Future decades will reveal whether resistance to the decline of Gilbert and Sullivan has secured the apparent immortality which more mainstream repertoire enjoys: it will be in no small measure due to the work of the Buxton festival if this succeeds.

Whereas the Buxton management saw the ageing of their participants as decidedly problematic, since it placed their favoured repertoire in jeopardy, Music in the Round audience members were more confident that future generations would share their enthusiasms. Several interviewees characterised chamber music as 'music for the third age', citing its concentrated and intellectual qualities as having greatest appeal to older listeners. There may be some truth in that, but it is contradicted by other evidence from this festival, not least that these same interviewees had been attending since the festival's inception twenty years previously, and admitted that the audience had 'aged with the performers' [MitRI 2]. There may be similarities here with the folk club audiences studied by Niall MacKinnon (1993), where the 'age bulge' was even more specific; his questionnaire survey of ten folk clubs around Britain revealed an absence of both teenagers and retired people, and around half the audience in their thirties (p. 42). MacKinnon considers whether this age-related interest in folk music represents a static bulge that moves down the population, or whether the 30-39 year olds currently attending clubs were part of the folk revival of the 1960s and so feel a particular affinity with the repertoire. Since most of the current members of clubs had joined in their 20s, and were not being followed by another generation displaying similar interests, he concludes that audiences overall are likely to age with this group of participants: 'the demographic profile does not indicate that the folk scene is necessarily in danger of disappearing, but does point to its appeal being no longer that of a youth sub-culture' (p. 43).

Folk club audiences will have several decades to judge whether MacKinnon's analysis is correct, and to decide on a course of action for bringing in a new audience for the future. For the Music in the Round audience, the need for regeneration is more urgent, as the concentration of interest is amongst a retired population who, as one (younger!) audience member put it, 'are going to snuff it around the same time' [MitRI 14]. It may be, as with the folk clubs, that there is a specific generational interest in chamber music amongst current audiences; the hope that 'chamber music suits the twilight years' [MitRI 2] has yet to be fully demonstrated. Little longitudinal data exists on the development of musical interest across the lifespan, but Carol Prickett's (1998) summary of the literature on music and ageing draws attention to the potential of music to assist in the transitions of later life, through activities ranging from performing to music therapy. A recent survey by Vernon Pickles (2003) focused on changes in music listening over the life-span; questioning respondents recruited through the 'university of the third age' (U3A) adult education scheme, Pickles found evidence of stable but developing tastes.   As with the Music in the Round audience members, well-established habits of listening and musical engagement contributed to the valuing of concert attendance in later life, which suggests that even if chamber music is indeed for the 'third age', the foundations for such enjoyment must be laid earlier. Pickles concludes that 'more than some other faculties, musicality resists the ravages of time or possible dementia. Third-agers who maintain their knowledge and understanding of music are storing up treasure for their future' (Pickles, 2003: 423). Certainly the Music in the Round concert-goers had invested considerable time and expense in developing their listening habits, and showed every intention of continuing this for as long as possible.

Since the resident string quartet had recently announced their retirement, the need for a rejuvenation of the Music in the Round festival and its audience was perhaps uppermost in respondents' minds. Many expressed sadness at the quartet's decision, whilst understanding the performers' desire to pursue new musical opportunities while they still had the energy. One interviewee recalled her own experience of the retirement of a musical ensemble, a chamber choir to which she and her husband had belonged for thirty years or more:

> We were all reaching about this kind of age, and so we had a meeting one night, with none of us really knowing what the likely outcome was going to be, and at the end of that meeting, we came to the unanimous decision that we should disband. So in some ways I can actually quite respond to what they're doing. [MitRI 17]

Memories of leaving behind a much-loved ensemble made this listener very sympathetic to the difficulties of retiring, and she was hopeful that the members of the quartet – as well as the Music in the Round audience – would find a new sense of direction and source of musical fulfilment. This hope was shared by many in the audience, prompting Simon Clements, a loyal audience member since the festival's inception, to write a short article for the Friends of Music in the Round Newsletter (Spring 2003), for which he interviewed around thirty 'Friends' by telephone. He reported that several audience members 'dared to admit that they suddenly felt liberated to go and live "where in the world they wished", now that the anchor was going to be lifted' (p. 1). While those few respondents seemed willing to retire with the quartet, others were keen to see the festival continue and many specified the need for a younger quartet, perhaps to recall the vitality of the first years of the festival, or maybe to avoid the trauma of another imminent retirement.

The need for regeneration amongst audience and performers alike seemed to be widely felt, although one interviewee noted that broadening the audience profile brought its own risks – 'if you try and do something too obvious about it then it just becomes patronising' [MitRI 4]. The available evidence supports this view that limitations in an audience's make-up are self-perpetuating: minority groups are unlikely to feel welcome and comfortable amongst an established arts community, as research with low-income families (Moore, 1997), Black and Asian arts consumers (Harris Research Centre, 1993), and young people (Hill, 1997) has demonstrated. Young people's attendance at live classical music is notoriously low, since a classical concert in its traditional mode of presentation fails to fulfil the criteria for a good night out – perceived value for money, enjoyable social interaction and so on – and bears little relation to the listening practices familiar to this age group from other genres and settings (see Pitts *et al.*, 1999 for a review of the literature on attendance at arts events). It is therefore unlikely that young people who do attend will find obviously like-minded company amongst a concert audience, with the result that arts events are seen to be for other people unless family, friends or educational initiatives intervene to encourage and sustain patterns of attendance (Mass Observation, 1990). Participants at Music in the Round frequently expressed concern about the limitations of their established and homogenous audience; as one put it, 'I would love to see the audience profile expand – not that I have anything against retired white middle class academics' [MitRQ 95]. The same tensions as were evident at Buxton are revealed; participants are caught between maintaining a situation that is personally enjoyable, and making changes to ensure its survival.

Seeking converts to musical participation

In lamenting the absence of a youthful audience, it would be easy to overlook the fact that the mid-life adult population was also under-represented: only 13 per cent of the audience at the Music in the Round festival were aged under 45. Many obvious reasons for this spring to mind – lack of time, other work and family priorities, cost of attendance and so on – but Julian Johnson would hold that these reasons themselves are indicative of the declining status of classical music:

> Adults overburdened with responsibility at work and home look to their leisure time as a space in which to stop being responsible – to play, to become childlike. We don't want our leisure activities to be intellectually demanding precisely because leisure is defined as a release from such activities. Our lack of engagement with serious art is by no means unconnected to our work lives, which impose a certain expectation about our leisure time. (Johnson, 2002: 122)

The assumptions of Johnson's argument and the findings of my case studies are in interesting conflict: the opportunity to 'play' was to be found in the musical activities that Johnson sees as being in decline, and the particular responsibilities that performance brings were keenly felt by Buxton and COMA participants. Rehearsals offered an escape from the routine demands of work and family life, but they brought with them new challenges which were entered into readily and actively. Similarly, Music in the Round audience members deliberately sought the intellectual engagement that Johnson claims 'we' avoid.

Given that the participants at all three case study events were leading fulfilling musical lives, having found supportive environments within which to develop their skills and interests, their collective anxiety to broaden access and opportunities might appear slightly puzzling. With the exception of the Gilbert and Sullivan fans' fear of extinction, arguments for widening participation seemed to be quite abstract, driven by ethical or moral convictions, or the simple desire to share experiences and enthusiasms with others. The COMA participants, particularly, spoke of feeling isolated in their musical tastes, and valued the opportunity to be among like-minded people for the duration of the summer school. Perhaps their hopes of increasing access are therefore connected with extending those feelings of musical compatibility, in the hope that being part of a 'larger minority' would be more comfortable. The students in Study 1 bring this assumption into question, however, having begun to doubt their musicality when they moved out of the isolated musician roles they had occupied at school. COMA participants, similarly, valued their self-perceived eccentricities, and might have been disappointed to find these diluted in a crowd.

There is a common thread amongst the case studies of wanting to convert others to participants' own tastes; an evangelism about musical styles, influential people, particular venues, and the events themselves was shared across the diverse musical settings. At a local level, case study participants took pride in introducing their friends to the events they valued; several Music in the Round members talked with pleasure of introducing new people to the festival, and COMA participants went home at the end of the summer school with the intention of telling friends what they had missed. Such personal conversions held many potential benefits: cementing friendships, making the events themselves more sociable and enjoyable for those participants, and increasing the connection between the musical event and other aspects of participants' lives. Enthusing about one's musical experiences seems almost instinctive, and offers points of contact with other people, illustrated in contexts as diverse as the peer-influenced listening behaviours of teenagers (North *et al.*, 2000), the shared fandom of Bruce Springsteen devotees (Cavicchi, 1998), and the extensive internet discussions of those Gilbert and Sullivan fans known as 'Savoynetters'.

The more abstract desire to share musical opinions and convert a broader population is also a well-engrained musical behaviour, as demonstrated in the critiques of performances and recordings to be found daily in newspapers and specialist magazines. From misunderstood music students to contemporary music enthusiasts, the case study participants illustrated a general desire to increase the number of people who held similar musical perspectives to their own. This tendency seemed partially motivated by a benevolent intention to share experiences that they had enjoyed, but also by a more self-interested need to be less obviously isolated in their musical preferences and behaviour. The musical events studied here are certainly minority interests; even the most optimistic recent data suggest that only 6 per cent of recorded music sold around the world is 'classical' (British Phonographic Industry, 2004), itself a genre in which contemporary music and Gilbert and Sullivan would find only a marginalized position. One could question whether this matters, given that the music remains unscathed by its minority status, and the participants find the sense of identity and difference that they may be seeking by resisting the musical mainstream. If musical participation was as commonplace as watching television, it might in fact lose some of its appeal for those who currently value it so highly. This is not an invitation to reinforce the elitism of which 'art' music has long been accused, but rather to recognise that musical needs can be fulfilled in a wide variety of ways, and the instinct to 'convert' others to that minority position may imply a failure to recognise alternative musical perspectives.

The impetus to widen access to the case study events was often expressed as a perceived deficit or lack of understanding in other people's lives, but is more persuasively read as a symptom of the high value placed upon their activities by the current participants. The urge to preserve or promote events and repertoire was coupled with an anxiety about their continued existence and success, bringing an element of self-interest to the otherwise philanthropic desire to share much-loved musical experiences with others. Audiences, in particular, looked to the future of their musical activities with some concern, aware of their dependency on the performers' decisions and continued commitment to the events. The next chapter will focus on audience experiences of musical participation, considering the part that listeners play in shaping a musical event, and analysing the impact of concert attendance on the lives of 'participant listeners'.

CHAPTER SIX

The Participant Audience:
Listening and Belonging

The inclusion of audience members in the category of 'participants' for this study challenges the notion of the passive audience, who gratefully receive whatever musical offerings are put before them, and demonstrate their reactions only in the extent of their applause and their repeat attendance. The roles fulfilled by an audience are constrained to an extent by concert-going conventions, but within those boundaries individual audience members engage with the musical and social aspects of the event in a variety of ways. Evidence from the two case studies featuring audience members – Study 2 at the Gilbert and Sullivan Festival, and Study 4 at Music in the Round – has revealed the high level of involvement and opinion prevalent amongst the audience, who often feel as great a commitment to the events they attend as do the performers. Regular attenders at the Music in the Round festival explicitly referred to themselves as 'participants rather than onlookers' [MitRQ 147], attributing this variously to the proximity to performers afforded by the 'in the round' venue, or to the feeling of involvement that their long-term attendance at the festival had generated. Those at Buxton, too, who saw the Gilbert and Sullivan festival as occupying a central role in their musical and social lives, demonstrated a far greater involvement and interest in the style and direction of their chosen event than has generally been recognised in discussions of concert-going practices.

Attending a concert demands a certain commitment from audience members; not just of time and money, but of the concentration and energy necessary to listen to live music for several hours. When listening takes place as part of a festival, these factors are all amplified to become an even greater statement of intent; further emotional and monetary investment is demanded, and attendance becomes either more appealing or more daunting to potential audience members. Like the performers discussed in previous chapters, audience members may come to concerts for a variety of reasons which are rarely articulated except in appreciation or recommendation of particular events or performers. In this chapter, the experiences of audience members at the Music in the Round chamber music festival are considered in more detail, and comparisons made with the views of performers discussed in earlier chapters.

Participating in listening: the experience of concert-going

The experience of attending live classical music events has been little researched, attention tending to focus on quantitative studies of audience numbers and profiles, rather than the individual perspectives of those in attendance (e.g. Mass Observation, 1990; Research Services of Great Britain, 1991). The historical assumption that the views of audience members can reasonably be overlooked has at least two potential roots: firstly the tendency of musicological research to emphasise the primacy of the text, to which the performers are subservient and the audience merely receptive; and secondly the classification of concert attendance as a kind of consumer behaviour, with success judged by the number of tickets sold rather than the experiences of the people who are present. By this model, concerts are done *to* – or at best *for* – an audience, such that the quantity of people in attendance is more important than the level of engagement and participation felt by individual listeners. The views of committed concert-goers in the case studies suggests that individual experience is in fact rich, varied and highly personal, bringing together elements of musical taste, preferred listening behaviours and social expectations.

There is greater emphasis on listener experience within the popular music literature, where 'fan' behaviour has been explored for the insight it offers on the ways people use and respond to music, although David Hesmondhalgh has pointed out that the amount of empirical evidence on popular music audiences is sometimes exaggerated and requires further work (2002: 118). Within the existing studies ,'fans' are usually considered to be extreme in their reactions to a specific band or singer, and are viewed with some suspicion by more moderate enthusiasts: 'common discourse conflates the word "fan" with "fanatic"' (Cavicchi, 1998: 6). Many of the Gilbert and Sullivan festival respondents (Study 2) were keen to distance themselves from 'fans' of the genre, viewing their own involvement as more controlled and rational. But fans, too, are dismissive of the behaviour of their counterparts in the 'temporary role of audience member' (ibid.: 91), for whom the necessity to attend concerts is less compelling:

> Fans see ordinary audience members as passively responding to the more obvious and superficial elements of rock performance, interested only in having fun, partying, and being entertained. But by strongly weaving their performance experiences into their daily lives, fans see their own participation in rock performance as far more active, serious, and interpretive, as shaped by something larger than the performance itself. (Cavicchi, 1998: 91)

The provision for pop and rock listeners to become fully participant 'fans' is more obvious than for classical audiences; and yet the 'Friends' of Music in the Round clearly valued their access to regular newsletters, and were often avid collectors of CD recordings by the performers. Their involvement was more measured and intellectual than that of the 'teenie fan' (Rhein, 2000), and so held greater respectability as a means of fostering connections between concert-going and everyday life:

The obsession of a fan is deemed emotional (low class, uneducated), and therefore dangerous, while the obsession of the aficionado is rational (high class, educated) and therefore benign, even worthy. (Jenson, 1992: 21)

Music in the Round participants tended to avoid the word 'fan' in describing their own behaviour or that of fellow audience members, referring to themselves as 'supporters' or 'groupies', a term used light-heartedly or pejoratively according to context. Devotion to the host string quartet was considerable amongst the regular audience, who wrote and spoke in highly enthusiastic terms about its influence on the festival and on their lives. Practical manifestations of this included membership of the supporting 'Friends' organisation, the rush to buy tickets as soon as advanced booking opened, and the cancelling of other engagements to ensure full attendance at the festival. Occasionally there was more overt 'fan' behaviour, and on two occasions during this festival, individuals brought flowers for the performers as a mark of appreciation; a bunch of lily of the valley given diffidently to one of the staff to pass on anonymously, and single yellow roses left on each of the performers' chairs for the second half of the final concert. Like the Bruce Springsteen fans studied by Cavicchi (1998), regular attenders at Music in the Round expressed a sense of solidarity through which they 'find validation by seeking out others with the same feelings and experiences' (p. 162). Links between chamber music listeners and Springsteen fans may seem far-fetched, but the traditional divisions of listening behaviour are potentially misleading, as each group engages in comparable activities within the conventions of their chosen musical genre and its notions of acceptable audience conduct.

Recent attempts to analyse the ritual of a Western classical concert have still assumed the role of the audience to be one of grateful receptivity, even while exposing the sociological oddities of such circumstances:

The concert hall [...] presents us in a clear and unambiguous way with a certain set of relationships, in which the autonomy and privacy of the individual is treasured, a stance of impersonal politeness and good manners is assumed, familiarity is rejected, and the performers and their performance, as long as it is going on, are not subject to the audience's response. (Small, 1998: 43)

Small is resistant to the hierarchical relationships implied by the one-way communication and ritual behaviour of the traditional concert hall, seeing these as an 'instrument for the reassurance of the industrial middle and upper classes' (p. 193) who seek to escape the distractions of the outside world in favour of the comforting repetition of the Western art music canon. Listeners, by this model, are 'spectators at a spectacle that is not ours', denied any relationship with the performers and organisers of the event, such that 'our only power is that of consumers in general, to buy or not to buy' (p. 44).

At a superficial level, the two events discussed in this chapter lack many of the features which cause Small such discomfort: performers at the Music in the Round festival engage in conversation with their audience; social interaction between audience members is encouraged through 'Fringe' events at the Buxton Gilbert and Sullivan Festival and by meals organised for the 'Friends' of Music in the Round;

and listening participants at both events give their feedback willingly and extensively to the organisers. Listeners are therefore more powerful and more socially connected than in Small's model of the standard orchestral concert, and indeed appear to value the distinctiveness of these events from that traditional 'stuffy "penguin suits in a drawing room" image' [MitRQ 130]. Small's concerns for the roles of listener are therefore partially addressed, but his deeper anxieties regarding the falsely reassuring relationships of the concert hall remain, and indeed are recognised by those members of the audience who have begun to fear for the survival of the events they currently enjoy so much. Such fears, for both audiences, tended to focus on the difficulty of recruiting new, younger listeners for their events, rather than questioning the repertoire and its contemporary relevance to the extent that Small does. Isolation from worldly distractions was seen as a positive feature of concert attendance by some listeners, just as the performers at Buxton and COMA relished being able to focus on some aspect of themselves or their lives that was distinct from everyday concerns. In this enjoyment they may confirm Small's misgivings about the social unrealism of concert life, but their experiences illustrate a greater range of musical and social encounters than he acknowledges, coupled with a fair degree of sensitivity to the implications of their chosen form of musical engagement. Audience members are shown here to engage in active, participant listening, whereby they are at least complicit in the relationships of the concert hall, rather than merely subjected to them.

Preparation and understanding: the skills of concert-going

Concert-going can easily be dismissed as a leisure option, demanding little effort from participants beyond that required to arrive on time and conform to concert hall etiquette; 'audience members are expected not to make a noise or to converse, and it would be profoundly odd – or even offensive – if people attending a concert … were to be found reading a book' (Abercrombie & Longhurst, 1998: 54). It has not always been assumed, however, that concerts could be approached with little educational input: guides to concert-going were abundant in the mid-twentieth century, as titles such as *The Orchestra Speaks* (Shore, 1938) and *The Enjoyment of a Concert* (Ulrich, 1951) promised to enlighten audiences and better prepare them for a concentrated listening experience. Ulrich begins with the charmless statement that 'had my wife been more musically educated this book would not have been written' (ibid.: xv), and there is a clear hierarchy of listeners in evidence in many of these books, beginning with amateur musicians and ending with 'the ordinary music lover' who, it is thought, 'will gain something from being one of a number of people concentrating, even subjectively, along the same lines' (Russell, 1942: 136). Some guides were directed at children, but although their tone might be different – 'please don't tap your feet in time to the music: you've no idea how infuriating it can be to other people' (Salter, 1950: 95) – the advice on concert preparation and etiquette was similar across the generations. Preparation with a miniature score or a piano duet arrangement, and the fostering of a critical mind through repeated listening and analysis were all recommended, since 'intelligent listening partly means trying to seize and understand the design of the work as it flashes by' (Salter, 1950: 143) and advance notice of themes and structures was likely to increase success in this endeavour.

The regular Music in the Round audience had done their most substantial preparation through attendance at the previous nineteen festivals, described by one as 'one of the major cultural influences of my life and a constant source of pleasure' [MitRQ 50]. Many made reference to the contribution that past concerts and talks had made to their musical knowledge, and saw the 'audience choice' festival as a celebration of that development. One diarist wrote that 'discussion about elements of the performances seems to me to have been more intense and perhaps shows that we have been learning a lot in the 20 years' [MitRD 10]. Levels of preparation for individual concerts varied amongst the audience, with some seeing them simply as 'a good way to have a break from work' [MitRQ 267] or 'a pleasant interlude in a mundane life' [MitRQ 277], while others engaged in more substantial preparatory work:

> I read a little bit about [the Messiaen] on the internet before I went to the concert, which helped me: it mentioned quite a lot about how it was written, where it was written, and the circumstances [...] I could hear quite a few elements in that music which were like birdsong. I mean, it's maybe just because I read it first and so it was in my mind, but I found it extraordinary that piece. [MitRI 13]

Often, too, the concerts sent listeners away with renewed interest in reading about or listening to the music they had encountered, so forging connections between their festival attendance and other aspects of their musical lives:

> Collecting the CDs or LPs cheaply from second-hand shops is an important dimension to the festival. They complement and fill out my listening. I get *so* much more listening out of each, and the CD/LP brings back memories of the live concert performance. [MitRD 6]

Not all participants were so enthused by the role of CDs in relation to live music, and some sought to preserve their concert memories by avoiding recorded listening, on the grounds that 'nothing can replicate what we have experienced this evening' [MitRD 2]. Ways of capturing and recalling concerts were clearly important, and several diarists expressed frustration at the difficulty of putting their musical experiences into words. One long-term participant had found his own strategy for full and lasting engagement with the concerts: he was to be seen at each concert sketching images of the performers in his programme, as he had done for the full twenty years of the festival:

> I draw and sketch during the performances, hoping and being careful not to bother or distract anyone near me. But it is my way of listening and however scrappy my sketches are, they do recall pieces. If I have a blank programme, I get bothered and years later cannot recall hearing that piece. I suppose I am drawing the relationship, and the drawings change as the week goes on. [MitRD 6]

Like the COMA participants in Study 3, Music in the Round listeners appeared to value the connections between their own artistic lives – whether as painters, poets or musicians – and the music-making they witnessed during the festival. While some listeners lamented their lack of musical performance skills, they were nevertheless willing to be actively involved in the concert, whether through the intensity of their listening or in the responses and reflections they made afterwards.

Participants seemed to have strong memories of past concerts, and relished the rediscovery of previously heard works through the audience choice festival:

> Sense of history with the Tippett: we were *there* at the first performance, and remember his presence in the audience (stripy jacket and socks). [MitRD 5]

> I loved hearing the Rachmaninov cello sonata again and understood it better after last year's Russian Festival. [MitRD 6]

Sometimes this revisiting of well-loved pieces of music brought its own pressures, as shown in these two diary entries from a listener who had nominated Messiaen's *Quartet for the End of Time* as his 'audience choice':

> When it was first performed in the Crucible, I think it was one of those experiences when everything becomes more than the sum of its parts. I know quite a few people who were there and who say things like "I will never forget it!". I'm worried tonight will not have the same magic.

> The *Quartet for the End of Time* took me off the planet; is there any other work quite like this? [...] They got the ultimate applause of seconds of silence. Personally I would have been content to just quietly get up and go home, but then you have to thank the players for such total commitment. I'll never forget it... [MitRD 13]

In their preparation, engagement and reactions, Music in the Round listeners showed themselves to be fully participant in the musical event. Perhaps more than for the other case study events, the relationship between individual audience members and the repertoire they heard was prominent in their discourse, with the social elements of participation less central to their enjoyment than at, for example, the COMA Summer School. Musical and social needs had to be carefully balanced, and while listeners often wanted to engage in conversation, they would occasionally avoid contact in order to preserve their feelings at the end of a particularly intense performance:

> On the way in I bumped into Ann who apologised for not speaking to me after last night's performance. Said she was so choked up she could not speak. I agreed I didn't want to talk to anyone either! [MitRD 2]

The conversations that took place – whether immediately or after some time for reflection has passed – seemed to be a valued part of the festival for many regular attenders, but those who had been involved for fewer seasons sometimes found contact with other audience members more difficult, matching Christopher Small's description of the concert interval:

The truth is that the interval is not a break in the event at all but an essential part of it, providing opportunity for social intercourse with members of one's own reference group, to crystallize one's response to the event by discussion (intervals seem interminable to those with no one to talk to) and even to be seen as present by those whose opinions matter (by no means as discreditable a reason as many seem to believe). (Small, 1987: 12)

At Music in the Round the 'friendliness' commented on by many participants seemed to be connected for most with the noting of familiar faces and exchanging of smiles, rather than with more substantial interactions: 'there is something about seeing a lot of familiar faces there [...] you know, there's a real kind of bond' [MitRI 15]. The 'in the round' venue may be partly responsible for this tendency, since it fosters the easy recognition of other audience members, but is rather lacking in comfortable spaces in which to socialise; comments about the poor catering facilities and cramped foyers featured heavily in responses to the 'what would you change?' section of the questionnaire. Such concerns are by no means unique to this festival: discussing plans for a new London concert venue after the second world war, Thomas Russell, viola player and administrator with the London Philharmonic Orchestra, noted the importance of provision for social interaction amongst the audience:

Both before and after a concert it is pleasant to meet friends in comfortable surroundings, and to discuss what we are about to hear or, better still, what we have just heard. To leave a concert hall after a vital experience and fight for a seat in a bus or train, to jostle for a place in a crowded café, surrounded by people not blessed with the same experience, is to become aware of an anti-climax. One does not want to dive into the cold bath of everyday life quite so rapidly. (Russell, 1942: 119)

Managing the transition between festival attendance and everyday life was recognised as a challenge by some participants, who held spontaneous parties or went for walks in the Peak District to overcome the feelings of 'bereavement' at the end of the festival [MitRI 3]. With these individual rituals added to the collective experiences of the festival, Music in the Round was 'an annual event to anticipate' [MitRQ 117], with long-term significance for regular participants:

The festivals have taken us to maturity, through our 'middle period' and have been part of the rhythm of our life. Meeting again and again in this intense, passionate atmosphere has cemented many friendships that continue throughout the year. [MitRQ 161]

The skills and experiences of concert-going have been shown to be emotional, musical and social for these participants, many of whom have long histories with the festival and feel it to be 'one of the best things in life' [MitRQ 87]. The next section will consider the motivations for concert attendance which have contributed to this lasting engagement with Music in the Round.

Motivations for concert-going

Individual motivations for attending live music events remain largely hidden in the published literature, save for the admission by some of Andy Bennett's respondents in a study of tribute bands in Newcastle, that 'a preference for the music of Pink Floyd is sometimes secondary to the novelty of seeing a relative or friend on the stage' (Bennett, 2000: 177). Ruth Finnegan, similarly, noted a prevalence of loyal friends and family amongst the audience for amateur music-making in Milton Keynes:

> Audiences for most amateur musical events comprised people attending in virtue of some connection with the performers ... Indeed many local audiences were made up mainly or wholly of the performers' friends, relatives and supporters (a few bands even had their own fan groups who followed them from performance to performance), and the experience of the audience was naturally coloured by these personal relationships. (Finnegan, 1989: 152)

Despite the large proportion of amateur performers at the Buxton Gilbert and Sullivan Festival, audience members with a personal connection were far outweighed by those attending out of loyalty to the festival or to the musical genre it celebrated. Similarly, although Music in the Round listeners valued the sense of familiarity with the performers that repeated attendance at the festival had brought them, relatively few cited this as a motivation for their concert-going, being far more likely to mention musically-related factors, as shown in Table 6.1. Support for live music and for the event itself emerge here as being more powerful than personal links with performers, although qualitative data from the questionnaires and interviews revealed that a sense of feeling comfortable and familiar with the event were also important to regular listening participants.

Table 6.1 Reasons for attending Music in the Round

	I enjoy hearing live music of high quality	I have been before and enjoyed the festival	I am a chamber music enthusiast	I know some of the performers	Other	I am performing during the festival
No.	329	296	217	62	46	4
(%)	(95%)	(85%)	(63%)	(18%)	(13%)	(1%)

Many respondents selected several options from the given list, wanting to include their specific liking for the event alongside more broadly musical motivations. In the 'other' category, participants mentioned their desire 'to support live/classical music' [MitRQ 167] and 'the cultural life of the city' [MitRQ 280], as well as giving more pragmatic reasons for their attendance, such as the reasonable price of tickets or the opportunity to visit friends in the nearby Peak District. An overwhelming picture of an enthusiastic and expectant audience emerges, along with a sense of collective motivation and shared interests.

The notion of being amongst like-minded people – a recurring theme across the four case studies – was another strong motivation for attendance, echoing Michael Argyle's suggestion that 'the group who make up the audience come to share an emotional experience; they may know some of the other members, or recognise them as members of the same social group, who share a set of attitudes, an identity' (1996a: 200). Argyle's description does not mention music at all, and he offers the stereotyped example of dinner-jacketed opera-goers to illustrate a heavier emphasis on the collective experience of attending a performance in the company of friends (or potential friends) rather than on the individual listening experience. There is some validity in the notion of shared attitudes and familiarity, which seems to be just as strong for audience members as it is for performers. However, for this enjoyment in the social aspects of concert-going to be sustainable, there must be some engagement with the music itself; and for Music in the Round participants, detailed knowledge of the chamber music repertoire showed this to be the case.

Participants' motivations for attending individual concerts within the festival were closely connected to their liking for particular repertoire: although 33 per cent of questionnaire respondents mentioned time, money and other restrictions on their attendance, 67 per cent saw musical reasons as more important in their decisions to attend particular concerts (see Chapter 5 for further discussion). Loyalty to the host string quartet meant that their concerts were invariably sold out first, and some participants felt 'ashamed of this a bit' [MitRQ 240], recognising the desirability of a more adventurous approach to concert selection. Attitudes to contemporary music revealed some dissent amongst the audience, a few stating unequivocally that they 'can't cope with modern music – give me the old stuff!' [MitRQ 255], while others were willing to trust the Artistic Director's judgement and 'risk something different' [MitRQ 105]. Previous festivals have deliberately addressed the challenges of recruiting audiences for contemporary music, and seem to have moved the Music in the Round listeners some way from this typical description of new music concerts:

> Contrast the prompt, often too prompt, surge of applause which greets the ending of a classical concerto with the brief, embarrassed silence and scatter of handclaps that acts as a prelude to the applause at an avant-garde première. Many of the more traditionally-minded among the audience will dislike an avant-garde work simply because 'you don't know where you are in it'. (Small, 1977/96: 26)

Music in the Round participants varied in the extent to which they were willing to engage with new works, often favouring the 'sandwich' programming approach where concerts have 'at least one item I know or believe I shall like' [MitRQ 51]. For every listener who would reject 'obscure works by composers I don't know' [MitRQ 104] there was another who avoided 'over-familiarity with the music' [MitRQ 185], suggesting that the audience as a whole balanced guaranteed pleasure with more educative opportunities. Since audience members were making informed choices about which concerts to attend, the proportion of listeners with a liking for or interest in the specific programme of each concert was high, perhaps resulting in the uniformly enthusiastic responses which at times proved wearisome to more critical listeners:

> At risk of sounding arrogant, I found an ever greater readiness than usual to respond exuberantly and – it seems to me – sometimes uncritically. All performances drew the same enthusiasm, perhaps justifiably, but there has been something a bit 'rote' about the constant cheering and stamping. [MitRD 1]

This ritualised response to each concert was indeed striking: applause began promptly after all but the most reflective pieces, and performers generally returned to the stage area three times to acknowledge the tumult of clapping and cheering around them. Loyal festival-goers were unlikely to comment on this aspect of the audience behaviour; only infrequent visitors found the atmosphere 'complacent, uncritical and unthinkingly responsive' [MitRQ 137]. For those firmly located within the audience community, the effect was rather to 'feel part of the whole wonderful experience' [MitRQ 129], valuing their role as one of a 'very sophisticated, broadminded and dedicated audience, which is not just a chance gathering of indifferent individuals' [MitRQ 186]. Some tensions in the audience's perceptions of one another begin to emerge in these descriptions, and so a closer investigation of the ethos of the festival is necessary to allow a clearer understanding of the listening experiences of both newcomers and veterans.

Creating a concert ethos

As may already have become apparent, Music in the Round is a festival of strong characteristics which are shaped by the venue, the host performers and their regular guests, and by the loyal and well-established audience (see also Pitts, forthcoming a). Participants spoke frequently of an 'intimate' and 'informal' atmosphere which was unique to the festival and in some cases had 'spoilt [them] for other kinds of concerts' [MitRI 12]. Performances take place in the Crucible Studio Theatre, in which performers occupy the floor area in the centre of the venue, while audience members sit around them, some only a few feet away and able to 'read the music over their shoulders almost' [MitRI 13]. As well as guaranteeing 'proximity to the performers and good acoustics' [MitRQ 82], this arrangement enables listeners to 'see other people enjoying the music' [MitRQ 136] as the audience are unusually visible to one another:

> If you do glance up occasionally and you see somebody with a slight smile [...] their involvement adds to your joy, your enjoyment, it does to me anyway; we're all really enjoying this, that's lovely, it's a nice feeling. [MitRI 11]

Participants referred frequently to the close connections between venue and ethos, valuing the 'feeling of togetherness with the performers' [MitRQ 159] which resulted in 'seriousness of purpose achieved through cheerful social interaction' [MitRQ 197]. Since for many listeners Music in the Round was the mainstay of their concert-going life, some were surprised that the atmosphere did not suit everybody:

> We brought a cousin of my partner and his wife (our guests for the weekend). They had been to the festival before – but find the intimacy, energy, emotion and enthusiasm of the audience and the performers hard to take. We realised afresh how privileged we are, how special the festivals are – and how sad and purist lots of other folks are! They will not be invited again: we have too many other friends who *do* want to come. [MitRD 11]

The small and tightly-focused venue could easily have been overpoweringly intense, but other elements of festival behaviour helped to lighten the mood and contribute to the informality that was also enjoyed by most participants. The casual dress code of the performers, for example, contributed to the 'relaxed presentation' [MitRQ 297], as T-shirts printed with the logo of the '20th anniversary' festival were worn by all performers, and were also on sale to the audience. The result was not always flattering, and a few audience members noted that 'not everybody looks quite right in those T-shirts' [MitRI 17], but enthusiasm for the convention clearly remained, as demonstrated by the number of audience members wearing T-shirts from previous festivals; visual symbols of their affiliation and long-standing attendance. Similar behaviour had been in evidence at the Buxton festival, where T-shirts with the logo of a performing society or the details of a particular production were also popular; people literally wearing their Gilbert and Sullivan affiliation on their sleeve. At Music in the Round, though, the connection between performers and audience members was reinforced by their access to a shared uniform, a marketing opportunity that appeared (perhaps surprisingly) to have been resisted at Buxton, where the organisers still appeared in dinner jacket and tie to make announcements at the start of each evening performance.

Another unspoken dress convention emerged on the last night of the festival, when seasoned Music in the Round participants were wearing hats: men in boaters and women in straw hats generated an 'English garden party' atmosphere, while others had decorated cardboard hats with images of the performers or other themed references. Music in the Round staff, selling CDs and programmes in the foyer as usual, joined in the tradition by wearing cardboard hats featuring logos cut from the brochures of past festivals. Not all audience members appeared to feel comfortable with the celebratory tone of the evening, with one (as already noted in Chapter 2) objecting to the decoration of the stage for the second half of the concert:

> I had to ask the Octet to remove the balloons before they started. That is one example of the festival getting in the way of the music. I'm afraid I don't go for the hats either. I like my musical experiences to be unadulterated. [MitRD 8]

Too much could be made of the minutiae of these festival rituals, which are bound to have built up over the twenty years of shared musical experience that was being celebrated in the 'audience choice' programme. Diarists were generally unabashed in their view that this festival, in particular, was directed to 'the faithful' [MitRD

5]; 'all of us who made our choices, those who have been to other/many festivals and want to relive the pleasures of either loved favourites or new enchantments' [MitRD 7]. It was quite clear from the overwhelmingly enthusiastic responses of that faithful audience that the festival had fulfilled this purpose admirably; but there were some guilt-tinged notes of disquiet amongst interviewees who perceived the dangers of catering exclusively for an established audience (see further discussion later in this chapter). Indeed, since generating new audiences for chamber music was one of the festival's initial aims, it is somewhat ironic that the first audience of twenty years ago are still in attendance, converted so completely that they leave little room for newcomers.

Contact between performers and audience members was also fostered through the spoken introductions given at each concert, which listeners found made the music 'accessible and therefore much easier to understand and appreciate' [MitRQ 337]. These talks served the dual function of relaxing the audience with in-jokes and light-hearted banter, as well as placing the music in context with explanations that used a minimum of technical language but assumed a considerable knowledge of repertoire:

> These festivals are for the initiated – people who already know these kinds of work and want to both re-hear things they know and discover new works. It's obvious that there are a lot of musically very well-informed people in the audience and the introductory talks assume that this is so – and this is *not* a criticism. [MitRD 2]

Comparison with the Buxton festival is interesting, since there the 'initiated' were also the target audience, but this fact seemed to render discussion of the works unnecessary. Introductions to each performance were made there too, consisting of one or other of the father and son team that organised the festival appearing in front of the stage curtain before the overture to the show began. Announcements there took the form of 'notices' and information, when again the assumption of previous attendance was made, and shared jokes were enjoyed; most memorably, 'could the swimmers who were singing *Yeomen of the Guard* in the park between five and seven o'clock this morning please return the ducks?'. Direct communication with an audience appears to foster the sense of familiarity and companionship that is valued by regular attenders, particularly where it offers insight on the creative processes that have contributed to the performance which is about to happen.

The aspects of the Music in the Round festival mentioned so far as contributing to its ethos are all within the control of the performers, or at least the host quartet, whose leader was also the Artistic Director of the festival. But the audience acknowledged too the effect that they have on one another, and were like the COMA participants and the Buxton performers in observing their similarities and shared interests, sometimes with a wry note of self-recognition. Where Buxton audience members had been rather reluctant to answer the questionnaire item which asked them to define a 'typical' member of the audience and then say how closely they fitted that definition, Music in the Round respondents approached the task with relish. There was strong agreement in their answers, too: audiences were perceived by the majority as being 'a bit wrinkly, with both sexes evenly represented' [MitRQ 15]; 88 per cent of respondents thought that the audience was generally over 50, and there were comments that the audience was 'getting older – there used to be many more young people' [MitRQ 41]. The potential problems of this ageing audience profile have been discussed in Chapter 5, but here it is worth noting that age was the criterion most likely to cause people to say that they did not fit the 'typical' profile of an audience member; usually because they felt themselves to be younger than average, but not always:

> Older than most, attention span more than averagely likely to wander. Have slept through a whole work. [MitRQ 76]

This candid admission allows me to mention in passing that the amount of snoozing in concerts was quite extraordinary, although such admissions of guilt were rare (– several more respondents noted their levels of 'tiredness' in particular concerts, which might be a euphemistic confession). Some listeners enjoyed spotting their less attentive companions across the auditorium: 'it's interesting if other people are reacting to the music and they are in one's line of vision. (And amusing if they've fallen asleep/irritating if they're snoring!)' [MitRI 6b]. In one lunchtime piano recital, the end of a slow movement was punctuated by a prolonged bout of loud, regular snoring, but sleeping habits were usually more discreet; a bowing of the head that could have been concentrated listening, but for the expressions of bewilderment when the applause started.

Guesses at the occupations and interests of the audience members were as clearly defined as their estimated ages, with the predictions of likely careers falling into only three main groups: professional (50 per cent), university/education (27 per cent), and retired (23 per cent). The questionnaires also asked participants to give their current occupation, and whilst the answers showed greater variety than was judged to be typical – including a gardener, several artists, some self-styled 'housewives' and others not in paid employment – the overwhelming profile was indeed of a population working in business, medicine, education and other professions. Responses from those who felt they did not fit this pattern sometimes listed other characteristics which were implicitly perceived to be standard:

> I fit a lot! However, I've not been through higher education, am not professionally qualified; don't own a car; am more unemployed than otherwise. [MitRQ 96]

> Half and half. I've been an academic, still do a bit of teaching at Sheffield Uni, but am not smartly dressed, am good at bar etiquette. I smoke in the interval and don't wear socks and sandals. [MitRQ 128]

Another respondent suggested that a question on postcode would have been a useful addition to the questionnaire [MitRQ 55], joining those who speculated that most of the audience was from the more affluent areas of this very socially divided city. A substantial number added the terms 'white' and 'middle class' to their definitions of the audience, and a few expressed concern about this, even while noting 'Who else do you see at concerts, recitals and operas?!' [MitRQ 36]. This endorses Christopher Small's description of the Western concert hall as 'a place where middle-class white people can feel safe together' (1998: 42); as discussed in Chapter 5, narrow audience profiles are self-perpetuating, since newcomers who feel themselves to be outside the 'norm' are unlikely to return (see Harland & Kinder, 1999). Whilst a notable proportion of the audience appeared to feel concerned by the apparently restricted appeal of the festival, some were more resistant to calls for wider accessibility:

> Excellence in any place or form is to be cherished and I get tired of hearing claims that classical music (or any other 'serious' art form) is elitist. I see no reason why everyone should like everything (it would make life extremely boring) and an enthusiasm for art is no more elitist than an enthusiasm for pigeon fancying. [MitRD 13]

The same problems of preservation and promotion that beset the Gilbert and Sullivan festival (see Chapter 5) were in evidence here, and there was an undercurrent of awareness that the festival could not survive indefinitely with its current audience. These concerns were heightened by the knowledge of the host string quartet's imminent retirement, leading to much speculation amongst the audience about the future of the festival. Most were keen to see a new resident string quartet – some specifying that younger and/or female performers would make a welcome change. The unity of the audience respondents on this point was quite striking, showing that a large body of people can form a shared opinion through only the most casual consultation with one another. Like the students in Study 1, the audience members held opinions that had no obvious forum in which to be heard, and so felt powerless to influence the future of events despite their strong personal interest in such developments.

Audience members' individual experiences of the festival were bound up with the roles that each listener played in contributing to its ethos and ensuring its continued success. The next section turns to these more 'outward' relationships with the festival, comparing them with the attitudes of performers at COMA and Buxton, and considering further the extent to which listeners view themselves as musical participants.

The roles of the audience: commitment and critique

Discussion in the previous chapter of the audience at the Buxton Gilbert and Sullivan Festival suggested that their demands and preferences had as much, if not more, effect on the character of the festival as did the views of the performers. The audience had apparently greater devotion to the repertoire, attending the festival as their primary source of Gilbert and Sullivan listening, whereas the performers saw the genre as one of many potential opportunities for accessible singing, enjoyable acting and general camaraderie. Audience members were strongest, too, in their commitment to traditional performances and to preserving the genre for future generations, so creating a demand for particular types of production which in turn restricted the performers' choices of performing style. Changes to the festival might have been welcomed by performers seeking new challenges and opportunities, but were likely to have been resisted by audience members wanting a reliable, even predictable, festival experience.

At Music in the Round, audience opinion was similarly vociferous; illustrated in the avoidance of vocal recitals and jazz concerts by otherwise regular concert-goers, and in some residual dissatisfaction at the shortening of the festival from two weeks to ten days a few years previously. Since 'chamber music' is a more open-ended category than 'Gilbert and Sullivan', audience members at Music in the Round seemed more receptive to new challenges and variety; the chamber music equivalent of Buxton's annual repetition of 'the canon' would soon cause interest to dwindle amongst those audience members who avoid music they know 'inside out' [MitRQ 41] or that they have heard recently [MitRQ 103]. The festival's Artistic Director has in previous years been overtly influential in selecting repertoire that is little known or rarely heard in close succession, programming 'themed' events that have explored the work of a particular composer, group of composers, or geographical region. Many of the audience testified to the educational value of this approach, caused by 'each concert adding to the appreciation of the whole, and one's musical knowledge' [MitRQ 57].

In May 2003, when this research was carried out, the festival had an 'audience choice' focus rather than a predetermined theme, an approach which celebrated the twenty year history of the festival by allowing audience members to nominate pieces, composers or performers they wanted to hear again. In the festival programme, the Artistic Director enthused about this departure from tradition:

> The first exciting part of this programme, for me, is that I hardly have to take any of the blame for the choices. The second is that we have played every piece before and we are really looking forward to playing them again. Each year there is normally some panic about making sure that we have learnt everything before the festival begins. I think this applies to everyone taking part, to all of whom I give a very warm welcome.

This brief introduction assumes a familiarity with the format and style of the festival that may be bewildering to newcomers, but which welcomes members of the established audience to an event in which they play a significant role. The introduction ends with a paragraph confirming this close relationship between the performers and their loyal following: 'Thank you all for your fantastic support over the last twenty years. You are the most wonderful audience to play for'. This sentiment was repeated in the spoken introductions that began each concert, the first of which started with the words 'I don't think twenty years ago any of us had any idea we'd still be doing festivals', interrupted by laughter from the audience. Those familiar with the festival clearly enjoyed being part of its shared history, but such behaviour risks excluding those who attend less frequently:

> The audience at the evening concert felt definitely cliquey. There was a large element of long-term festival supporters who wore hats etc. I can understand the motives behind that, but it could be off-putting to newer members of the audience. [MitRI 7]

Given that the small venue for the concerts was often sold-out, with even regular attenders struggling to book all the tickets they wanted, the danger of alienating newcomers could be seen as irrelevant, since there would be little room for them anyway. The festival serves a highly valued and significant role for those who do attend regularly, and so attempts to market it more widely might be considered tokenistic and superfluous. A very few respondents were of this rather exclusive opinion; the majority, however, felt concerned at the 'closed' nature of the event and were keen to market it to a more varied audience, within and beyond Sheffield.

The strength of audience commitment built up through twenty years of festivals effectively separates the experiences of loyal listeners and relative newcomers, such that the same conventions and practices hold familiarity or novelty for different sections of the audience. Although the strongest voice amongst my questionnaire sample was from the established Music in the Round audience, other groups were represented too, and 26 people identified themselves as never having attended before. Isolating their views from the sample shows a population that is still diverse, ranging from students attending one concert because they had been given a free ticket, to a woman in the 76+ age bracket who stated her occupation as 'keeping going' and was attending 'all of it, except the social bits' [MitRQ 35]. Respondents in this group were more likely than average to be visiting Sheffield and so able to have only a casual acquaintance with the festival, although one cited 'apathy' as a reason for not attending concerts as he admitted that 'it's the first time I have been despite living in Sheffield all my life' [MitRQ 293]. Characterisations of other audience members were consistent with those of the broader sample; the majority were seen as ageing, knowledgeable professionals who 'listen with genuine understanding and interest' [MitRQ 287]. There was a roughly equal split between those who felt themselves to fit well with the general audience profile, and those who shared nothing 'except the same love of classical music' [MitRQ 321].

The passionate support for Music in the Round that characterised the responses of regular audience members was more muted amongst these first-time attenders, with most enthusiasm expressed by visitors from other cities:

> As an audience member coming to the festival from out of Sheffield I can only be envious of the venue and the population which can sustain this. It looks like a festival tailored for a local clientele and which has nurtured that support. [MitRQ 315]

Those who did enthuse about their first experience of the festival mentioned its excellence, intimacy and informality – the same qualities valued by long-term participants. However, few of the 26 newcomers seemed overwhelmed by their experience in the way that was typical of more established listeners, and only one expressed the intention of returning for future festivals. It seems that the first impressions formed of the festival are consistent with the values of the regular audience, making it relatively easy to 'drop in' to the festival; harder perhaps to form a lasting sense of connection given that the established nature of the audience was also immediately evident to newcomers.

The festival is a relatively closed community, not just in its well-established audience, but also in its strong local connections. Most of the audience were residents of Sheffield or the surrounding area, and whilst the international profile of the performers was respected and admired, the accessibility of 'high quality music on my doorstep' [MitRQ 71] was a significant part of the festival's appeal for many. Where the other events studied imported their performers and audience to the region, Music in the Round featured a string quartet who were active in the local community, and was described by some audience members as 'the jewel in the Sheffield musical crown' [MitRQ 69]. The cultural and economic history of Sheffield partly contributes to this strong local awareness, since the city has suffered in recent decades from the decline of its once-prosperous steel industry, and has been slower than its neighbouring cities, Leeds and Manchester, to embrace the architecture and ideals of city centre regeneration. Investment and development in the city is therefore particularly noticeable, and locals are alert to any signs of cultural renewal that invite favourable comparisons with 'rival' cities.

Long-term residents are often 'very proud of Sheffield and also a bit proprietorial about it' [MitRI 11], and some attributed the success of the festival to this collective pride in the community: 'I think it partly relates to the idea of Sheffield as "nobbut a big village", you know, so I wonder if it would ever have developed this way in larger cities' [MitRI 18]. A few others were more scathing about their home city, echoing the sentiments of the local music critic who started his programme essay with the words 'not many remarkable things have happened in Sheffield over the past twenty years' (Bernard Lee, programme essay 2003), and went on to express surprise at the audience reaction and the success of the festival. The festival 'makes it worthwhile to live in Sheffield' [MitRQ 58] for some regular attenders, but the audience was apparently divided on whether the festival is an oasis in a cultural desert [MitRQ 326], or a contribution to a much-loved, vibrant city. Either way, its character was agreed to be in part a function of its location, removed from the more varied concert life of London, and offering a rare opportunity to 'hear world class musicians [...] without having to travel too far' [MitRQ 117].

Despite the strong identification with the festival evident amongst participants, 'audience choice' nominations were fairly limited, with 355 votes cast in total, by fewer than 100 people in the audience [MitRI 4]. Only four works received ten or more votes, making individual votes very powerful and so increasing the pleasure for those who found that their request had been included in the programme: 'I mean it was a real thrill them playing something that you'd chosen, because I got quite a few choices, so that was a buzz, you know' [MitRI 10]. From audience questionnaire responses, it was clear that the proportion of non-voters (80 per cent) far outweighed the voters (20 per cent) with a fair number saying they had not been asked, and so revealing that they had not bought the previous year's programme which had included a nomination form. Some had refrained from voting because they 'couldn't choose a favourite' [MitRQ 81], because they 'guessed sufficient others would' [MitRQ 12], or because 'knowing the choice was coming from the past festivals I cannot think of anything I would not value re-visiting for at least a second hearing' [MitRQ 48]. A few found the concept of selecting 'best' pieces more deeply problematic, 'an unwelcome artificiality' that trivialised the listening experience:

> The voting thing – it occasionally irritated me this year when people said, 'ah, this must be the most important piece of chamber music in the twentieth century', and I'm thinking 'music is essentially a subjective experience, so you can tell me what you think is good for you, but I don't want that'. [MitRI 1]

This same interviewee had missed the 'educative' aspect of the more usual themed festivals, and certainly the feeling of celebration, perhaps even nostalgia, was noted by other audience members, often with greater indulgence or enthusiasm: 'it hasn't got an overriding obvious theme but it's allowed new themes/ideas to emerge; it also allows one to remember the original performances of the favourites if we can' [MitRQ 46].

The 'audience choice' festival appeared to have heightened feelings towards Music in the Round, increasing the enjoyment and sense of belonging experienced by the majority of participants, but also highlighting the discomfort others felt with the 'annoyingly cliquey atmosphere' [MitRQ 108]. One diarist described the first night ethos as one of 'self-congratulation but mainly great pride and gratitude towards the quartet and their commitment to Sheffield' [MitRD 7]. Once again, the strong sense of participation is clear, and although one listener joked that 'I'm sure they managed without me on my days off' [MitRD 13], others felt as if their 'presence was significant' [MitRD 10] and took their contributing role more seriously:

> I think that is part of the magic of it – that you feel that you are, as the audience, you're involved in some way, and you actually have a responsibility to be there with them. I don't know what it is, but it's something about feeling that you, as the audience, are important, and how you react is important to they way they perform, they react – respond, perhaps a better word. [MitRI 17]

This feeling of contributing to the musical event appears not to be transferable: many respondents mentioned their dissatisfaction with other, more formal concerts and were loyal to the particular festival and its main performers, rather than to the notion of live music in general. Building up a communicative relationship with an audience demands the long-term investment of time and commitment that these players and listeners have given one another. Whilst regular Music in the Round listeners could find similar musical pleasures at other events, they evidently value the familiarity and friendliness of the festival context, such that the social elements become difficult to separate from the musical experience. It seems that for listeners, just as much as for performers, the collective focus on a musical activity holds high value, and increases both expectation and enjoyment.

Listeners as musicians

The roles and experiences of participant listeners have been shown to be varied and complex, shaped by the expectations and attitudes of individuals, and affected by their social and musical context.   Music in the Round participants, like their counterparts in the Buxton audience, demonstrated a strong sense of commitment to their chosen event, and to the repertoire or performers that were featured there. The role of music in their lives was undeniably significant, and strong patterns of regular and active listening emerged, often coupled with past musical learning or ongoing amateur performing activities.   Like the students in Study 1, however, participants at both events showed some doubts about whether such behaviour could reasonably be described as 'being a musician'.   Questionnaire responses from Music in the Round participants showed a high level of musical involvement beyond the festival, with many amateur performers and singers, several learning instruments as adults, and a large number having played in earlier life.   Despite this, few were prepared to declare themselves 'musicians', although the criteria for inclusion varied between participants, as shown in Table 6.2:

Table 6.2   Music in the Round audience answers to 'Would you describe yourself as a musician?'

Categories	Sample responses
No (69%)	[MitRQ 131] No. It implies more than my almost non-stop listening to music, very occasional singing and past flute playing – a 'musician' would be more dedicated, skilled, 'professional' about it.
	[156] No. I like to play the piano to understand how the music works, but can't play it for anyone else to listen with pleasure. But it's made me a better and keener listener to real musicians.
	[160] Good heavens no! I get a tremendous amount out of listening and attempting to play music – but that doesn't make me a musician.
Yes (20%)	[87] Yes. Music is a central part of my life – both listening and playing.
	[154] Yes. Have been professional teacher/performer/composer on and off for the last 20 years.
	[171] Yes. Playing and listening is the main thing I do and what gives me the greatest pleasure.
Uncertain (11%)	[84] I wouldn't but others probably would. It does play a significant part in my life.
	[222] Probably not any more – too out of practice!
	[326] My only claim is teaching myself to play the recorder (and to read music) quite late in life.

As regular concert-goers, these participants seemed particularly sensitive to the criteria of quality and professionalism, often highlighting the gap between their own enjoyment of musical activity and their appreciation of performances given by more accomplished players. Quantity of involvement seemed less important than it was for the school and university students in Study 1; one respondent spending at least eleven hours a week playing the viola nevertheless qualified his description of himself as a musician as follows:

> A very coarse musician – seldom practice unless I expect to have to play for a first violin part. Usually second violin or viola. Play instrumental and chamber music only for own enjoyment and *never* for an audience – not even friends or family: they know to approach no nearer than the next room! [MitRQ 76]

The emphasis for these participants was on quality of involvement, and unequivocal claiming of the 'musician' label was most likely to be justified in terms of some external validation of this; musical qualifications, experiences or professional work. 'Amateur' was used as a modifying label within all three categories, serving variously to make claims to be a musician more modest, or to explain why participants felt unable to include themselves in that definition:

> Yes – but as regards performance standard, pretty amateur! [MitRQ 49]

> No, because I have never taught or performed except as a chorus member as an amateur. But I have some claim now to be a connoisseur and listen to live and recorded music a very great deal. [MitRQ 106]

There were no respondents who felt that attendance at Music in the Round was sufficient to class them as musicians, but many followed the participant quoted above in seeking other words to describe their listening: these included 'music lover' [MitRQ 20], 'appreciative listener' [MitRQ 98], 'life-long accomplished listener' [MitRQ 121], 'avid listener' [MitRQ 159], 'musical and with a good knowledge of music' [MitRQ 188], and 'enthusiastic audience member' [MitRQ 225]. Rather like the Bruce Springsteen fans in Daniel Cavicchi's (1998) study, there are levels of 'listener-ship' amongst these participants, who recognise their own development and increasing skills as listeners and search for the language to express that.

Participants sometimes expressed regret at their lack of playing skills, feeling that a lack of opportunities in childhood had left them 'very sympathetic to music but sadly [with] little talent' [MitRQ 197]. The number of adult learners, particularly pianists, was nonetheless striking: several noted recent successes in graded performance examinations or were 'trying to find time to improve with the burden of work' [MitRQ 275]. Ignoring the troublesome 'musician' label and including all those who mention past or current playing experiences, 63 per cent of the audience reported having some experience of playing an instrument or singing (there may have been more, since the question asked about current involvement, and information about discontinued participation was unsolicited). This evidence provides some support for Julian Johnson's (2002) speculation over the high level of musical interest to be found amongst classical music audiences:

> Those who have engaged most profoundly in classical music have almost always practised it themselves. Scratch the surface of most music lovers and you will often find

an amateur musician, however lapsed their actual involvement. Amateurs, not professional musicians, keep classical music alive. (Johnson, 2002: 119)

The number of amateur musicians was certainly higher than those declaring themselves to be professionals, but there were some strong counter-examples to Johnson's argument, including some regular attenders who felt themselves to be 'fond of music but no expert' [MitRQ 84]. These participants demonstrate through their differentiated experiences the unreliability of generalised theories about concert attendance; to suggest that those without experience of performing engage less 'profoundly' would be to deny the significance of Music in the Round to a substantial proportion of the audience. Indeed, those with higher levels of performing expertise were most likely to be resistant to the festival 'hype' and the idiosyncratic nature of the performances themselves, and so were arguably less engaged with the event by virtue of this emotional and intellectual distance.

Lucy Green (2002) and Paul Berliner (1994) show that 'purposive listening' is a valued learning strategy in pop and jazz performance, but Green, particularly, notes a lack of similar cultural exchange amongst classical musicians. The absence of professional performers in the Music in the Round audience supports this idea that listening is an activity largely reserved for amateurs and non-performers; those who are able to perform do so, those who are not listen to the professionals. Of course there may be many other reasons why professional musicians in Sheffield choose not to attend the festival (or elect not to fill in questionnaires), and further research would be necessary to corroborate fully the notion that listening to peers is more common in other musical genres. The Buxton Gilbert and Sullivan Festival, however, provided some support for this view, in that performing groups were unlikely to go and see one another's productions, using the festival as an opportunity to perform, rather than to gain inspiration from seeing others do so. There may have been many pragmatic reasons for this, not least that the competitive nature of the festival meant that comparisons with other societies were likely to focus on quality rather than ideas, and so might have detrimental effects on the confidence of individuals or groups who were yet to perform. Again, Lucy Green suggests that this tendency to pay attention to 'relative skill or ineptitude' (p. 212) is in part a product of classical music training, where excessive emphasis on assessment means that comparisons with more skilled performers are often de-motivating rather than being a source of musical stimulus.

Amongst the audience at the Buxton Gilbert and Sullivan Festival, 49 per cent of the questionnaire sample mentioned some current or past musical involvement; a lower figure than at Music in the Round, but nonetheless signifying an audience with considerable practical experience. Of those 49 per cent, the majority were or had been singers, often in church or cathedral settings as well as in Gilbert and Sullivan groups. Like the adult piano learners and chamber music players of the Music in the Round audience, these listeners' performing interests echo those displayed on stage, and some saw their listening as a direct source of inspiration, attending shows 'which my own society will be performing soon' [BUXQ 1]. Whilst groups performing during the festival avoided comparisons between their own and others' performances, audience members without the imminent pressure of performance seemed more able to engage with the ideas presented by other societies.

Performances seem to have their strongest motivating force on susceptible listeners when they are slightly removed from the listeners' own performing opportunities; whether physically, such as visitors to the Buxton festival taking ideas back to their own societies, or conceptually, as with the Music in the Round listeners beginning piano lessons in order to get some sense of what it feels like to play an instrument they have enjoyed hearing. Listeners who seek to mimic exactly the standard and style of the performances they have heard will inevitably become frustrated; those who seek a more abstract link with the experience of performing that they have witnessed stand more chance of finding a useful connection between their participation as listeners and players. This is in some ways the opposite of 'purposive listening' – still a valid possibility for classical music audiences, but not demonstrated convincingly amongst my sample. Rather, this desire to emulate, however partially, the performers on stage might be called 'aspirational listening', in that listeners become resolved to seek greater involvement than their audience role currently allows. Playing or singing is only one route to this greater participation: those listeners at Music in the Round who engaged in further listening or reading to enhance their concert attendance were also showing this desire for deeper involvement that seems to be characteristic of the participant listener.

Buxton audience members were less likely to call themselves 'musicians' than were the Music in the Round respondents, perhaps because being primarily singers they faced more doubts about their musical credentials than did the instrumentalists in the chamber music audience. Singers had often learnt their skills in the group settings of school, church or amateur performing societies, and so seemed less conscious of their own 'musicianship' than those instrumental performers who had taken individual lessons or engaged in sustained practice. Appraisals of their own sense of being a musician showed the majority of Buxton audience members excluding themselves from this category, as illustrated in Table 6.3.

Enthusiasm and enjoyment were more obviously present in the Buxton audience answers than in those from Music in the Round participants; again, perhaps, because of the prevalence of singers, who are more likely to have experienced the pleasures of group rehearsal and performance. The word 'professional' occurs only once in the Buxton responses, although 'amateur' status was mentioned frequently: this is revealing of the participants' musical context and experiences, as the Music in the Round listeners compared themselves with the professional performers they saw during the festival, whereas the comparison for Buxton listeners was mainly with other amateur groups. Music in the Round audience members therefore mentioned skill, professional status and quality more than their Buxton counterparts, who tended to focus on current involvement (many having retired from active participation) and evidence of training.

Table 6.3   Buxton audience answers to 'Would you describe yourself as a musician?'

Categories	Sample responses
No (72%)	[BUXQ 57] No – just doing it for fun; level not very high. [75] No – I am completely self taught, do not read music. [122] No – high knowledge level (and appreciation) of choral music; dedicated (rusty) amateur.
Yes (16%)	[49] Yes – attend Guildhall School of Music and Drama. Love music. [62] Yes. I spend a large amount of my leisure time playing music and earn a small amount of money from music (but have a non-musical full time job). [82] Yes, because I enjoy playing and listening to music, chiefly classical.
Uncertain (12%)	[70] One who is extremely fond of music. [83] More enthusiastic than proficient; started singing in cathedral choirs at age of 8, developing an ability to read music. [172] Only in the sense of choral singing.

The dilemmas facing the school and university students in Study 1 are once again in evidence; being a musician appears to be a multifaceted concept, dependent on context, status and attitude as much as on skill and experience. Comparisons with others are shown to be largely detrimental to a sense of 'self as musician', usually being used to illustrate an absence of certain defining qualities in the respondent, rather than for positive reinforcement. For Music in the Round participants, lack of musical involvement was often a source of regret, despite the high levels of engagement demonstrated through dedicated attendance at the festival. Buxton respondents were less likely to express such disappointment in their own musical experiences, perhaps because the activities on stage seemed more accessible to them, and their non-participation more a matter of choice than lack of opportunity.

This chapter has shown listeners to be fully participant in the musical events studied, shaping their ethos and direction through their attendance and behaviour. Regular attendance brings with it a high level of loyalty and commitment, and fosters connections between social and musical elements of concert-going, which are more tenuously linked for first-time participants. There are broad similarities here with the experiences of performers, who need the sense of continuity and belonging that membership of a performing society affords. Whether such participant listening experiences could be achieved at concerts that were not part of a festival or series is still open to question; listeners would possibly make connections between independent events for themselves (cf. Cavicchi, 1998: 92), but the sense of being part of a larger and established event seemed to be important to these participants. Music in the Round listeners speculating about the future of the event emphasised the need for a host ensemble, since 'if there is no core of that kind, it's difficult to see how it will be distinguished from any other series' [MitRI 18].   Contributing to a distinctive event appeared to be part of the listeners' enjoyment at both festivals, and allowed individuals to feel actively involved in ensuring the future of the music-making that brought them such pleasure. Many respondents also expressed the view that some responsibility for nurturing future audiences and performers lay outside the events, specifically with schools and education projects. The next chapter considers the potential for fostering musical participation in schools and more widely, drawing on the personal histories of some Music in the Round audience members, and proposing some educational implications from the case study research.

CHAPTER SEVEN

Fostering Musical Participation: Educational Perspectives and Implications

This project began in institutional settings, where music students were found to be insecure about their sense of musical ability and identity. The research then turned to concert halls and rehearsal rooms in search of people who felt a greater confidence and enjoyment in their musical activities. Performers and listeners in the three event-based case studies sometimes had their own doubts about their musical skills, particularly where they compared themselves with others who appeared to be more educated, more active, or more respected in their field. For the most part, however, those engaging with music in their everyday lives did so predominantly for the sheer pleasure of musical participation, and the closeness this brought with the repertoire and with others who shared their enthusiasms.

The relationship between skill, knowledge and enjoyment surfaced in each of the case studies: COMA participants were keen to increase their skills within a supportive environment; Music in the Round audience members attended primarily for pleasure, of which extending their knowledge was an important part; and the Gilbert and Sullivan performing groups each struck their own balance between the public demonstration of their skills and the within-group generation of enjoyment and fun. Only in the study of music students in transition did self-doubt dominate discussion of their current musical experiences and self-concept. This finding presents a clear educational challenge: to lessen the gap between institutional and 'real world' musical experiences, and to bring some of the enjoyment experienced by case study participants into educational contexts.

This chapter considers the educational implications of the case study findings, and presents additional evidence to inform discussion of the relationship between teaching, learning and musical development, including a second round of interviews with Music in the Round listeners. Two related projects are also discussed: one focusing on the educational outreach work of *Powerplus*, which brings professional players and student composers together for performances of new works, and the other on the experiences of undergraduate music students, asked to predict the educational qualities and approaches that will best support their learning during the first term at university. The need for more effective links between musical participation in education and in adult life is considered, and some implications for school and higher education are proposed.

Music education and the 'real' world

Participants in the case studies often struggled to articulate their reasons for engaging with musical activity, but tended to emphasise the enjoyment, the sense of social connection and belonging, and the broadening of musical awareness and skills that resulted from their membership of performing groups or attendance at festivals and concerts. These elements assumed different levels of importance according to the needs and perspectives of the participants; some focusing more on their own musical and personal development, some seeking to expand their knowledge of a particular repertoire, and others valuing most highly the supportive and friendly groups within which their music-making was located. Whatever the emphasis, though, enjoyment was the critical factor, sustaining participants in activities which could at times be demanding, expensive and frustrating, but which always yielded some element of satisfaction and pleasure.

Given the centrality of enjoyment for adult participants, its absence in much educational discourse on music is striking. Whilst teachers have long known the importance of fun and enjoyment in the music classroom, theoretical writings and official publications have rarely acknowledged this, perhaps because such an apparently trivial concern would weaken their impact and seriousness. Peter Cope's (2003) discussion of a school inspection which criticised a secondary school music department for 'an over-emphasis on fun' (p. 309) shows how an excessively serious approach can become dangerously embedded in official policy. Part of the difficulty may be that music has always struggled to find a comfortable place in the curriculum, having been seen throughout the last century as less essential than English and maths, more frivolous than history and geography, and not so widely accessible as art and physical education (cf. Pitts, 2000a/b). Writers on music education have therefore devoted considerable energy to justifying music's contribution to a truly comprehensive education. Reasons put forward for the inclusion of music in the curriculum have ranged from the assertion of the morally uplifting character of the classical repertoire, the encouragement of self-expression and creativity through composing, to the modern interest in extra-musical benefits, whether these be improved behaviour and concentration or more effective functioning in specific mental tasks. Yet enjoyment, fun and pleasure are the driving factors in adult participation in musical activities, and surely worthy of a central place in thinking about musical education.

The long-term aims of music education

The notion that music in schools lays foundations for musical participation in adult life features briefly in the National Curriculum for England, which states that 'teaching in music … encourages active involvement in different forms of amateur music making, both individual and communal, developing a sense of group identity and togetherness' (DfEE, 1999: 14). Given the obsession with 'measurable outcomes' in current educational directives, this assertion is surprising, since it credits music education with an influence that may not become evident until pupils enter adult life. This aim for music education is not in itself a new line of thought, as this extract from the work of the influential schools inspector Percy Scholes illustrates:

> Throughout the whole of the musical activities in school or college the students' future musical life must be kept in view. The teacher of mathematics can hardly expect that many of his *[sic]* pupils will carry to a more advanced point what they have learnt under his instruction, but the teacher of literature or music whose pupils' progress stops dead on the day they leave his classroom has failed. (Scholes, 1938: 319)

The National Curriculum document is written as if the benefits of adult musical participation will automatically follow from the inclusion of music in the curriculum, which seems optimistic but rather unlikely. David Aspin (2000) suggests that more systematic links with community arts organisations are necessary if music in schools is to ensure 'the conception, construction and launching of individual learners into a responsible and fulfilled life' (p. 83).

Whilst music in education undoubtedly has some role to play in fostering adult participation, Ruth Finnegan rightly contests the view that young people's musical activities are entirely preparatory: 'schools are something more than just channels to lay the foundation for "proper" musical participation in later life; they are *themselves* organised centres of music – a real part of local musical practice' (Finnegan, 1989: 206). In this conviction she echoes the ideals of the Calouste Gulbenkian Foundation report on the arts in schools, published a few years previously:

> To see education only as a preparation for something that happens later, risks overlooking the needs and opportunities of the moment. Children do not hatch into adults after a secluded incubation at school. They are living their lives now. (Calouste Gulbenkian Foundation, 1982/89: 4)

Musical learning needs to have both current value and sustainability, such that teachers are faced with the challenge of enthusing young people about musical participation as well as equipping them with the learning strategies and critical awareness to pursue their interests independently. Few longitudinal studies exist to measure the success of past approaches, and it is too early to judge the long-term effects of the educational reforms of the late twentieth century. The question of how much influence music education exerts on lifelong engagement with music is, however, an intriguing one.

The lasting effects of music education

To investigate the effects of school education on the musical lives of case study participants, I conducted a second round of interviews with Music in the Round audience members, asking them about the influences on their current musical interests, and in particular about the effects of their school musical experiences. Four participants chose to be interviewed in person, and three others responded by e-mail; a small but well-informed sample, several of whom were or had been professionally involved in education. The school experiences of these respondents were varied, ranging from a boys' public school in the 1940s to a Yorkshire comprehensive in the 1960s, and there was consequent variety in the musical emphases; singing and 'music appreciation' for the older generations, and the influence of the folk revival for those now in mid-life. All but one of the respondents had learnt a musical instrument at school, all had participated in school concerts as singers or instrumentalists, and most recalled attending occasional concerts either with parents or as part of a school expedition. Beyond this factual recall, respondents described the ethos and attitudes of their school in relation to music, and here too there was considerable variation:

> Although she clearly loved her subject, [my music teacher] appeared to be quite a timid soul, not really charismatic or inspiring. If it had not been for the influence of my parents I do not think I would have my current interest in classical music. [MitRI 15b]

> I went to a very musical comprehensive school in the East Riding of Yorkshire, which had a really well-established string orchestra and had a really excellent string peripatetic teacher, and a well-established brass band, and probably some good wind teachers as well, and also a dynamic school music teacher. So it was a happening place for music, which was great for me. [MitRI 1b]

These memories show the importance of energetic and inspiring music teaching in fostering a child's interest, as personality and skill appear to be intertwined in the responses and experiences of these participants. One interviewee stated explicitly that he had not been well taught, having experienced 'rather deadly instruction' [MitRI 2b] in his abortive attempts to learn the flute and piano. However, all acknowledged the residual learning that their musical education had brought them, valuing the opportunities that had resulted from, for example, playing in the orchestra, even where hindsight suggested that 'it really wasn't of a high standard at all' [MitRI 17b].

Memories of specific pieces of music performed by the school orchestra or choir were also vivid: learning Schubert songs in German at the age of 10; being one of five soprano boys singing in unison 'With verdure clad' from Haydn's *The Creation*; playing the St Matthew Passion in the newly-built Coventry Cathedral with the school orchestra; and performing in a school production of Britten's *Noye's Fludde* a year after its 1958 premiere in Aldeburgh. This last experience, particularly, illustrates the effects of early exposure to musical repertoire and opportunities:

> It did not occur to me that this music might be thought to be difficult to perform or listen to. But once the sound world of Britten impinges on the subconscious it can't be eradicated, nor would I want it to be. He is always a vital, joyous, thought-provoking composer and he has sent me off into so many musical directions. [MitRI 7b]

Childhood experiences of music or performers that had proved to be influential in later life had left several of the interviewees with a conviction that all children should be taken to concerts in the hope of fostering similarly lasting interests: 'even if they don't understand it or even if they don't like it, I'm convinced that something will come back to them one day, and I think that's really the story I would take out of my own experience' [MitRI 2b]. Another respondent had reacted more strongly to the underlying messages of her school musical experience, that all children should have the opportunity to participate in music, even where their skills are apparently limited: 'choral music was the big thing, and that was open to everybody regardless of whether you played an instrument, so you know, you could join in, and that was the thing that I think I remember most' [MitRI 17b]. These attitudes, although different in their detail, both support the widespread access to music that participants had either valued or missed in their own experience, and amongst all respondents there was a clear determination that music should be part of young people's lives, preferably through the multiple avenues of school, home and concert attendance.

The memories of school music discussed so far were closely intertwined with home influences, and these were impossible to separate for several respondents, who spoke fondly of listening to records, playing chamber music, or hearing parents playing instruments in the home. For some, this home environment had brought the same sense of inevitability to their own musical participation that was experienced by the music students in Study 1; several spoke of it having been 'natural' for them to learn a musical instrument because siblings were already doing so, or because parents expected and encouraged it. Even where families were described as 'not very musical', participants' parents appeared to have had clearly defined musical preferences, and for many there were clear memories of fathers, in particular, playing gramophone records with their children; one 'a terrific enthusiast for the Beethoven quartets' [MitRI 18b], another sharing his collection of Wagner 78s [MitRI 2b], and another playing Bartók quartets on the record player and leaving his young son 'really puzzled' by them [MitRI 1b]. Only one interviewee recalled an absence of recorded music at school and at home, which had left her feeling disadvantaged later in life:

> Because it was after the war and we hadn't a lot of money, there was not actually music going on in the sense of radios playing music, so I realised when I got to university that I was actually quite poverty-stricken in a way, as to actually knowing a wide range of music, and that's something that only gradually came. [MitRI 17b]

For those who were listening in the home, classical repertoire was dominant, sometimes to the extent that other genres were hardly acknowledged: 'oh, we used to sing folk songs at school, and jazz I thought was a bit wild [...] so I was a typical snooty boy, who thought only classical music would be proper' [MitRI 2b]. Parents' and teachers' classical tastes were challenged more by the younger respondents, whose interests in folk and pop music bridged the divide between home and school:

> In the sixth form, some friends and I formed the School Group (!) with various uncool instruments (my self-taught guitar never quite matched Hank Marvin of Shadows fame – this was around 1966) and we played at wet playtimes and messed around in the music room for our own fun. These are about the only happy memories I have of otherwise fairly hateful schooldays. [MitRI 13b]

It was an era where there was a sort of folk revival going on, and playing an acoustic guitar was quite a high status thing to do, socially. So it was quite easy to start groups up, playing, so we played vigorously right through secondary [school]; initially with some support from the music teacher and then not with his support, I think when we got more interested in playing things that he wasn't interested in. [MitRI 1b]

For the second interviewee quoted above, the cultural influences of the time, his mother's Irish musical heritage, and the 'tacitly supportive context at the school' combined to foster his enthusiasm for folk performance, which continued after school with banjo and fiddle playing in pub sessions while at university, and into later adulthood with an ongoing busy schedule as a fiddle player in a ceilidh band. He was amongst those respondents for whom school music education had a 'supportive, continuing effect', and indeed most appear to have come to their school music lessons already receptive to opportunities and ideas that had been valued in the home. Several expressed doubt that school music could entirely overcome a lack of family musical interest, seeing a partnership of home and school musical support as being most conducive to lasting involvement.

Where interviewees were now parents themselves, the difficulties of fostering musical participation in their own children were readily acknowledged, and they were self-critical of their attempts to encourage instrumental practice, judging their success by the adult musical behaviour of their offspring:

When they were at primary school I encouraged them to have goes at things, and they both volunteered [... Now] they both tell me that my parenting was less than helpful in terms of them carrying on. They haven't explained quite to me what I should have done, and it's still a great mystery to me – I don't know. It's a terrible frustration, you know; how to balance encouragement, support and laissez-fairism on the one hand, and oppressiveness on the other hand. [... They] laugh at me and say 'I don't play the fiddle any more because you were too critical'. And that might be true – aarghh! [MitRI 1b]

Playing through school and then 'giving up' was not an uncommon experience for parents to report, and although several of them seemed disappointed by this outcome, they acknowledged that the experience of learning had at least fostered an interest in music in their children. In two cases, participants' sons were attempting to learn the guitar as adults and finding it difficult; one son admitting he wished he had 'learnt his scales better' [MitRI 17b], and the other possibly suffering from learning habits acquired as a young 'cellist:

Because he's got no background in practising, in other words application, discipline, the daily drudge – if that's what it is – that has never been there and so it's very difficult for him to find it now as an adult. I would find it hard as an adult; I mean I keep trying to learn the piano, but I can't sustain it on a regular basis, so I lose it. [MitRI 2b]

Reflecting on their children's experiences, as well as their own, these adult concert-goers, performers and musical enthusiasts perceive a close connection between a supportive family context for music, and the receptivity of a child to the musical opportunities available at school. Attitudes formed in the home appear to be robust in the face of poor quality music teaching, but will flourish when opportunities for instrumental learning, musical performance and the acquisition of skills and knowledge are provided in school. Participants expressed doubt that the reverse could also be the case, and felt concerned for children who did not get musical support and exposure in the home, suspecting that school music would have a hard task in overcoming this absence. For most participants, the specific nature of their parents' musical interest had corresponded closely with the focus of the school curriculum; whether this was the music teacher's interest in opera picking up a father's enthusiasm for Wagner, or the inclusion of folk music in the school curriculum matching an Irish mother's love of traditional music. The greater diversity of music in the lives of today's parents and children might make these coincidences less reliable, and certainly the dominance of classical music in the lives of these participants cannot be assumed to be as widespread as it was in their youth. They readily acknowledged the challenges for music teachers in responding not only to the musically able and interested, but also in the need 'to hunt out those who are not as good and bring them on' [MitRI 2b]. Music education, it seems, holds a great deal of responsibility for later musical attitudes and behaviour, but is not solely influential, a fact which makes the music teacher's task even more challenging.

Learning from and through musical participation

The experiences of the case study participants reported here go some way to answering Michael Mark's (1996) call for research with adults who 'receive enough satisfaction from music participation to invest themselves in it' (p. 121) and whose behaviour might, therefore, hold valuable insights for institutional learning:

> We could well learn something about teaching and learning that the study of music instruction in schools can't tell us. And we might be able to apply some of this knowledge to school music. (Mark, 1996: 119)

The case studies illuminate some critical features in the informal acquisition of musical skill and knowledge, showing how closely related are enjoyment, participation and learning. In the rehearsals of the Gilbert and Sullivan performers, for example, the combination of fun and hard work that was frequently referred to offers an appealing model for the acquisition of musical skill. The high standards of peers and rivals motivated performers to sing well in rehearsals, and the performance itself provided a clear aim which generated group responsibility and cohesion.

Listeners at Music in the Round and Buxton were similarly motivated by the desire to gain full value from their experiences, often bringing a substantial knowledge of the repertoire to their concert attendance. Memories or current experience of musical participation informed listeners' evaluations of the music they heard and, particularly at Music in the Round, led to independent listening and study between concerts. Once again, interest in music proved to be self-perpetuating, as the experience of being part of a well-informed and appreciative audience encouraged individuals to extend their own knowledge and reinforce their commitment to the repertoire and performers. Far from being passive listeners, these live music supporters were active and involved in their chosen events, sometimes seeming more committed than the performers to the preservation and promotion of the repertoire.

The most obvious commitment to musical education was to be found in the third case study, where COMA participants were eager to learn from tutors, respecting their experience and 'hero' status within the contemporary music world. They fitted established profiles of adult learners in their tendency to be 'more highly motivated than traditional students, more accustomed to thinking of learning as occurring in both informal and formal settings, and more capable of bringing a rich variety of experiences to the classroom material' (Datan *et al.*, 1987: 171). However, they were not averse to criticising tutors' teaching or management skills, and several instances of dissatisfaction were reported by diary participants, including problems with an 'autocratic' tutor (discussed in Chapter 4), and with another who allowed his composing class to be 'taken over ... by some new participants' [CMD 13]. The balance of tutor control and participant intervention was finely tuned, with the participants proving unwilling to accept a lower level of involvement in workshops than they had anticipated. In each case, the musical outcome was not in itself sufficient to ensure satisfaction and pleasure; their sense of involvement and contribution to the musical processes was an essential part of the experience.

In school and university settings, students are rarely so vociferous in articulating their educational needs and preferences, although the growing body of research on student perspectives in higher education shows that they often have clear and useful suggestions that simply lack a forum for discussion (e.g. Young, 2000; Drew, 2001; Pitts, 2003). Similarly, Patricia Shehan Campbell's research with primary school children includes a vivid description of how the children demonstrate greater musical understanding between the tasks in their class music lesson than is demanded of them by their teacher:

> When Mrs Bedford used the claves to play one pattern to a sixth-grade group, it erupted into a full-fledged rhythmic improvisation as a lead boy took the pattern and three others layered over him, patting their rhythms on their legs and on the choir tiers. ... During these rhythmic occurrences, Mrs Bedford took one of two strategies: she stopped, stared, and waited for the children to cease their rhythms, once sternly asking 'Are you finished?', or she moved toward them while continuing the lesson, which typically (although not always) brought the musical improvisation to a close. (Campbell, 1998: 51)

Campbell is a sympathetic observer as Mrs Bedford attempts to keep to her lesson plan in the face of apparent insubordination, but she wonders gently whether the teacher 'might do well to spin an occasional lesson from children's creative (rather than solely imitative) responses' (p. 51). Listening closely to the experiences of learners at all levels of music education is still a relatively new trend in research, although it has long been at the heart of good teaching practice. Faced with large classes and multiple external pressures on their methods of teaching and assessment, teachers in schools can easily be forgiven if the individual voices of their pupils are not always heard. Universities, particularly in the relatively small classes that are typical of music departments, have fewer excuses. The remainder of this chapter will present some additional evidence from students in secondary and higher music education, and will consider the potential for more deliberate interactions between musical learning, teaching and participation.

Challenges and implications for music in schools

Since music in schools cannot claim an exclusive role in shaping the attitudes, behaviours and preferences of adult life, schools are perhaps best seen 'not as transmitters of culture but as complex cultural exchanges' (Calouste Gulbenkian Foundation, 1982/89: 43). The provision of musical opportunities in schools is vital in ensuring that all pupils have the chance to develop musical interests and expertise. However, it is difficult in the current educational climate for teachers to acknowledge that not all pupils will experience these opportunities with the same depth of engagement and enthusiasm as their peers. To suggest that music education serves different needs for different pupils is to invite familiar accusations of élitism; and yet it is accepted in adult life that responses to music will vary across the population. There are certainly ethical charges to answer if young people's access to musical activities is dictated by ability, financial support, or family encouragement – as is often the case with instrumental tuition – but so long as equality of access is ensured, then a variety of responses should not only be acceptable, but even encouraged.

It has long been recognised that 'out of school, adolescents are enthusiastically engaged in musical self-education' (Ministry of Education, 1963: 70), but the challenges of connecting that independent learning with the aims and constraints of formal education have proved difficult to resolve. Lucy Green's (2002) study of popular musicians offers insight on the kinds of learning strategies employed by those who are self-taught, including 'purposive listening' to recordings and live performances, and shared rehearsals in which they learn from and with their peers. Green hypothesises that 'young musicians who acquire their skills and knowledge more through informal learning practices than through formal education may be more likely to continue playing music, alone or with others, for enjoyment in later life' (p. 56); the logic being that those who are self-motivated enough to learn independently are also likely to ensure that their performing opportunities continue into adult life. There is an implicit critique of the opposite function of formal education in that argument: maybe the choirs, orchestras and school productions that are organised by music teachers protect their young participants too much from the practicalities of the performing world, whereas the band members interviewed by Green have full responsibility for every aspect of their performing. Involving senior students in the planning and preparation of school productions might raise their awareness of the broader tasks associated with musical performance, as well as increasing their sense of responsibility and contribution.

More experienced students could also act as 'musical mentors' for those new to the traditions of school performances, sharing their expertise and so developing the skills of communication and support that were valued across the case study events.

Lucy Green advocates greater use in the classroom of the informal learning strategies of popular musicians, whilst noting the difficulties of overcoming the habits of teacher-directed learning: 'Many teachers would feel guilty and irresponsible if they found themselves sitting for even ten minutes outside the classroom whilst pupils worked at copying their favourite recordings through peer interaction and without any intervention on teachers' parts!' (Green, 2002: 204). Teachers are accustomed to holding the role of 'expert', and it takes courage to relinquish the status and sense of certainty that this provides. Indeed, Green found that the self-taught popular musicians whom she interviewed reverted to the traditional apprenticeship methods of classical instrumental tuition when taking on their own pupils, demonstrating that 'it is one thing to experience a way of learning, and another thing to recognize its feasibility as a teaching method' (p. 178). Music teachers sometimes seem reluctant to bring their own musical expertise and experiences into the school context, so limiting their impact as accessible live musicians who might be role models or sources of inspiration for their students. Instrumental tutors, similarly, could usefully contribute to the life of the school by performing alongside their students, and it is likely that some staff members beyond the music department will have musical skills that could be brought to light through informal concerts and ensemble playing. Links could be further extended to include parents, former students and the wider community, all of whom have a role to play in illustrating that musical participation can be a significant and rewarding feature of adult life.

Recent research on music teachers' awareness of different genres and musical practices has suggested that 'school music culture tends to be introverted and avoids looking for models of current practice from the art of music' (York, 2001: 1). The sociologist Howard Becker notes that without this awareness of the musical world beyond the classroom, schools teach a version of the arts that can never be fully up-to-date, 'except when, rarely, the training institution is an integral part of the art world' (Becker, 1982: 59). Bringing the techniques of informal learning into the environment of formal education is not a straightforward process, and it is quite possible that the element of rebellion and 'otherness' is part of the satisfaction of musical knowledge acquired away from school. Music teaching in schools needs to be compatible with, but distinctive from, the musical learning in which students are engaged beyond the classroom, so that students are encouraged in their independent learning by teachers who retain a credible and supportive role.

Making music education part of the art world

Educational outreach programmes such as those run by many orchestra and opera companies in Britain arguably have a head start in ensuring that their activities are rooted in the wider social world of musical participation. One such project in Sheffield, *Powerplus*, makes explicit connections between young people's musical compositions and the professional concert world, by enabling young people to write music that is then performed by members of the Northern Chamber Orchestra at a public venue in the city. The students on the project attend rehearsals of their work and discuss the details of their pieces with the performers, and then hear their music played live to an audience of families and friends. For the young people involved, the experience of a live contemporary music concert is often unknown, and is made more approachable by the fact that their own music and that of their friends and peers is being performed.

Questionnaires completed by the students and their parents after a concert in January 2004 showed that the format described by one parent as 'professional musicians taking the children seriously and performing brilliantly' was highly successful. The experience of the venue, the expertise of the performers, and the presence of an audience gave a validity to the students' work that it could not have acquired so fully within the confines of the school environment. Students gained in rehearsal and performance from listening to their own work and that of their peers, and several made reference to hearing their pieces 'in real life', as opposed to the computer-generated performances that were more familiar to them. The opportunity to work with professional musicians was highly valued, and developed not only the students' skills in writing idiomatically for a variety of instruments, but also their confidence and self-esteem as composers (cf. Pitts, forthcoming b).

The students had also enjoyed classroom visits from players, 'because it was great to hear qualified musicians explain how to get the full benefit from the instrument and how to write the music better'. Contact between students and 'real world' performers quickly established different working relationships than those which generally exist between teachers and students, where the performing or composing expertise of the teacher is unlikely to be acknowledged to the same extent. Players from the orchestra were often pedagogically untrained and so reliant on intuitive teaching approaches; students were therefore faced with some blunt criticisms as well as some genuine enthusiasm, but overall were treated as equal partners in a musical process, with their compositions given full respect and attention by the players. Under these circumstances, the students were able to behave as composers, with their activities focused towards an authentic performing goal rather than being constrained by the standard pressures of assessment.

In contrast with many of the outreach programmes that have been established by British opera companies and orchestras over the last twenty years (cf. Winterson, 1994; 1996; Knussen, 2003), *Powerplus* has the advantage of being embedded in classroom practices; the contribution of the regular class teacher is vital, and one of the project's explicit aims is staff development, since this offers the potential for longer-term impact on the schools involved. Rather than giving students a glimpse of the musical world 'out there', the project brings that world into their classroom and values the contribution that they make to it. This offers a useful model for other similar initiatives, which deserve to be more widely supported and available in schools, rather than being seen as a novel or temporary diversion from the established curriculum. The satisfactions and pleasures of musical participation are best understood from the inside; and that, perhaps, is the compelling argument that educational debate so often skirts around – young people cannot *know* whether they feel an affinity with musical activities if they have not had sufficient, varied and authentic opportunities to experience them.

Challenges and implications for higher education

The potential connections between the case study events and the musical communities of university departments ought to be stronger than for schools, given the greater similarity of conditions: adult participants who have chosen to pursue their musical activities beyond school, working at a high level of performance amongst like-minded people. However, music in higher education shares some constraints with the secondary sector, not least the compulsion to assess and validate certain kinds of learning, and the tendency to be somewhat marginalized within the larger institution.

Comparisons can most obviously be made with the COMA summer school, in which participants took charge of their own learning and ensured that tutors were aware of their hopes and expectations for each workshop. The participants' mature approach to resolving difficulties in small group learning drew on their high levels of motivation, and made full use of their tolerant attitudes in resolving conflict and respecting one another's perspectives (see Pitts, 2004a). Within the short time-scale of the summer school, participants were determined to be fully involved in their workshop activities, and so perhaps experienced a greater urgency to remedy difficulties than would be the case in an institutional setting. Nevertheless, there are lessons for universities in the active involvement demonstrated by these participants; students in seminar groups, for example, may be less willing to contribute to the direction and style of group activities, but could be encouraged in this, so developing a sense of independence and control over their learning.

COMA participants demonstrated another characteristic that is desirable but not always present in institutional music education: their willingness to learn from one another rather than depending entirely on tutor input. In addition to the wide-ranging and challenging conversations that took place throughout refreshment breaks (see Chapter 3), participants made deliberate attempts to draw on one another's expertise; consulting with more experienced composers, exchanging ideas about repertoire, and comparing strategies for developing regional COMA ensembles. Once again, this approach came from participants' attitudes rather than being contrived, and its replication within formal music education might lose some of the spontaneous sense of community that was an essential part of the summer school. However, recent research and practice in peer assessment and group learning – in music education and more generally – has begun to erode some of the boundaries that have traditionally made students more competitive than co-operative (see e.g. Cheng & Warren, 2000; Daniel, 2004; Blom & Poole, 2004).

Understanding students' perceptions of music in higher education is a fundamental step in developing their learning and attitudes, but in practice this is often neglected amongst more 'strategic' striving for research excellence and the funding associated with that. Empirical evidence to inform university teaching and learning is therefore patchy and often carried out at a local level, with all the ethical and methodological limitations which that implies. There remains a substantial need for careful definition of the purposes of university music education, in order that the transition from school, through higher education, and into music-related professions can be a stimulating and rewarding experience.

Changing perceptions of university music education

Students begin their university education with attitudes inherited from their school experiences, and so it is not surprising that the undergraduates interviewed in Study 1 were still struggling, several months into their degree course, to find new ways of approaching their musical learning (see Chapter 2). A brief study conducted with another group of first year undergraduates in the music department at the University of Sheffield further illustrated some of the expectations, hopes and anxieties that accompanied the transition from school to university. As part of their introductory meeting at the start of the academic year, students were asked to complete a short questionnaire, designed to increase staff awareness of the challenges facing new students. For the 52 students who responded, improving in their instrumental performance was the dominant priority, along with acquiring a 'diverse understanding and knowledge' of music. Students wanted to be known individually by their lecturers, who should have 'enthusiasm, dedication and originality' in their teaching, in order to help students 'distinguish and develop personal strengths'. One student expressed the hope that university should be 'one of the most memorable and creative times in my life', whilst another aimed for 'a good social aspect with a wide variety of friends'. These new first years had a wide range of musical abilities and interests, along with a willingness to develop new ones. Their expectations of their lecturers were high; staff were expected to be approachable 'at all times and for whatever reason', and to have 'a desire to help people achieve their best'. The students themselves were resolved to be receptive to opportunities and ready to 'try everything available'; open-mindedness, a willingness to accept criticism, confidence and versatility all emerged as desirable qualities in the ideal music student.

In their introductory meeting, students expressed high hopes for their university education, whilst showing somewhat limited imagination about how it might differ in content and approach from their school experiences. At the end of their first semester, responses from 20 students participating in a follow-up survey revealed that the idealistic thoughts of their first week had been partially subsumed amongst more immediate, practical concerns. These second responses demonstrated considerable self-awareness, with one student stating explicitly that 'the transition from A Level to degree is quite daunting', whilst others could point to specific developments (or lack of) in their own musicality: for one student 'participating in ensembles has improved my sight-reading and helped me to listen to others more', for another 'my knowledge has been broadened to incorporate aspects of music I have not considered before', whilst another admitted 'I've not improved as a performer – mostly lack of time/effort on my part'. Perceptions of the lecturer's role had clearly been affected by individual experiences, with attitudes ranging from a feeling that 'lecturers have helped me to learn more by expressing musical knowledge with a lot of enthusiasm', to an anxiety that 'some of the lecturers are difficult to approach when I get stuck because I think they will look down on me (this may not be true, but it's what I think)'. The variety of students' experiences and perceptions illustrates the need to investigate and listen to these more closely than is generally the case, in order that the independence and enthusiasm demonstrated by some students might be fostered and made more widespread. The foundations for positive attitudes to learning are present amongst these responses, but the danger also exists that the limitations of school learning strategies – an excessive focus on assessment, for example – might be compounded by the new difficulties faced in the university context.

These first year students echo the responses from Study 1 in experiencing particular difficulties connecting their formal learning with their other musical activities, perhaps because these had previously been separated for them through the notion of 'extra-curricular' music at school. One student in the original study candidly admitted, 'I don't do as much private practice now that I'm not made to' [UGQ 5], and several others commented that their increased involvement in music paradoxically meant a reduction in its value:

> Music is less important to me now; maybe this is because now it is pretty much the only thing I study, so it has become less of a treat compared to other things. [UGQ 6]

> More and less important. More because virtually all my time is spent linked to music and less because all my time *has* to be linked to music. Because I have less choice, my enjoyment of music has slightly decreased. [UGQ 7]

There is an obvious contrast here with the attitudes of the COMA participants, who were keen to cram as much music-making as possible into their summer school, and saw strong connections between their week at Bretton Hall and the independent musical development that would sustain them in the year ahead. Participants left making resolutions to practice more or find increased time for their composing, which (regardless of whether they would be fulfilled when the intensity of their enthusiasm wore off) showed that the summer school had reinforced their commitment to musical involvement.

University lecturers might hope that their undergraduate students would display similar independence of musical thought and activity, but it is clear from the attitudes reported above that the students' expectations are rather different. This seems fundamentally to be a problem of communication, since students at the end of their music degree courses have been shown to be more readily able to work independently and pursue musical opportunities without staff intervention (Pitts, 2003). Some lecturers may perceive a certain old school charm in this process of gradually understanding – as if by osmosis – the quirks of university education, but there are undoubtedly more effective ways of ensuring that students gain full benefit from their undergraduate experience.

Further research is needed into students' perspectives and expectations; but more urgently, better systems of communication between lecturers and students would facilitate smoother transition into university life, and a greater likelihood of independent learning within and beyond the degree course. First year students' definitions of what it is to be a 'musician' are likely to have been shaped predominantly by their school experience and their often well-established performing lives. These understandings need to be respected and built upon, rather than being presumed inferior to the narrow academic constructions of musical behaviour that have historically characterised music in higher education.

Recognising the value of musical participation

This book has shown that while musical participation may be a minority activity, its value to those who do participate is immeasurable, and generates a desire to share such enjoyment more widely. Much the same could be said of music in education, where instances of imaginative and stimulating teaching abound, but institutional recognition and support remains limited. Just as the enthusiasts for Gilbert and Sullivan, contemporary music and chamber music sought to convert those who could not understand their particular musical pleasures, so the urgency for change in music education is focused more on attitudes than on practice, since the task of music educators would be greatly facilitated by increased recognition and support for their existing work.

The teachers and students who participate in school concerts and productions are fully aware of the contribution that such activities make to students' personal, emotional and musical development. The A Level and university students interviewed in Study 1 all made enthusiastic reference to their experiences of extra-curricular performing at school, recalling the 'fantastic buzz' [Y13I 11] generated by the school musical, or the 'special attention' [UGQ 5] they received as part of a close-knit performing group. Colin Durrant (2003) and Mary Kennedy (2003) report similar reactions from the students they have worked with, but research is scarce on this topic, and further evidence is needed to help persuade educational managers and policy-makers of the impact that musical participation can have in young people's lives. Performance opportunities in schools are largely dependent on the goodwill and energy of music teachers, who typically receive little recognition or reward for this demanding aspect of their work. Greater acknowledgement of the value of performing opportunities might help to place them more securely within the remit of music teachers, to be given equal weight with classroom music provision when decisions about staffing and funding are being made.

Alongside increased support for performing opportunities in schools, a braver transformation of attitudes and values needs to take place: the acknowledgement that musical participation – in school as in adult life – does not fulfil the same needs and purposes for everyone. Musical involvement should certainly be available and accessible to all, since children need regular and varied chances to engage with music and discover its potential contribution to their lives. The exclusion of children from musical activities, whether on the grounds of finance, ability or musical preference should be avoided at all costs. But involvement in music for some students may turn out not to be immediate or contained in school provision, and this variation in response should not be taken as a reflection of music's educational validity.

The music departments in many schools are filled with energetic activity, and should be supported in their attempts to bring students of all backgrounds into contact with musical experiences that will be lastingly meaningful. Such activity deserves to be evaluated for its consonance with the real world behaviour evident in the case study responses, where participants were fully aware of the wide-ranging effects and implications of their musical lives. Music education should have a central, long-term aim: that all students should leave school knowing enough about music to be able to pursue it further through independent learning and involvement in adult life. This view is embedded in the best current practice, but is rarely recognised in wider educational discourse, where musical provision is undermined by the need to conform to standardised measures of educational achievement. Musical engagement and satisfaction is hard to put into words, even for people as active and committed as my case study participants. There would be great educational potential in placing such unquantifiable experiences at the heart of the learning process, and worrying rather less about how they might be measured.

University music departments in Britain are beginning to feel the pressures that have long weighed upon colleagues in secondary music education, and the need to resist the constraints of educational bureaucracy is a timely concern. Universities and conservatoires are in many ways closer than schools to 'real world' musical life, since students in higher education are pursuing independent adult lives that bring them into contact with many more musical influences than are contained within the institutional curriculum. Nonetheless, recognition of these additional influences on students' musical development is limited and the tendency to assume that only certain types of knowledge can be accredited pervades this level of education as much as earlier stages. The traditional musicology curriculum, where proficiency in Western, tonal music is the main priority, is slowly being opened to scrutiny and challenge, and this change offers some potential for broadening the scope of musical experience and learning at degree level. However, assumptions about the musical backgrounds and interests of students have so far taken little account of changes in school music education, and admissions processes are rarely equipped to recognise independent musical learning that has not been validated through conventional examinations. Students' transition out of higher education is also affected by an insularity that fails to recognise the connections between formal learning and the wider musical world, such that students a few months away from leaving music conservatoires feel excessively dependent on their teachers and so ill-equipped for the difficulties of a 'precarious and unpredictable career in music': 'Having a passion for your instrument, that's idealistic; and having to earn a living, that's realistic. We must learn how to combine the two' (Rogers, 2002: Appendix C). Once again, a willingness to make links between education and the wider musical community or 'art world' (Becker, 1982) offers a more sustainable route into musical participation for young adults, and should be sought at every opportunity by students and staff in higher education.

The behaviour of the participants in the three event-based case studies shares a vital characteristic: it is largely the result of independent learning, rather than being dependent on direct and systematic teaching. Music educators therefore need to be humble about their role in fostering musical participation, whilst being alive to the opportunities which they can bring to their students. Just as the COMA summer school participants felt personally responsible for the satisfaction they derived from their attendance, and the Music in the Round listeners felt concern for the future of the festival, so too should music students at all levels be encouraged in their sense of individual development. Teachers have a vital role to play in enabling such development to flourish, using their greater musical and educational experience to support students' learning, whilst being receptive to emerging interests which may be different from their own. Schools, universities and conservatoires have the potential to become true musical communities, in the sense experienced by the case study participants. This may not have measurable educational validity, but the long-term impact can be substantial, and makes a vital contribution to the sustaining of musical life well beyond educational settings.

CHAPTER EIGHT

Conclusions:
Understanding Musical Participation

Through case studies of specific musical events and communities, this book has illustrated the importance of musical participation in the lives of those who are involved, and highlighted the potential for further research in different contexts. This chapter will evaluate the methods and findings of the case studies, and investigate the prospects for future research.

Investigating musical participation

The task of understanding participants' motivations for and experiences of making music has illuminated a number of tensions in researching musical behaviour in local communities. Investigating events without disrupting them is a familiar challenge from many fields of social and ethnographic research, and it is inevitable here that my own musical experiences and sympathies will have shaped the questions I put to participants and my interpretation of their responses (cf. Barz & Cooley, 1997). I have made no claims to objective or generalisable truths in this book, but rather have aimed to represent participants' views clearly before commenting upon them, distinguishing my interpretation from theirs through the use of direct quotes wherever possible. This section of the concluding chapter will evaluate the methodological and interpretative strengths of the various approaches used in the case studies, and will suggest future directions that could help in overcoming their limitations.

The first case study, carried out with school and university music students whom I had taught for at least one academic year prior to the research, brought with it the challenges of researching 'close to home'. There is ample precedent for this approach in educational research, and whilst it has drawbacks which must be acknowledged, it offers a valuable opportunity for students to voice opinions and ideas which might otherwise lack a forum for discussion. In this and other projects that I have carried out in my own institution (cf. Pitts, 2003; forthcoming c), I have found both educational and research benefits in listening to students more carefully than is generally the case, and have received feedback from them that the process is mutually beneficial. The strategy of using a questionnaire to ask general and introductory questions and an interview to follow these up worked well in this context, perhaps reducing the inhibitions that students might have felt if potentially sensitive topics of discussion were broached for the first time in interview.

With its dual focus on expectations of music in higher education and perceptions of what it is to be a musician, the first case study has led to further investigation of both of those aspects (cf. Pitts, 2003), with the focus here being on notions of musical identity and self-confidence. Asking the question 'Do you consider yourself to be a musician?' revealed in this and the other case studies a general level of uncertainty that at times felt like a rather fruitless direction for research. However, persisting with the question proved to be thoroughly worthwhile in illustrating the importance of context and continuity in fostering a secure musical self-image. Listeners in the Music in the Round audience (Study 4), for example, discounted high levels of past or ongoing involvement in their reluctance to claim the 'musician' label for themselves, and so the value judgements of that term were confirmed in ways that might not have emerged through a question that focused in abstract on its meaning.

Having decided to focus my next investigation of musical behaviour on a community rather than institutional setting, the Gilbert and Sullivan festival was an ideal choice in so far as it enabled me to gather the views of people who were actively involved in a clearly-defined musical genre, and who would be likely to hold ready opinions about their motivations and experiences. The main challenge of this study was a personal one: as may have become apparent in earlier discussion, my liking for the Gilbert and Sullivan repertoire is almost non-existent, despite (or perhaps because of) my involvement as a rehearsal pianist in a number of productions in the past. My discomfort with the genre was both a motivation and a hindrance: I wanted to understand the disjunction between my own views and those of devotees of the genre, and yet found it necessary to keep my opinions concealed in the interests of ethnographic research. This dilemma reveals a hidden assumption that is prevalent in musicological research, where writers are often implicitly championing the music that they investigate, arguing for its place in the canon or its validity as an analytical subject. Existing writing on Gilbert and Sullivan, to continue that example, often has a defensive or overtly celebratory tone, echoing the attitudes that were prevalent at the Buxton festival (e.g. Eden, 1986; Wren, 2001). In researching the Gilbert and Sullivan festival, I found my distance from the repertoire to be helpful in retaining my focus on participants' views of their musical activities, and I have been careful to communicate their enthusiasm alongside a more questioning stance, which I found to be present amongst the performers but largely absent in the audience questionnaire responses.

From my observations and informal discussions with audience members at Buxton, I am confident that my interpretation of their greater commitment to the genre – compared with the more varied views held by performers – is a fair and accurate representation. The second case study highlighted, however, the value of closer connections with respondents, whether through interviews, participant observation, or even just visibility in conducting the research. Comparing the second and fourth case studies, which were designed to be complementary, I feel that the closer focus on the audience at Music in the Round (Study 4) allowed greater understanding of the diversity of their views than was possible at Buxton. In that fourth case study, the smaller venue and high level of repeat attendance amongst the audience meant that my research assistant and I became familiar figures at the festival, and were often approached by audience members with ideas or questions relating to the research. This may have increased both the amount and depth of questionnaire responses, and although some interviews were conducted with people I had not met during the festival, our shared experience of concert attendance certainly facilitated discussion.

A similar sense of connection developed with participants at the COMA summer school (Study 3), who were very tolerant of my presence as an observer at their workshops and rehearsals, and often initiated conversations with me, keen to share their perceptions of COMA, contemporary music or more wide-ranging topics. Engaging in the one day summer school gave me an opportunity to compare the experience of participant observation with the more interventionist methods of questionnaires and interviews, and I found the advantages and disadvantages to be equally weighted. My fieldnotes include reflection on the difference this made to my understanding of the day: 'I have more of a sense of emotional engagement, but have also forgotten many of [the tutor's] quotable sentences and remember mostly my experiences rather than those I have observed'. My day as a participant appeared to satisfy the summer school members that I was 'one of them', as the questions about which instruments I played and whether I was interested in contemporary music stopped after that point, and were replaced with light-hearted compliments on my performances at the evening concert. Despite the centrality of participant observation to ethnomusicological research, however, I remain convinced that questionnaires and interviews have their place too, particularly in research that is concerned with the perceptions and interpretations of participants, which are not always demonstrated through observable behaviour. I would acknowledge, though, that my greater involvement in the COMA summer school and the Music in the Round festival gave me a deeper understanding of the pace of events there, and possibly made participants more forthcoming in their desire to share ideas and contribute to the research than was the case amongst the Buxton festival audience.

The final case study at the Music in the Round festival generated the greatest amount of research data, including a high level of questionnaire responses and some detailed and lengthy interviews. The festival was significant in this study primarily for the comparisons it enabled between audience and performer perspectives on musical involvement, offering insight on the experiences and perceptions of committed concert-goers, who viewed their listening as a valuable, often central, part of their musical lives. Some initial attempts to include the views of performers at the festival were made, and a number of interviews took place, but these were mainly disregarded in this context as focusing too much on the festival as a phenomenon and insufficiently on the role of attendance in the lives of regular participants. The wealth of material generated by this audience shows the potential for further investigations of the concert-going experience, questioning what makes an audience feel satisfied and involved in their listening (cf. Pitts, forthcoming a). Chamber music audiences offer only one example of the broad range of live listening that frequently takes place around the country; some further evidence is to be found in ethnomusicology and popular music studies, but there remains a need for closer investigation of the extent to which feelings of social compatibility and comfort affect listeners' enjoyment of different genres. Greater understanding of this aspect of live listening might help to generate some solutions to the problem of widening participation and securing future audiences, which was a real preoccupation for audiences at both festivals (Studies 2 & 4).

The decision to draw on all four case studies throughout the book, rather than making each one the subject of a separate chapter, was a deliberate one, designed to allow any differences in focus and intention between participants to emerge more clearly. Being different in kind, with its focus on institutions rather than events, the first study inevitably became separated, but remained a source of comparison, particularly with adult participants' views of themselves as musicians (or not). By illustrating the effect of context on musical confidence and self-perception, the first study also highlighted the supportive networks in evidence across the three event-based studies, so emphasising that shared musical interests are not sufficient to ensure an enjoyable experience of participation. The need to be amongst like-minded people was recognised by all participants, but the university students showed that shared goals and co-operative intentions are also vital in overcoming the urge to make comparisons with others which can undermine the sense of 'self as musician'. More deliberate investigation of this aspect of music in education might help to bring the valuable features of voluntary participation into the classroom, by increasing understanding of shared musical processes and reducing the emphasis on judging and assessing musical outcomes.

The diverse musical contexts of Studies 2 to 4 were helpful in illuminating concerns which transcended differences of musical preference and clientele. Each event focused on a musical genre that was recognised to be a minority interest, but which participants felt should be more widely promoted and accessible, particularly for younger people. Conversely, the collegiality gained from being part of a select group was part of the events' appeal, providing a supportive environment within which shared interests could be assumed and allowed to flourish. Previously published studies have tended to disguise such similarities of intention and practice, limiting their scope by being located within particular academic disciplines or musical genres. The breadth of literature and behaviour included in this study has been an advantage in understanding the complexities of musical participation, and clearly there is potential for complementary investigations of a wider range of musical settings. In particular, the longitudinal study of membership of a performing group would be able to consider the variable nature of musical participation reported by some of the participants, tracing more closely the peaks and troughs of preparing a performance and coping with the completion of a long-awaited musical event.

There is also potential for investigating the barriers to musical participation, in order to answer some of the participants' own questions about why more socially diverse membership of performing groups seems to be so difficult to secure. Understanding musical participation from the 'outside', listening to the perspectives of those who feel unable or unwilling to participate, would inform discussion of the future of musical events and groups and perhaps suggest strategies for more effective communication between participants and the wider public. Once again, educational settings would be a useful target for investigation, since the close-knit communities referred to by the school and university students in Study 1 must surely have had an impact on the attitudes of students in the rest of the school. Music has often been accused of being an elitist or off-putting curriculum subject, and greater understanding of the factors which shape such attitudes could inform educational debate and policy, and hopefully challenge the perceptions themselves.

This project has increased the available evidence on musical participation, and has analysed this through comparisons across events and in reference to relevant theoretical and empirical literature. It has given voice to the experiences of participants who engage with music for a variety of reasons, but who share a love of belonging to a like-minded group of enthusiasts, and who gain satisfaction from using and developing their musical skills. The book closes by revisiting the themes that have dominated this discussion, through which the participants' understanding and valuing of their musical experiences have been revealed.

Valuing musical participation

Musical participation both generates and solves a variety of musical, personal and social challenges, such that its demands and rewards are finely balanced. From the university students struggling to assert their musical identity amongst a new group of peers, to the Gilbert and Sullivan audience eager to preserve the music they love for future generations, music can easily become a source of frustration or anxiety, and yet the resolution of these difficulties lies within further participation. Involvement in music is a process of defining and fulfilling ambitions: performers and audience members alike question their abilities and credentials with varying levels of self-doubt, but are driven on by the multiple satisfactions of their participation – personal, social and musical. Participants mention the strains of musical involvement quite frequently, but these are far outweighed (at least for those who persist with musical activity) by transcendent moments of enjoyment, achievement and fulfilment, felt to be unattainable by other, 'everyday' means.

It is easy to become too serious and theoretically-minded in a discussion of musical participation, which is after all an activity entered into for largely straightforward reasons: having fun, exercising a valued and pleasurable skill, and spending time with like-minded friends. Walter Podilchak (1991) might feel that 'fun has been under-theorized' (p. 134), but the search for a theory of fun would rightly give academic research a bad name, and will not be attempted here. Participants themselves are active in making sense of their musical involvement, finding meanings and justifications for their behaviour through reference to broader musical and social concerns. Concluding by revisiting the themes of their discourse (first outlined in Chapter 1) therefore seems the most appropriate way of drawing together the diverse but interconnecting experiences I have observed.

Musical participation has been shown to fulfil the following roles for case study respondents:

♦   *Musical participation as a potential source of confirmation and confidence*

The role of music in participants' self-perception and confidence was most clearly in evidence in Study 1, when the university music students revealed the process of questioning their musical abilities that had accompanied them in the transition from school to university.   Those who had resolved this difficulty most satisfactorily had done so by focusing their sense of 'self as musician' more precisely, thinking of themselves as composers, academics or future teachers.   For performers in the other studies (2 & 3), success within their peer group was highly valued, but recognised to be transitory: it seems that the acquisition of musical confidence is an ongoing process, needing to be reinforced by continued activity and achievement.   This element of continuity in musical life was important too for audience members (Studies 2 & 4), who often expressed anxiety about the future of their favoured repertoire, and were strongly aware of the extent to which their musical enjoyment was dependent on the activities of others.

♦   *Musical participation as an opportunity to demonstrate or acquire skills*

Learning and enjoyment were closely allied across the four case studies, confirming the notion that continued development has a central place in musical participation.   Performers in the Gilbert and Sullivan societies (Study 2) enjoyed the opportunities afforded by that repertoire for substantial chorus parts and principal roles, just as players at the summer school (Study 3) supported COMA's mission to make contemporary music more accessible to amateur performers. Most participants were also keen to broaden their musical skills and awareness, although there was a strong conservative presence amongst the Buxton audience (Study 2) and some resistance to contemporary music within sections of the Music in the Round audience (Study 4).   Nonetheless, across the case studies there was a recognition of music's intellectually stimulating function, illustrated through the open-minded and wide-ranging conversations of the COMA participants, and the eagerness of many Music in the Round listeners to prepare for and respond to concerts in order to extract full value from them.

♦   *Musical participation as a way of promoting and preserving repertoire*

With the exception of the school and university settings (Study 1), each case study had a clearly defined musical focus, such that participants often felt themselves to be championing a particular cause, often contrasting their own devotion to a genre with a perceived lack of appreciation in the broader community.   Gilbert and Sullivan devotees (Study 2) were most obviously concerned with preserving a potentially endangered repertoire, although this zeal was most widespread amongst the audience and organisers, with the performers more prepared to find their musical pleasures in a variety of contexts.   Other participants felt themselves to be a misunderstood minority; performers taking some delight in that role while audience members apparently felt more anxious about the implications for their listening future. The need for greater recognition, particularly amongst young people, of the value of music and musical participation was commonly expressed, and education and outreach projects were felt to hold an important role in sustaining musical life for future generations.

♦ *Musical participation as an opportunity to perform with others*

Most participants found the opportunity to perform with others a great source of enjoyment, although attitudes varied amongst performers (Study 2) as to whether group solidarity or individual contribution should be allowed to dominate a performing society's aims. Being part of a performing group gave participants confidence and opportunities that would be denied to them as solo performers; an option considered to be feasible by very few. Performance was central to musical enjoyment for many, although the process of rehearsal and preparation also needed to be satisfactory; excessive tutor interference in group compositions at COMA, for example, was strongly resisted as denying participants a sense of connection with their work.

♦ *Musical participation as a forum for social interaction and friendships*

The demands of musical participation make it difficult to sustain in isolation, as the COMA participants (Study 3) illustrated through their resolutions to practise or compose more after the summer school. Performers spoke of the tolerance and friendship within their society, where all could find a welcome, and be freed from the 'worldly' comparisons of status, wealth and success that operate in other spheres of life. Rehearsals, in particular, fostered close-knit groups amongst the performers, evident to a lesser extent in the audiences (Studies 2 & 4), where a pervading sense of friendliness sometimes compensated for a lack of real connection with fellow listeners. The experiences of COMA workshop members showed that the social interactions between musical participants were not always straightforward, sometimes requiring considerable interpersonal skills in a effort justified by the need to keep a group focused on an intended musical outcome.

♦ *Musical participation as a way of enhancing everyday life*

Rehearsing, performing and listening all offered added dimensions to the lives of participants, allowing them to explore interests and behaviours that were distinct from their work or family roles. Finding the time and energy to attend rehearsals and concerts brought its own demands, but was recognised as being worthwhile; the experience of leaving a musical event feeling revitalised was frequently mentioned. Again, the shared interests of other performers or audience members gave participants a sense of belonging to something that went beyond everyday concerns and gave their lives a new depth of meaning and purpose.

◆   *Musical participation as a way of escaping from everyday life*

It was less usual for participants to talk about music as an escape; most of them perceived connections with other aspects of their lives and valued the continuity between their performing and everyday selves. For some, however, the physical escape from work and family pressures was a motivation in itself; being able to concentrate solely on the music helped to clear other thoughts from their minds, and contributed to the rejuvenation that musical involvement could bring. COMA summer school participants (Study 3) experienced a literal escape that most enjoyed; a week away from families and work allowed them to concentrate on their music-making in a way that was not routinely possible. And for performers on stage, assuming the clothes and character of a given role allowed them to feel liberated from their everyday persona, or to be noticed in a way that was novel and welcome.

◆   *Musical participation as a source of spiritual fulfilment and pleasure*

Closely connected with the enhancement of everyday life, the concept of 'spirituality' was used – sometimes with reservations – to encompass the indescribable pleasures of musical involvement. Belonging to an audience was compared by several Music in the Round listeners (Study 4) to church attendance, where a similar sense of shared purpose and values was known or assumed to be important. Musical involvement, like religious conviction, is difficult to put into words, and can result in an evangelical zeal that is resisted by those who lack an existing involvement or sympathy in either sphere. Participants across the case studies struggled to articulate their experiences of music, whilst feeling a need to persuade those in positions of educational or social influence of the value of musical participation. The spiritual dimension of music therefore brought individuals a sense of peace and fulfilment, but raised its own tensions when the focus turned to ensuring the future of such valued activities.

Over-riding themes of balance and satisfaction emerge in each of these perspectives, such that musical participation can be seen as a process of disturbing and restoring equilibrium. Participants are able to define and pursue individual challenges within a supportive group context, bringing together in musical activity the pleasures of friendship, shared goals and mutual interests which are all valued highly in daily life. Empirical research into such experiences offers new perspectives on engagement with music, increasing understanding of motivations and behaviour by revealing the complex human interactions that contribute to musical events. Musical participation deserves to be more widely recognised and understood by researchers, policy-makers and funding bodies: in short, to be valued as highly as it is by the case participants and many others like them.

References

Abercrombie, N. & Longhurst, B. (1998) *Audiences: A Sociological Theory of Performance and Imagination*. London: Sage.

Allmendinger, J., Hackman, R. & Lehman, E. V. (1996) 'Life and work in symphony orchestras', *The Musical Quarterly*, 80 (2): 194–219.

Argyle, M. (1996a) *The Social Psychology of Leisure*. London: Penguin.

Argyle, M. (1996b) 'Subjective well-being', in A. Offer (Ed) *In Pursuit of the Quality of Life* (pp. 18–45). Oxford: Oxford University Press.

Aspin, D. (2000) 'Lifelong learning: the mission of arts education in the learning community of the 21st century', *Music Education Research*, 2 (1): 75–85.

Averill, G. (2003) *Four Parts, No Waiting: A Social History of American Barbershop Harmony*. New York: Oxford University Press.

Bailey, B. A. & Davidson, J. W. (2002) 'Adaptive characteristics of group singing: perceptions from members of a choir for homeless men', *Musicae Scientiae*, 6 (2): 221–56.

Barz, G. F. & Cooley, T. J. (Eds) (1997) *Shadows in the Field: New Perspectives for Fieldwork in Ethnomusicology*. Oxford: Oxford University Press.

Baumgardner, A. H. (1990) 'To know oneself is to like oneself: self-certainty and self-affect', *Journal of Personality and Social Psychology*, 58: 1062–72.

Becher, T. & Trowler, P. R. (1989/2001) *Academic Tribes and Territories*. Buckingham: Open University Press.

Becker, H. S. (1982) *Art Worlds*. Berkeley: University of California Press.

Bell, C. (2002) 'It tolls for thee', in J. L. Walters (Ed) *Bloody Amateurs* (UP14) (pp. 9–16). Reading: Unknown Public.

Bennett, A. (2000) *Popular Music and Youth Culture: Music, Identity and Place*. London: Macmillan.

Berliner, P. F. (1994) *Thinking in Jazz: The Infinite Art of Improvisation*. Chicago: University of Chicago Press.

Berlyne, D. E. (1971) *Aesthetics and Psychobiology*. New York: Appleton-Century-Crofts.

Bhatti, M. & Church, A. (2000) '"I never promised you a rose garden": gender, leisure and home-making', *Leisure Studies*, 19: 183–97.

Blacking, J. (1995) *Music, Culture, and Experience: Selected Papers of John Blacking* (ed. R. Byron). Chicago: University of Chicago Press.

Blake, A. (1997) *The Land Without Music: Culture and Society in Twentieth Century Britain*. Manchester: Manchester University Press.

Blom, K. & Poole, K. (2004) 'Peer assessment of tertiary music performance: opportunities for understanding performance assessment and performing through experience and self-reflection', *British Journal of Music Education*, 21 (1): 111–25.

Blum, D. (1986) *The Art of Quartet Playing: The Guarneri Quartet in Conversation with David Blum*. Ithaca, New York: Cornell University Press.

Booth, A. (1997) 'Listening to students: experiences and expectations in the transition to a history degree', *Studies in Higher Education*, 22 (2): 205–20.

Booth, W. (1999) *For the Love of It: Amateuring and Its Rivals*. Chicago: University of Chicago Press.

Born, G. (1995) *Rationalizing Culture: IRCAM, Boulez and the Institutionalization of the Musical Avant-Garde*. Berkeley: University of California Press.

Born, G. & Hesmondhalgh, D. (2000) (Eds) *Western Music and its Others: Difference, Representation, and Appropriation in Music*. Berkeley: University of California Press.

Borthwick, S. J. & Davidson, J. W. (2002) 'Developing a child's identity as a musician: a family "script" perspective', in R. A. R. MacDonald, D. J. Hargreaves & D. Miell (Eds) *Musical Identities* (pp. 60–78). Oxford: Oxford University Press.

British Phonographic Industry (2004) Classical trade deliveries 2003. *BPI Market Information*, No. 223, March 2004. Downloaded 8 April 2004 from www.bpi.co.uk.

Bull, M. (2000) *Sounding Out the City: Personal Stereos and the Management of Everyday Life*. Oxford: Berg.

Burr, V. (1995) *An Introduction to Social Constructionism*. London: Routledge.

Butterworth, T. (1990) 'Detroit String Quartet', in J. R. Hackman (Ed) *Groups That Work (And Those That Don't): Creating Conditions for Effective Teamwork* (pp. 207–24). San Francisco: Jossey-Bass.

Calouste Gulbenkian Foundation (1982/89) *The Arts in Schools: Principles, Practice and Provision*. London: Calouste Gulbenkian Foundation.

Campbell, P. S. (1998) *Songs in Their Heads: Music and its Meaning in Children's Lives*. Oxford: Oxford University Press.

Cavicchi, D. (1998) *Tramps Like Us: Music and Meaning among Springsteen Fans*. New York: Oxford University Press.

Chanan, M. (1994) *Musica Practica: The Social Practice of Western Music from Gregorian Chant to Postmodernism*. London: Verso.

Cheng, W. & Warren, M. (2000) 'Making a difference: using peers to assess individual students' contributions to a group project', *Teaching in Higher Education*, 5 (2): 243–55.

Clarke, E. F. (2003) 'Music and psychology', in M. Clayton, T. Herbert & R. Middleton (Eds) *The Cultural Study of Music: A Critical Introduction* (pp. 113–23). London: Routledge.

Clift, S. & Hancox, G. (2001) 'The perceived benefits of singing: findings from preliminary surveys of a university college choral society', *Journal of the Royal Society for the Promotion of Health*, 121 (4): 248–56.

Coffman, D. D. & Adamek, M. S. (1999) 'The contributions of wind band participation to the quality of life of senior adults', *Music Therapy Perspectives*, 17: 27–31.

Cohen, S. (1991) *Rock Culture in Liverpool: Popular Music in the Making*. Oxford: Clarendon Press.

Cohen, S. (1998) 'Sounding out the city: music and the sensuous production of place', in A. Leyshon, D. Matless & G. Revill (Eds) *The Place of Music* (pp. 269–90). New York: The Guilford Press.

Cohen, S. & Taylor, L. (1976/92) *Escape Attempts: The Theory and Practice of Resistance to Everyday Life*. Routledge: London.

Cook, N. (2003) 'Music as performance', in M. Clayton, T. Herbert & R. Middleton (Eds) *The Cultural Study of Music: A Critical Introduction* (pp. 204–14). London: Routledge.

Cooke, M. & Morris, R. (1996) 'Music making in Great Britain', *Journal of the Market Research Society*, 38 (2): 123–34.

Cope, P. (2002) 'Informal learning of musical instruments: the importance of social context', *Music Education Research*, 4 (1): 93–104.

Cope, P. (2003) 'OFSTED, fun and learning: a case study of a school music inspection', *British Journal of Music Education*, 20 (3): 307–16.

Cottrell, S. (2002) 'Music as capital: deputizing among London's freelance musicians', *Ethnomusicology*, 11 (2): 61–80.

Cottrell, S. (2003) 'The future of the orchestra', in C. Lawson (Ed) *The Cambridge Companion to the Orchestra* (pp. 251–64). Cambridge: Cambridge University Press.

Cottrell, S. (2004) *Professional Music-Making in London: Ethnography and Experience*. Aldershot: Ashgate.

Crafts, S. D., Cavicchi, D., Keil, C. and the Music in Daily Life Project (1993) *My Music*. Hanover: Wesleyan University Press.

Cross, S. & Markus, H. (1991) 'Possible selves across the life span', *Human Development*, 34: 230–55.

Csikszentmihalyi, M. (1990) *Flow: The Psychology of Optimal Experience*. New York: Harper & Row.

Dane, C., Fiest, A. & Manton, K. (1999) *A Sound Performance: The Economic Value of Music to the United Kingdom*. London: National Music Council.

Daniel, R. (2004) 'Peer assessment in musical performance: the development, trial and evaluation of a methodology for the Australian tertiary environment', *British Journal of Music Education*, 21 (1): 89–110.

Datan, N., Rodeheaver, D. & Hughes, F. (1987) 'Adult development and aging', *Annual Review of Psychology*, 38: 153–80.

Davidson, J. W. & Good, J. M. M. (2002) 'Social and musical co-ordination between members of a string quartet: an exploratory study', *Psychology of Music*, 30 (2): 186–201.

Dempster, D. (2000) 'Wither the audience for classical music?', *Harmony: Forum of the Symphony Orchestra Institute*, 11: 43–55.

DeNora, T. (2000) *Music in Everyday Life*. Cambridge: Cambridge University Press.

Department for Education and Employment (DfEE) (1999) *Music: The National Curriculum for England*. London: DfEE/QCA.

Dews, C. L. B. & Williams, M. S. (1989) 'Student musicians' personality styles, stresses, and coping patterns', *Psychology of Music*, 17: 37–47.

Drew, S. (2001) 'Student perceptions of what helps them learn and develop in higher education', *Teaching in Higher Education*, 6 (3): 309–31.

Dunsby, J. (1995) *Performing Music: Shared Concerns*. Oxford: Oxford University Press.

Durrant, C. (2003) 'Cultural exchanges: contrasts and perceptions of young musicians', *British Journal of Music Education*, 20 (1): 73–82.

Durrant, C. & Himonides, E. (1998) 'What makes people sing together? Socio-psychological and cross-cultural perspectives on the choral phenomenon', *International Journal of Music Education*, 32: 61–70.

Eden, D. (1986) *Gilbert and Sullivan: The Creative Conflict*. Cranbury, New Jersey: Associated University Presses.

Erikson, E.H. (1959) 'Identity and the life cycle', *Psychological Issues*, 1:1–171.

Everitt, A. (1997) *Joining In: An Investigation into Participatory Music*. London: Calouste Gulbenkian Foundation.

Felski, R. (1999) 'The invention of everyday life', *New Formations*, 39: 15–31.

Finnegan, R. (1989) *The Hidden Musicians: Music-making in an English Town*. Cambridge: Cambridge University Press.

Finnegan, R. (1997) 'Music, performance and enactment', in H. Mackay (Ed) *Consumption and Everyday Life* (pp. 114–46). London: Sage/Open University Press.

Finnegan, R. (2003) 'Music, experience and the anthropology of emotion', in M. Clayton, T. Herbert & R. Middleton (Eds) *The Cultural Study of Music: A Critical Introduction*. New York: Routledge.

Finney, J. & Tymoczko, M. (2003) 'Secondary school students as leaders: examining the potential for transforming music education', *Music Education International*, 2: 36–50.

Frith, S. (1996) 'Music and identity', in S. Hall & P. du Gay (Eds) *Questions of Cultural Identity* (pp. 108–27). London: Sage.

Frith, S. (2003) 'Music and everyday life', in M. Clayton, T. Herbert & R. Middleton (Eds) *The Cultural Study of Music: A Critical Introduction* (pp. 92–101). London: Routledge.

Gabrielsson, A. & Lindström Wik, S. (2003) 'Strong experiences related to music: a descriptive system', *Musicae Scientiae*, 7 (2): 157–217.

Green, L. (2002) *How Popular Musicians Learn: A Way Ahead for Music Education*. Aldershot: Ashgate.

Hargreaves, D. J. (1986) *The Developmental Psychology of Music*. Cambridge: Cambridge University Press.

Hargreaves, D. J. & Marshall, N. A. (2003) 'Developing identities in music education', *Music Education Research*, 5 (3): 263–74.

Harland, J., Kinder, K. & Hartley, K. (1995) *Arts in Their View: A Study of Youth Participation in the Arts*. Slough: National Foundation for Educational Research.

Harland, J. & Kinder, K. (Eds) (1999) *Crossing the Line: Extending Young People's Access to Cultural Venues*. London: Calouste Gulbenkian Foundation.

Harland, J., Kinder, K., Lord, P., Stott, A., Schagen, I., Haynes, J. with Cusworth, L., White, R. & Paola, R. (2000) *Arts Education in Secondary Schools: Effects and Effectiveness*. Slough: National Foundation for Educational Research.

Harré, R. (1998) *The Singular Self*. London: Sage.

Harris Research Centre (1993) *Black and Asian Attitudes to the Arts in Birmingham*. London: Arts Council of Great Britain.

Haslam, D. (1999) *Manchester, England: The Story of the Pop Cult City*. London: Fourth Estate.

Headington, C., Westbrook, R. & Barfoot, T. (1987) *Opera: A History*. London: Bodley Head.

Hendry, L. B. & Kloep, M. (2002) *Lifespan Development: Resources, Challenges and Risks*. London: Thomson Learning.

Hesmondhalgh, D. (2002) 'Popular music audiences and everyday life', in D. Hesmondhalgh & K. Negus (Eds) *Popular Music Studies* (pp. 117–30). London: Arnold.

Hill, R. (1997) *The Arts, Commercial Culture and Young People: Factors Affecting Young People's Participation in Artistic and Cultural Programmes*. Strasbourg: Council of Europe Directorate of Education, Culture and Sport.

Hills, P. & Argyle, M. (1998) 'Musical and religious experiences and their relationship to happiness', *Personality and Individual Differences*, 25: 91–102.

Hughes, M. & Stradling, R. (2001) *The English Musical Renaissance 1840–1940: Constructing a National Music*. Manchester: Manchester University Press.

Hunter, B. C. (1999) 'Singing as a therapeutic agent, in *The Etude*, 1891–1949', *Journal of Music Therapy*, 36 (2): 125–43.

Jenson, J. (1992) 'Fandom as pathology: the consequences of characterisation', in L. A. Lewis (Ed) *Adoring Audience: Fan Culture and Popular Media* (pp. 9–29). London: Routledge.

Johnson, J. (2002) *Who Needs Classical Music? Cultural Choice and Musical Value*. New York: Oxford University Press.

Kaemmer, J. E. (1993) *Music in Human Life: Anthropological Perspectives on Music*. Austin: University of Texas Press.

Kelly, J. R. (1983) *Leisure Identities and Interactions*. London: George Allen & Unwin.

Kemp, A. E. (1996) *The Musical Temperament: Psychology and Personality of Musicians*. Oxford: Oxford University Press.

Kennedy, M. (2003) 'The Experience of Noye's Fludde: a church and community adventure in music-making and learning', *Music Education Research*, 5 (1): 29–44.

Kingsbury, H. (1988) *Music, talent and performance: a conservatory cultural system*. Philadelphia: Temple University Press.

Knussen, S. (2003) 'Educational programmes', in C. Lawson (Ed) *The Cambridge Companion to the Orchestra* (pp. 239–50). Cambridge: Cambridge University Press.

Kubey, R. & Csikszentmihalyi, M. (1990) *Television and the Quality of Life: How Viewing Shapes Everyday Experience*. Hillsdale, NJ: Lawrence Erlbaum Associates.

Lamont, A. (2002) 'Musical identities and the school environment', in R. A. R. MacDonald, D. J. Hargreaves & D. Miell (Eds) *Musical Identities* (pp. 41–59). Oxford: Oxford University Press.

Lamont, A., Hargreaves, D. J., Marshall, N. A. & Tarrant, M. (2003) 'Young people's music in and out of school', *British Journal of Music Education*, 20 (3): 229–41.

Levine, S. & Levine, R. (1996) 'Why they're not smiling: stress and discontent in the orchestra workplace', *Harmony: Forum of the Symphony Orchestra Institute*, 2: 15–25.

Levitt, R. & Rennie, R. (1999) *Classical Music and Social Result*. London: Office for Public Management.

Leyshon, A., Matless, D. & Revill, G. (Eds) (1998) *The Place of Music*. New York: The Guilford Press.

MacDonald, R., Hargreaves, D. & Miell, D. (Eds) (2002) *Musical Identities*. Oxford: Oxford University Press.

MacKinnon, N. (1993) *The British Folk Scene: Musical Performance and Social Identity*. Buckingham: Open University Press.

Mackerness, E. D. (1974) *Somewhere Further North: A History of Music in Sheffield*. Sheffield: J. W. Northend.

McIlveen, R. & Gross, R. (1999) *Adolescence, Adulthood and Old Age*. London: Hodder & Stoughton.

Manturzewska, M. (1990) 'A biographical study of the life-span development of professional musicians', *Psychology of Music*, 18: 112–39.

Mark, M. (1996) 'Informal learning and adult music activities', *Bulletin of the Council for Research in Music Education,* 130: 119–22.

Markus, H. & Nurius, P. (1986) 'Possible selves', *American Psychologist*, 41 (9): 954–69.

Markus, H. & Ruvolo, A. (1989) 'Possible selves: personalized representations of goals', in L. A. Pervin (Ed) *Goal Concepts in Personality and Social Psychology* (pp. 211–41) New Jersey: Lawrence Erlbaum.

Maslow, A. (1968) *Towards a Psychology of Being*. New York: Van Nostrand Reinhold.

Mass Observation (1990) *Arts in London: A Survey of Users and Non-Users*. London: Greater London Arts.

Matarasso, F. (1997) *Use or Ornament?: The Social Impact of Participation in the Arts*. Stroud: Comedia.

Merriam, A. P. (1964) *The Anthropology of Music*. Evanston: Northwestern University Press.

Mills, J. (1996) 'Starting at secondary school', *British Journal of Music Education*, 13 (1): 5–14.

Ministry of Education (1963) *Half Our Future [The Newsom Report]*. London: HMSO.

Moore, J. (1997) *Poverty: Access and Participation in the Arts*. Dublin: Combat Poverty Agency/Arts Council.

Murnighan, J. K. & Conlon, D. E. (1991) 'The dynamics of intense work groups: a study of British string quartets', *Administrative Science Quarterly*, 36: 165–86.

Negus, K. & Román Velázquez, P. (2002) 'Belonging and detachment: musical experience and the limits of identity', *Poetics*, 30: 133–45.

Nettl, B. (1983) *The Study of Ethnomusicology*. Urbana: University of Illinois Press.

Nettl, B. (1989) *Blackfoot Musical Thought: Comparative Perspectives*. Kent, Ohio: Kent State University Press.

Nettl, B. (1995) *Heartland Excursions: Ethnomusicological Reflections on Schools of Music*. Urbana: University of Chicago Press.

Nissel, M. (1998) *Married to the Amadeus: Life with a String Quartet*. London: Giles de la Mare.

North, A. C. & Hargreaves, D. J. (1999) 'Music and adolescent identity', *Music Education Research*, 1 (1): 75–92.

North, A. C., Hargreaves, D. J. & O'Neill, S. A. (2000) 'The importance of music to adolescents', *British Journal of Educational Psychology*, 70 (2): 255–72.

Oddey, A. (1999) *Performing Women: Stand-ups, Strumpets and Itinerants*. London: MacMillan.

O'Neill, S. A. (2002) 'The self-identity of young musicians', in R. A. R. MacDonald, D. J. Hargreaves & D. Miell (Eds) *Musical Identities* (pp. 79–96). Oxford: Oxford University Press.

O'Neill, S. A. & Sloboda, J. (1997) 'The effects of failure on children's ability to perform a musical test', *Psychology of Music*, 25 (1): 18–34.

Opie, I. (1993) *The People in the Playground*. Oxford: Oxford University Press.

Paynter, J. (1997) 'The form of finality: a context for musical education', *British Journal of Music Education*, 14 (1): 5–21.

Peggie, A. (2002) 'Bloody amateurs', in J. L. Walters (Ed) *Bloody Amateurs* (UP14) (pp. 29–31). Reading: Unknown Public.

Pickles, V. (2003) 'Music and the third age', *Psychology of Music*, 31 (4): 415–23.

Pitts, S. E. (2000a) *A Century of Change in Music Education*. Aldershot: Ashgate.

Pitts, S. E. (2000b) 'Reasons to teach music: establishing a place in the contemporary curriculum', *British Journal of Music Education*, 17 (1): 31–40.

Pitts, S. E. (2002) 'Changing tunes: musical experience and self-perception amongst school and university music students', *Musicae Scientiae*, 6 (1): 73–90.

Pitts, S. E. (2003) 'What do students learn when we teach music? An investigation of the "hidden" curriculum in a university music department', *Arts and Humanities in Higher Education*, 2 (3): 281–92.

Pitts, S. E. (2004a) 'Lessons in learning: learning, teaching and motivation at a music summer school', *Music Education Research*, 6 (1): 81–95.

Pitts, S. E. (2004b) '"Everybody wants to be Pavarotti": The experience of music for performers and audience at a Gilbert and Sullivan Festival', *Journal of the Royal Musical Association*, 129: 143–60.

Pitts, S. E. (forthcoming a) 'What makes an audience? Investigating the roles and experiences of listeners at a chamber music festival', forthcoming in *Music and Letters*.

Pitts, S. E. (forthcoming b) 'Twenty-nine world premieres in two hours: the story of *Powerplus*', submitted to *International Journal of Education and the Arts*.

Pitts, S. E. (forthcoming c) '"Testing, testing..." How do students use written feedback?', forthcoming in *Active Learning in Higher Education*.

Pitts, S. E., Harland, J. & Selwood, S. (1999) 'A review of the literature', in J. Harland & K. Kinder (Eds) *Crossing the Line: Extending Young People's Access to Cultural Venues* (pp. 19–38). London: Calouste Gulbenkian Foundation.

Podilchak, W. (1991) 'Distinction of fun, enjoyment and leisure', *Leisure Studies*, 10: 133–48.

Policy Studies Institute (1991) 'The amateur arts and crafts', *Cultural Trends*, 12: 31–52.

Political & Economic Planning (1949) *Music: A Report on Musical Life in England*. London: Political & Economic Planning.

Prickett, C. (1998) 'Music and the special challenges of aging: a new frontier', *International Journal of Music Education*, 31: 25–36.

Rapoport, R. & Rapoport, R. N. (1995) 'Leisure and the family life cycle', in C. Critcher, P. Bramham & A. Tomlinson (Eds) *Sociology of Leisure: A Reader* (pp. 66–70). London: E. & F. N. Spon.

Research Services of Great Britain (1991) *RSGB Omnibus Survey: Report on a survey of arts and cultural activities in Great Britain*. London: Arts Council of England.

Rhein, S. (2000) '"Being a fan is more than that": fan-specific involvement with music', *The World of Music*, 42 (1): 95–109.

Rice, T. (1994) *May it Fill Your Soul: Experiencing Bulgarian Music*. Chicago: University of Chicago Press.

Rink, J. (Ed) (2002) *Musical Performance: A Guide to Understanding*. Cambridge: Cambridge University Press.

Roberts, B. A. (1991) *A Place to Play: The Social World of University Schools of Music*. Faculty of Education: Memorial University of Newfoundland.

Roe, K. (1987) 'The school and music in adolescent socialization', in J. Lull (Ed) *Popular Music and Communication* (pp. 212–30). Newbury Park: Sage.

Rogers, R. (2002) *Creating a Land with Music: The Work, Education and Training of Professional Musicians in the 21st Century*. London: National Foundation for Youth Music. Downloaded 6 November 2002 from www.youthmusic.org.uk.

Rosen, C. (2002) *Piano Notes: The Hidden World of the Pianist*. London: Allen Lane.

Ross, M. (1995) 'What's wrong with school music?', *British Journal of Music Education*, 12 (3): 185–201.

Rusbridger, A. (2002) 'On not being able to play the piano', *The Guardian Saturday Review*, 5 January 2002. Downloaded 29 November 2002 from www.guardian.co.uk.

Russell, T. (1942) *Philharmonic: A Future for the Symphony Orchestra*. London: Penguin.

Salter, L. (1950) *Going to a Concert*. London: Phoenix House.

Scholes, P. A. (1935) *Music, The Child and The Masterpiece*. London: Oxford University Press.

Scholes, P. A. (1938) *The Oxford Companion to Music* (10th Edn, 1970: ed. J. O. Ward). Oxford: Oxford University Press.

Service, T. (1999) *Practising Participation: The Repertoires and Relationships of Contemporary Music-making for Amateurs (COMA)*. London: COMA.

Seth, V. (1999) *An Equal Music*. London: Phœnix.

Sheldon, K. M. & Bettencourt, B. A. (2002) 'Psychological need-satisfaction and subjective well-being within social groups', *British Journal of Social Psychology*, 41: 25–38.

Shera, F. H. (1939) *The Amateur in Music*. London: Oxford University Press.

Shore, B. (1938) *The Orchestra Speaks*. London: Longmans, Green & Co.

Skelton, A., Bridgwood, A., Duckworth, K., Hutton, L., Fenn, C., Creaser, C. & Babbidge, A. (2002) *The Arts in England: Attendance, participation and attitudes in 2001*. London: Arts Council of England.

Sloboda, J. A. (2001) 'Conference Keynote: Emotion, functionality and the everyday experience of music: where does music education fit?', *Music Education Research*, 3 (2): 243–53.

Sloboda, J. A., O'Neill, S. A. & Ivaldi, A. (2001) 'Functions of music in everyday life: an exploratory study using the Experience Sampling Method', *Musicae Scientiae*, 5 (1): 9–32.

Small, C. (1977/96) *Music–Society–Education*. London: University Press of New England.

Small, C. (1987) 'Performance as ritual: sketch for an enquiry into the true nature of a symphony concert', in A. L. White (Ed) *Lost in Music: Culture, Style and the Musical Event* (pp. 6–32). London: Routledge & Kegan Paul.

Small, C. (1998) *Musicking: The Meanings of Performing and Listening*. Hanover: Wesleyan University Press.

Stebbins, R. A. (1976) 'Music among friends: the social networks of amateur musicians', *International Review of Sociology*, 12: 52–73.

Stebbins, R. A. (1992) *Amateurs, Professionals, and Serious Leisure*. Montreal: McGill-Queen's University Press.

Stebbins, R. A. (1996) *The Barbershop Singer: Inside the Social World of a Musical Hobby*. Toronto: University of Toronto Press.

Stebbins, R. A. (1997) 'Casual leisure: a conceptual statement', *Leisure Studies*, 16: 17–25.

Stebbins, R. A. (1998) *After Work: The Search for an Optimal Leisure Lifestyle*. Calgary: Detselig Enterprises.

Stebbins, R. A. (2001) 'The costs and benefits of hedonism: some consequences of taking casual leisure seriously', *Leisure Studies*, 20: 305–9.

Stedman, J. W. (1980) 'From dame to woman: W. S. Gilbert and theatrical transvestism', in M. Vicinus (Ed) *Suffer and Be Still: Women in the Victorian Age* (pp. 20–37). London: Methuen.

Stock, J. P. J. (2003) 'Music education: perspectives from ethnomusicology', *British Journal of Music Education,* 20 (2): 135–46.

Sudnow, D. (1978/2001) *Ways of the Hand: A Rewritten Account*. Cambridge, MA: The MIT Press.

Swanwick, K. (2001) 'Conference keynote: Musical development theories revisited', *Music Education Research*, 3 (2): 227–42.

Swanwick, K. & Tillman, J. (1986) 'The sequence of musical development: a study of children's composition', *British Journal of Music Education*, 3 (3): 305–39.

Thornton, S. (1995) *Club Cultures: Music, Media and Subcultural Capital*. London: Polity Press.

Ulrich, H. (1951) *The Enjoyment of a Concert*. London: Herbert Jenkins.

Walser, R. (1993) *Running With the Devil: Power, Gender and Madness in Heavy Metal Music*. Hanover: Wesleyan University Press.

Waterman, D. (2003) 'Playing quartets: a view from the inside', in R. Stowell (Ed) *The Cambridge Companion to the String Quartet* (pp. 97–126). Cambridge: Cambridge University Press.

Wegman, R. C. (2003) 'Historical musicology: is it still possible?', in M. Clayton, T. Herbert & R. Middleton (Eds) *The Cultural Study of Music: A Critical Introduction* (pp. 136–45). London: Routledge.

Williams, A. (2001) *Constructing Musicology*. Aldershot: Ashgate.

Williams, C. (2001) 'Does it really matter? Young people and popular music', *Popular Music*, 20 (2): 223–42.

Wilson, G. (1985) *The Psychology of the Performing Arts*. London: Croom Helm.

Winterson, J. (1994) 'An evaluation of the effects of London Sinfonietta projects on their participants', *British Journal of Music Education*, 11 (2): 259–70.

Winterson, J. (1996) 'So what's new? A survey of the education policies of orchestras and opera companies', *British Journal of Music Education*, 13 (3): 129–42.

Woodward, K. (1997) 'Concepts of identity and difference', in K. Woodward (Ed) *Identity and Difference* (pp. 7–50). London: Sage.

Wren, G. (2001) *A Most Ingenious Paradox: The Art of Gilbert and Sullivan*. Oxford: Oxford University Press.

York, N. (2001) *Valuing School Music: A Report on School Music*. University of Westminster & Rockschool Ltd.

Young, P. (2000) '"I might as well give up": self-esteem and mature students' feelings about feedback on assignments', *Journal of Further and Higher Education*, 24 (3): 409–18.

Young, V. M. & Colman, A. M. (1979) 'Some psychological processes in string quartets', *Psychology of Music*, 7 (1): 12–18.

Index